Jared I
6-17-06

In honor of your Bar Mitzvah
from the Hertogs

# THE
# DAWN

Also by the Author

*The Jewish State:*
*The Struggle for Israel's Soul*

# THE
# DAWN

*Political Teachings of
the Book of Esther*

YORAM HAZONY

SHALEM PRESS
JERUSALEM

First published by Genesis Jerusalem Press, 1995

Revised edition, Shalem Press, 2000, 2003

Printed by: Top Print Ltd., Tel-Aviv
Printed in Israel

10 9 8 7 6 5 4 3 2 1


Distribution:
The Shalem Center, 22A Hatzfira Street
Jerusalem 93102, Israel
Tel.: (02) 566-0601
North America: (202) 887-1270
E-mail: shalemorder@shalem.org.il
www.shalem.org.il

ISBN 965-7052-06-8

*for Aba*

RABBI YOSEF YITZHAK LIFSHITZ
HA'ETZEL 9
JERUSALEM

יוסף יצחק ליפשיץ
ישיבת רבי יצחק יחיאל
ירושלים עיה"ק

מוצש"ק פרשת יתרו
כא' בשבט תשנ"ה

על ספר קהלת נאמר "שתחילתו דיברי תורה וסופו דיברי תורה ... דכתיב 'סוף דבר
הכל נשמע, את האלקים ירא, ואת מצוותיו שמור כי זה כל האדם'. מאי כי זה כל
האדם, אמר רבי אלעזר כל העולם כולו לא נברא אלא בשביל זה". (שבת ל:)

ספר קהלת מלמדינו, ע"פ גמרא זו, שהסתירות שבקיום, קיימות רק כאשר אין יראת
אלוקים. יראת אלוקים היא תכלית הבריאה, שהעולם עומד עליה. והיא אבן הבוחן
לכל ערך, ולכל אידאה.

כך מצווים אנו ללמוד את התורה, למצוא את השפעת יראת השמים על הכתוב בה.
וכך עשה תלמידי יקירי וחביבי, דר' יורם חזוני נ"י, שבספרו על מגילת אסתר הראה
שהעוולות הפוליטיות, מקורן בגאוה וחסר יראת שמים. והצלחה פוליטית מקורה
באמונה ובטחון בה', ובירואה בו.

אין לי אלא לברכו, שיפוצו מעינותיו החוצה.

יצחק ליפשיץ

# Contents

# Acknowledgments

Although the pages that follow are the work of my pen, it is humbling to recognize how much the ideas contained in them owe to the efforts of others. I am grateful to have the opportunity to draw attention to these contributions, without which nothing that appears here would have been written.

Since my first steps in the thought and politics of the Jews, I have benefited from teachers whose instruction served to unlock the many doors that stood before me. Yosef Yitzhak Lifshitz of Yeshivat Rabbi Yitzhak Yehiel in Jerusalem guided me in both Jewish and Western philosophy, sharing with me his methods and ideas in a way that molded not only my scholarship, but also my life. Gordon Schochet of Rutgers University navigated me through the uneasy straits separating Judaism and philosophy from academia, offering me wisdom and support of every possible kind, and enabling me to emerge from my schooling a stronger individual. I was also assisted by Aaron Wildavsky of Berkeley, may his memory be blessed, whose work on the Joseph narrative provided important insights. Finally, my father, Yehonathan Hazony of Boston University, laid the foundations upon which all of my efforts have been built, and I think his spirit can be felt throughout these pages.

The ideas in this book are, in the more immediate sense, the product of the unique bond of learning and friendship that came into being in February 1990 with the founding of the Israel Academy of Liberal Arts, later incorporated into the Shalem Center in Jerusalem. All of the central figures at the Academy, Joshua Weinstein, Gavriel Danzig, Daniel Polisar, and my wife Yael, devoted endless hours to helping me and others recognize the meaning and consequences of our nature as men and Jews. Josh has been my regular study partner of many years and countless subjects. Since he and I first took up the book of Esther sometime in 1992, he has contributed a great deal to my understanding of this text, and his insights can be found all through the present work. As Director of the Academy until 1994, Gavriel provided me with the opportunity to teach the course in which my thoughts on Esther were subjected to their first trial by fire. Others who devoted countless hours to making the Academy a reality include Dan and Yael Goldstein, Douglas Goldstein, Evelyn Gordon, Julie Irwin, Danny Reed, Gidon Reich, Abigail Wisse and Seth Young.

*The Dawn* came to be written at the initiative of Jay Marcus of Genesis Jerusalem Press, who has for years been waging a relentless campaign to bring Jewish thought to new constituencies and subjects. He enthusiastically talked me through the original conception of the work, and persistently held me to the task despite my wholesale deviations from the publication schedule. The staff at the Shalem Center, Ofir Haivry, Joseph Gelb, and Ayala Graicer, graciously covered for me during the final stages of the composition and editing. The manuscript was read by Jay Marcus, Ari Marcus, Yitzhak Lifshitz, Yechiel Leiter, Daniel Polisar, Joshua Weinstein, my brother David Hazony and my wife Yael, each of whom offered important criticism and suggestions. David Hazony handled design, layout and production. Proofreading, indexing and other technical assistance were provided by Heather Gelb, Joseph Gelb, Abigail Hazony, Jodi Lev, Jocelyn Polisar and Faye Reich. I would also like to thank Mesorah Publications for granting permission to use their edition of the Esther text in Hebrew.

Finally, I would like to express my gratitude to those friends who have assisted me and my compatriots in all our endeavors since the founding of the Academy, including Barry Klein, Barry Liben, Andre Marcus, David Messer, Irving Moskowitz, D. Michael Scharf, Steven Schneier, Michael Siegal, David Weinstein and Ruth Wisse.

Above all, I would like to extend my deepest thanks to Ronald S. Lauder, whose inspiration continues to lift us all to new heights.


Yoram Hazony
Yishuv Eli
December 31, 1994

# INTRODUCTION

EVER SINCE THE INCLUSION of the book of Esther in the biblical canon two thousand years ago, there have been those who have asked what place such a work can have in the Bible at all. And their question must be well taken, for at first glance Esther appears to contradict all that we colloquially consider "biblical." Esther is a tale of kings and queens and evil grand viziers, which cannot help but strike one as a romance or a fairy story. Nowhere in its ten terse chapters can one find the cascading moral imperatives of Isaiah and Jeremiah, and even less in evidence are the sober laws of Moses. The term "God" appears nowhere, and one is hard-pressed to find any trace of theology amid the hairpin turns of the tale. Moreover, the Jewish heroes of the story seem to display little piety and negligible concern for Jewish law: Mordechai the Jew guides and advises his cousin, Hadassa, as she hides her heritage, marries a non-Jewish potentate, and, in a realm apparently rife with anti-Semitism, presumably gives up on any aspect of her Jewish observance that would betray her past so that she may remain in the palace. The book even refers to the young Jewish heroine by the Persian name of Esther, meaning "star"—and the stars were themselves part of the cult of idolatry in Persia—a fact that cannot but suggest assimilation and capitulation to the surrounding civilization.

Yet for all this, when the rabbis of the Talmud looked back across Jewish history, seeking to grant it coherence and permanence by assembling its teachings into a canon, they understood Esther to be of the utmost significance in concluding the Bible. When the rabbis spoke of the giving of the Tora to the Jewish people, they argued that it had been accepted not once but twice, once at Sinai at the beginning of the scriptures, and then again at the end, during the time of Esther.[1] And when they considered the eternity of the Bible's teachings, they asserted that there were two sections which could never be abolished, the books of Moses and the book of Esther.[2] And while they taught that the other scriptures could bring understanding of piety, wisdom, consolation and greatness, it was only the book of Esther which they thought offered the key to the miraculous.[3] To the rabbis, this little story of persecution and court intrigue was something precious, powerful, exceedingly important. It was a writing thought worthy of being the Bible's last words to man—in a sense, God's last words to man.[4]

To begin unraveling the riddle of Esther's meaning we must first recognize that Esther is a book about exile. That is, unlike most of the other writings in the Bible, which depict the Jews in their efforts to come to the land of Israel and build a Jewish nation there, Esther describes a world in which the Jews are distant from their land, their tradition and their God. When sovereign in the land of Israel, the Jews are confronted directly with questions of national morality: How to govern justly, how to obtain security and peace, how to establish the pious and good society in the face of the terrible obstacles encountered by any realistic appraisal of the proclivities and aptitudes of men. But in Israel the Jews at least have the advantage of sovereign authority: The government may muster vast material resources and promulgate laws in the service of the public interest; the intellectual leaders may freely study, teach and write in the pursuit of truth; and the leaders of the spirit may go about inculcating a love of justice and peace among the people. In sum, when sovereign in their own land, the Jews at least possess the *power* needed to determine and implement an ideal according to their own lights, whether they choose to make appropriate use of this power or not. And it is no coincidence, either, that it was when the Jews possessed this power, living on the land and fighting for it, that they also found themselves directly confronted by their God.

In exile, whether in ancient Persia or in a more contemporary one, Jewish life must somehow persist without the immense resources made available by independent, sovereign power. In exile, the Jews must live in dispersion, their institutions weak, their concerns wandering far from Jewish things, and their politics alienated from every obvious source of cohesiveness, direction and strength. It is clear at the outset that under such conditions there is no possibility of freely seeking and implementing any Jewish ideal. To live in a society ruled by others means that the government and the laws are not the product of a Jewish concern for the general public interest, and that they are certainly not the result of an interest in the well-being of the Jews as a nation; that Jewish intellectual endeavors are under constant pressure, whether overt or implicit, to conform to alien norms; and that Jewish leadership, if it is capable and effective, is perpetually viewed with a certain measure of suspicion and even fear—both by the community of non-Jews, and by members of the Jewish community concerned that Jewish success may be interpreted by the gentiles as a challenge to their authority. Thus exile, while never precluding entirely the possibility

of Jewish power, nevertheless establishes a formidable presumption
against it—a presumption which has ominous theological echoes in
the fact that even the most devout come to feel that the way has been
lost, and begin to speak as though in winter, of God having "hidden
his face" from his people.

It is to such a setting that we are introduced in the book of
Esther. Never before have the Jews experienced anything like it,
unless it was in Egypt, a thousand years earlier. Persia is an archetypal
Oriental tyranny, in which the peoples live by grace of the despot's
wishes, and in which the physical survival of the Jews implicitly
remains an open question, even when, as at the beginning of the
tale, the waters seem untroubled. Under these circumstances, the
narrative of Esther is faithful to the tenor of the times, seeming to
bypass issues of theology and religious observance to cope with the
more burning issue of the actual physical survival of the Jews. For
this reason, the book of Esther deals first and foremost with the
problem of a Jewish politics in exile: How the Jews, deprived of
every sovereign institution of power, may nevertheless participate
in, and in the last resort make use of, the authority of an alien
government in ensuring their own vital interest, and in this case
their lives. Esther offers its readers a choice between two antithetical
conditions—the one being a nightmare of impotence, in which "it
was written ... in the name of the king Ahashverosh ... to annihilate,
to kill and to destroy all the Jews, the young and the elderly,
children and women, in one day," and there is nothing to be done;
and the other in which Mordechai the Jew rises to a position of
great power with the ability to act in defense of the Jews, being, as
it says in the closing chapter, "second to the king Ahashverosh, ...
seeking the good of his people and speaking peace to all his
descendants." The nature of this utterly *political* choice—and how
it is to be made in practice—is the principal concern and teaching
of the book of Esther.

At the same time, Esther also moves to assert itself against that other, more subtle opponent, which had loomed over Persian Jewry for years before Haman had plotted against it. Persia in Esther's time is a cosmopolitan world-empire, which offers success and wealth to those among the Jewish exiles who will give up on the past and play by its rules. In Persia, as elsewhere, the Jews begin to disappear into the fabric of the empire, some of them changing their names and their dress, and arguing with self-confidence against the possibility and desirability of a continuation to Jewish history. What argument can be made as against these, to a defeated and dispirited Jewry, scattered to the corners of the world and no longer privy to the word of God? In making its political argument, the narrative of Esther consciously responds on these historical, religious and theological battlegrounds as well, offering answers which are among the most daring, and ultimately the most successful, in Jewish history.

Yet these deadly serious messages tend to be lost when the book is read today. Its association with the activities now surrounding the festival of Purim, the Feast of Esther, has rendered such themes obscure, since Esther is seldom read in a context in which it may be taken seriously on its own terms. As a consequence, many read the book only in a cursory fashion, believing that the plot pivots on "coincidence" or "luck." But a closer examination reveals that there is no coincidence in the tale: The political events leading to the salvation of the Jews of Persia are planned by Mordechai and Esther, and come to succeed by virtue of their shrewd understanding of the principles of politics, their courage and their faith in the face of an apparently Godless world. How these elements can work to produce the greatest of political events, in which "the enemies of the Jews hoped to rule them, but the situation reversed itself and it was the Jews who asserted rule over their enemies," this is the true tale of Esther, whose teachings demand our attention and our interest so many centuries later.

# ESTHER
# ONE
[1:1 – 1:22]

It came to pass in the days of Ahashverosh, the same Ahashverosh who reigned from India to Ethiopia, over 127 provinces: In the days when the king Ahashverosh would sit on his royal throne, which was in Susa the capital. In year 3 of his reign he made a feast for all his princes and his servants, the military power of Persia and Media, the nobles and princes of the provinces being before him, during which he displayed the riches of his glorious kingdom and the honor of his excellent majesty for many days — 180 days.

When these days had run their course, the king made a feast for all the people present in Susa the capital, from the highest to the most lowly, lasting seven days in the court, in the garden of the king's palace. There were hangings of white, of fine cotton, and blue, suspended with cords of fine linen and purple from silver rods and marble columns, divans of gold and silver on a floor of alabaster, marble, pearl and precious stone. And drinks in vessels of gold, and vessels, each one differing from the others, and the royal wine aplenty, from the hand of the king. And the drinking was in accord with the law that none should be compelled, for so the king had instructed all the officers of his house, that they should do according to each man's will.

Vashti the queen made a feast for the women as well, in the royal house of the king Ahashverosh. On the seventh day, when the heart of the king was merry with wine, he commanded Mehuman, Bizzeta, Harvona, Bigta and Avagta, Zetar and Karkas, the seven chamberlains who served in the presence of the king Ahashverosh: To bring Vashti the queen before the king wearing the royal crown, to show the peoples and the princes her beauty, for she was fair to look upon. But Vashti the queen refused to come at the king's command as communicated by the chamberlains, and the king was exceedingly angered, and his rage burned within him.

*The king turned to his advisers, who understood the precedents, for such was the king's habit before all who knew law and judgment — Those who were close to him were Karshena, Shetar, Admata, Tarshish, Meres, Marsena and Memuchan, the seven princes of Persia and Media, who saw the king's face, and who sat first in the kingdom —*

"*According to the law, what should be done to Vashti the queen, who has not performed the word of the king as communicated by the chamberlains?*"

*Memuchan said to the king and the princes:* "*It is not the king alone who has been wronged by Vashti the queen, but all the princes, and all the peoples in all the provinces of the king Ahashverosh. For this deed of the queen will become known to all the women, and their husbands will become contemptible in their eyes, when they tell: The king Ahashverosh commanded that Vashti the queen be brought before him but she came not. And this day the princesses of Persia and Media who have heard of the queen's deed will be telling it to all the king's princes, and there will be much contempt and anger. If it please the king, let a royal decree be issued, and let it be written among the laws of Persia and Media, so that it should not fail, that Vashti come no more before the king Ahashverosh, and let the king give her royal estate to someone better than she. And when the king's edict which he will issue is heard throughout all of his kingdom, vast though it be, all the wives will give honor to their husbands, from the highest to the most lowly."*

*The idea pleased the king and the princes, and the king did as Memuchan advised. He sent letters to all the king's provinces, to every province in its own script and to every people in its own language, that every man should rule in his own house and speak in the language of his own people.*

# I

# SUBMISSION
# AND RULE

ESTHER BEGINS WITH A PARTY in which Ahashverosh, king of Persia,[1] entertains his ministers and legions, drinks himself into a tantrum, fights with his wife the queen, consults with his advisers, and then has his consort humiliated and deposed. The whole sordid scene takes place without mention of the Jews or of their enemies, the subject of the book of Esther, so that one has to ask why the narrative should not have begun with the second chapter or even with the third, when the plot against the Jews breaks into the open. It was this question which moved the rabbis of the Talmud to argue that the Jews of the capital must have been present at the feast, and that something that took place there—either the misbehavior of the king towards the Jews, or their own misbehavior—must have served as the provocation which triggers their subsequent persecution.[2] But the purpose of the party in the book of Esther is not to add to an otherwise dense plot. It is to acquaint us with its host, with the manner in which he rules his empire. It is this empire which inherited those who destroyed the kingdom of the Jews; dispersed in its midst live their remnant. And one cannot understand what has become of them there, nor whom they will have to fight and why, nor the dangers before them, nor the greatness of their triumph, without first understanding Ahashverosh and his party, and the appetite for rule which throbs there drunk among the revelers from a hundred lands, so that the rabbis said that the Satan danced there himself.[3]

Ahashverosh is the ruler of most of civilization, from Ethiopia to India, and one might think that his time would be taken up with the responsibilities of governing more than a hundred provinces, or of securing them against external threats. Nevertheless, Esther begins by informing us that by the third year of his reign, the principal concern to which he dedicates himself is an ongoing carnival of drinking, which occupies the attention of the political, military and administrative elite of the empire for no less than six months. Moreover, even the lowest of commoners is given the run of the palace for a week of popular merrymaking, in which they have the chance of a lifetime to drink "royal wine aplenty, from the hand of the king" out of gold vessels, in surroundings of marble and pearl, no less. (1:6–7)

The point of this venture is hardly altruism. Ahashverosh pointedly seeks to display "the riches of his glorious kingdom and the honor of his excellent majesty" (1:4)—that is, to create a setting in which the entire empire can see the immense financial and administrative power which he, the king, can muster and dissipate at whim. This is a setting in which gratitude and flattery are lavished upon him from every corner of the empire, a show calculated to heap honor on him, and to create the impression, in the eyes of his subjects, as well as his own, that he is in control of the world.

When we try to understand this Ahashverosh, we have no choice but to suspect that the empire has not yet been suitably impressed with his virtues as a leader—for if he had governed well, there would be little need for such grotesquerie to assure the people's affections.[4] Yet in the absence of genuine rule, and of actual control over his millions of subjects, he is immensely concerned with the appearance of such rule and of such control. To be more precise, it is the *feeling* of control which he desires. For rule is an appetite, and power is a hunger, which the rabbis compared to a crocodile that would consume the world, and into which one could throw country after country and yet not sate it.[5] Ahashverosh is a glutton of power, in an empire which is sick with the yearning to extend itself, to swallow others, to control every thing. Lacking the talents to secure such power through political prowess and actual leadership, Ahashverosh believes he can move towards the same end by bribing his empire with profligacy and drink. In holding this belief he is, of course, neither the first nor the last.

The contemporary Western reader, immersed in the rationalism and materialism of our age, has a difficult time recognizing who and what this Ahashverosh is. We now tend to assume that men are motivated by self-interest, and that reason for the most part suffices to get along with our neighbors, and to feed the small stable of our occasionally unruly physical appetites. Absent, in this theory, is any motive for wanting to rule others. And good men, or even most men, are therefore supposed to have no such desire for rule, while the few who are undeniably preoccupied with such things are conveniently considered abnormal. Behavior such as that displayed by Ahashverosh is usually interpreted as a "mistaken" pursuit of "rational self-interest"—as though he and his advisers had reasoned it through and concluded that spending the taxes of the empire in this way would be more prudent than the pursuit of other policy options—without the possibility arising that there might be nothing rational in his motives whatsoever. Yet this last is precisely the case. The key to the motives of the king lies in recognizing that he is neither rationally self-interested nor, as we see again and again, particularly concerned with the more material desires for money, food or sex. The king appears in Esther as a representation of something else, something we are unaccustomed to recognizing in ourselves and others: The appetite for rule, the essential ingredient in the character of every ruler, in this case unenlightened, unchanneled and unrestrained.

It is worth considering the appetite for rule and control more closely, the better to understand this king and all others. The desire for rule—which the philosophers called *thymos*, and the Jews knew as man's *ruah*, or "spirit"—is a primary aspect of man's nature, the first quality mentioned in the books of Moses with respect to mankind: "God said: Let us make man in our image, after our likeness, and they will rule over the fish of the sea, and over the birds of the skies, and over the cattle, and over all the earth...."[6] Every person at all times strives to rule and control that which comprises his world: To find everything in its place as expected; to find his hungers soothed; to find that his friends are trustworthy, his wife faithful, his children obedient; to find others willing to do his bidding; to find those beliefs he holds confirmed and those causes to which he subscribes victorious; to find that his superiors are solicitous, and his opponents, if not utterly vanquished, at least held harmlessly at bay. Such a world is one in which he may move with unlimited freedom, unobstructed and unchallenged; it is a world of perfect stability and security, physical and emotional. Such a world is a fantasy, but it is one for which man strives from the day he is born, as surely as he strives for physical sustenance. As the appetite for food drives him towards his supper, so too does the appetite for control drive man to rule his world, or if he cannot, to find someone who can rule it in his place and provide him with the stability for which he yearns.[7]

Like all desires, the appetite for rule serves a crucial and life-sustaining purpose when it is held within bounds. It is the spirit that urges that the uncertain, threatening and challenging be made certain, benign and beneficial. Every healthy person experiences the tides of the spirit in some measure: Self-confidence, dedication, enthusiasm, magnanimity and a sense of purpose when control and rule are at hand; anger, fear, jealousy, guilt and aimless depression when they are lost. Together, these feelings map the boundaries between that which has already been achieved and that which has not, allowing man to build his life from one achievement to the next, driving him to extend the frontiers of the controlled, of that which is as it "should" be: To invest in shelter for winter, to resolve a difficult problem, to uncover a lost object, to master an elusive skill, to invent a much-needed device, to excel in one's profession, to win a recalcitrant love, to save a drowning child, to defend against a threat to one's life, to right injustice.

And there are also men of exceptional spirit, in whose soul all of these passions and more appear not so much as events but as cataclysms, as eruptions of sensation, direction and strength, and who are capable for this reason of achievements on a scale which others can hardly imagine. In this regard, the Bible speaks of "men of spirit"—administrators such as Joseph, warriors such as Caleb and Joshua, and artists such as Betzalel, to name a few[8]—the most outstanding of individuals, whose tremendous desire for rule is directed by reason or the command of higher authority towards tasks of which only they are capable.[9] For in all things, greatness requires two characteristics: An exceptional spirit, which provides a man with the power, dedication, intensity and boldness needed to control, to order, to achieve and to build; and reason—whether that of superiors or advisers, or his own—which provides man with right and consistent aims towards which he can divert the power of the spirit.

When it is not so directed, however, the exceptional spirit becomes a monstrous growth, whose eruptions drive the individual in arbitrary or ill-conceived directions, consuming all that stands in its way without being of profit to anyone: A man will be an overly spirited fool, given over to excessive excitements regarding the objects of his desire, to childish dependence on those who pander to these fetishes, to paranoid overreactions at the slightest hint of weakening in his rule, and, above all, to uncontrollable humiliations and rages when he feels that he has lost control—which in turn lead him to every kind of desperate action to restore it. Such a man is Ahashverosh, king of Persia, who, for want of the feeling of power over others, devotes half a year of his life to filling the nobles and commoners of his empire with drink, showering them with gifts, and boasting to them of his wife, that they might better recognize his greatness.

And being such a one, Ahashverosh is the archetype of the political ruler: All spirit, he will do anything to feel that he has control over others. But having no reason of his own to speak of, he has no idea what to do with this rule. Indeed, Ahashverosh never makes a decision of substance on his own in the entire book of Esther. Instead, he is, as one rabbinic commentator has it, "an axe in the hand of the wielder,"[10] initiating neither evil nor good, but applying the full force of his authority in whatever direction will make him feel most in control at a given moment. The result is that despite having vast powers at his disposal, Ahashverosh is at all times propelled by the pressures and manipulation of those around him— as is the state itself.

With this in mind, let us return to the king's party. In the entire stew of ostentation, excess and flattery which comprises the description of the feast, perhaps the most interesting detail is the liberty which the king accords the merrymakers: "And the drinking was in accord with the law that none should be compelled, for so the king had

instructed all the officers of his house, that they should do according
to each man's will." (1:8) That the king had seen fit to issue such an
order itself indicates how unusual it was for his government to
concern itself with the will of his subjects. The presumption, of
course, was that if one were invited to a royal carnival for six months,
one came; and if one were given wine to drink in abundance, one
drank wine in abundance—and the king's officers would ensure that
this was the case. The great rabbinic exegete R. Levi emphasized the
point by suggesting that normally the officers would have preferred
to kill a guest rather than let him offend the king by abstaining:
"They had a great flagon and would pour out of it for every individual.
Even if he died, even if he went insane, they would not let him be
until he had drunk all of it."[11] In this figure, Persia is the party: And
the king's officers were themselves the flagon, pouring the king's rule
down the throats of his subjects, even unto insanity, even unto
death.

Ahashverosh, however, makes an instructive exception. He knows
that he may demonstrate his power by issuing commands and having
them obeyed, yet he senses that he can achieve more by granting a
small measure of freedom. For the spirit seeks a control over others
which is not sated by mere physical obedience. Certainly, Ahashverosh
wants to feel that his subjects fear him and will do his bidding. But
he wants much more: To truly feel he controls his people, he needs
to rule their emotions first and foremost; he needs for them to love
and respect him, and to desire his rule. There is no better way of
gaining the gratitude of others than by using power to bestow
liberty—for this means granting a gift of power to another. For those
whom Ahashverosh has invited into his palace, accustomed as they
are to submitting to the wishes of the king, this microscopic, one-
time grant of power can win their gratitude as no material gift can. It
is no coincidence, either, that the material gift of choice is alcohol, an
agent whose action is directly on the spirit, "releasing inhibitions,"

"steadying the nerves," "making the heart merry," all of these affectations deriving from a chemically enhanced sense of power and control.[12]

The climax of the festival, and of Ahashverosh's show of power, is his flaunting of Vashti the queen before the people. Her husband merry and drunk, the queen is to be escorted out by his servants "to show the peoples and the princes her beauty, for she was fair to look upon." (1:11) We are told nothing of their relationship other than this, but on the basis of Esther's treatment later on, it is safe to surmise that there is not much to it. The queen is cloistered away in a distant corner of the palace, constantly subjected to a grueling regimen of treatments to improve her appearance, texture and scent, and able to see the king only when it pleases him to summon her. And when she appears in public with him for the first time during six months of festivities, it is not as his partner in ruling, nor as his partner in life, but as another accouterment in his demonstration of total power: The empire is to admire her object beauty, and to be impressed that the king has—as the Talmudic scholar Rav depicts Ahashverosh as saying—such a "vessel" for his "use."[13]

But Vashti prefers not to serve this purpose and refuses to appear, exposing his weakness before the entire aristocracy and even before the commoners of the empire. One can hardly think of a greater humiliation: For six months he has devoted himself to the systematic elaboration of his control, seeking to extract gratitude and honor from every man whom it is within his power to reach, a meticulously orchestrated show of omnipotence. And yet on the last night, at the last moment, he is proven impotent in his own house before the eyes of the throng he has labored so long to impress. In a moment, Ahashverosh is transformed into a laughingstock, and control over his world slips through his fingers.

Anger is the emotion of the spirit which moves men to muster all of their energies and facilities and focus them on the reassertion of

control. In a situation of helplessness, one can expect to feel an
enduring shame; but where there is the possibility of recourse, the
result is rage. Thus behaved Pharaoh, when time and again he felt
himself defeated, but then out of shame was born anger once more
("Pharaoh's heart hardened"), and he turned to re-enslave the Jews
whom he had been forced to liberate.[14] Here, too, Ahashverosh seeks
a way of reasserting his power, and he turns demonstratively to the
assembled princes and wise men, as they hold back smiles of pity and
embarrassment, and asks them to name that punishment which they
would find fitting for publicly humiliating the king of all the Persians
and Medes.

Ahashverosh's move is a masterstroke. At once he turns his
personal shame into an issue of state, with himself at the helm of an
entire empire which has been insulted, inviting those assembled to
join him in doing justice and reestablishing the honor of the king.
And at least one among their number is ready to seek favor by
helping Ahashverosh escape the trap he has set for himself. Memuchan,
from among the king's ministers sitting in the first rank, hastens to
point out that the interest of the ministers and indeed of all men in
the kingdom is identical to that of the king: "It is not the king alone
who has been wronged by Vashti the queen, but all the princes, and
all the peoples in all the provinces of the king Ahashverosh. For this
deed of the queen will become known to all the women, and their
husbands will become contemptible in their eyes ... and there will be
much contempt and anger." (1:16–18)

With this, Memuchan takes up the king's cause, turning the
royal family's domestic spat into an empire-wide battle of the sexes,
with Ahashverosh representing all men against the constant challenge presented by the women in their homes. He assures the king
that, far from laughing at him, every man in his kingdom is in
sympathy with him, since women, following the queen's lead, will
leave no man safe from similar humiliation in his own home. Now

Memuchan, who "knows the precedents," decrees what must be the punishment for a wife who challenges the authority of her husband: "That Vashti come no more before the king Ahashverosh, and let the king give her royal estate to someone better than she." (1:19) The queen should be stripped of all property, position and honor, and forever banished from the sight of the king.

For challenging the power of the king, Vashti is doomed to remain a widow to a living husband, deprived of every material or emotional asset she has or could have for the rest of her life; nothing is to remain save her life itself. Such a complete annihilation of the person of the queen, publicly forcing her into permanent, complete and degraded submission, should be understood to be the natural consequence of a deed such as hers. In this way, avers Memuchan, "when the king's edict which he will issue is heard throughout all of his kingdom, vast though it be, all the wives will give honor to their husbands, from the highest to the most lowly." (1:20)

Memuchan therefore offers the king a response calculated perfectly to reassert his battered sense of his power: Ahashverosh will at once (i) prove to Vashti and all his kingdom that he alone rules, and absolutely; (ii) annihilate the queen's challenge to his control forever by ensuring that she is never in a position to shame him again; and (iii) cement the adherence, gratitude and honor of the people by promulgating a decree which amounts to a gift of power to every adult male in the kingdom—that same gesture Ahashverosh wished to achieve through the free drinking of the king's wine. Thus vindicated by law and handed back the leadership of all Persia, Ahashverosh responds enthusiastically. The king issues the decree as proposed, publishing it in every language spoken in the empire and in every province, "that every man should rule in his own house." (1:22)

With this, "the rage of the king Ahashverosh had subsided." (2:1) He has for the moment regained his precious, perfect control over his home, his kingdom and his world.

But for the more sober among the onlookers, it is impossible to feel at ease with the abrupt termination of the queen's reign, and with the leer of juvenile satisfaction which creeps across the king's features when the deed is done. In this moment the intoxication of the carnival dissipates, leaving an unobstructed view of the partymaster and the forces which move him. Gone is the king's pursuit of his subjects' affection, gone the flattering gifts of freedom and power. It becomes clear that the person of the king is a fiction, a name and a face, under which riots the crocodile spirit, devouring until it controls. Where is his reason, that he might consider and reconsider his own interest, before destroying his wife the queen for a passing slight? Where is his reason, that he might consider and reconsider the interests of his empire, before feeding pieces of it to the reptile in his breast, devouring until it controls? But the ruler is not reason, but something else. For those who recognize this, the party is a revelation, and the harbinger of far worse to come.

# ESTHER
# TWO
[2:1 – 2:23]

After these things, when the rage of the king Ahashverosh had subsided, he remembered Vashti, and what she had done, and what had been decreed against her.

The king's youths, who attended him, said: "Let fair young virgins be sought for the king. Let the king appoint officials in all the provinces of his kingdom, that they may gather together all the fair young virgins to Susa the capital, to the house of the women, to the custody of Hegai the king's chamberlain, keeper of the women, to be given their ointments. Let the young woman who pleases the king be queen in Vashti's place."

And the idea pleased the king, and he did so.

Now in Susa the capital there lived a Jew whose name was Mordechai, the son of Jair, the son of Shimi,

the son of Kish of the tribe of Benjamin: Who had
been exiled from Jerusalem among those expelled with
Jechonia, king of Judah, who had been exiled by
Nebuchadnezzar, king of Babylonia. He had raised
Hadassa, that is Esther, his uncle's daughter, for she
had neither father nor mother; the young woman was
beautiful and fair to look upon, and when her father
and mother had died, Mordechai had taken her for a
daughter.

It came to pass that when the king's commandment and his law were heard, and when many young
women were gathered together to Susa the capital,
into the custody of Hegai, that Esther was also brought
into the king's house, into the custody of Hegai, keeper
of the women. The young woman pleased him, and
she found grace before him, and he hurried to give her
her ointments and her special rations, and the seven
maids chosen to be given her out of the king's house,
and he advanced her and her maids to the best place
in the house of women. Esther had not made known
her people and her kindred, for Mordechai had instructed her that she not tell. Each and every day,

Mordechai would walk before the court of the house of women, to know how Esther fared and what was to be done with her.

Now when each young woman's turn came to go in to the king Ahashverosh after she had been twelve months under the regimen for the women — for such were the periods of anointing, six months with oil and myrrh, and six months with sweet odors and other women's ointments — This is how the young woman would come to the king: Whatever she requested would be given her to bring with her from the house of the women to the king's house. In the evening she would come, and in the morning she would go to the second house of the women, into the custody of Sha'ashgaz, the king's chamberlain, keeper of the concubines, and she would come in to the king no more, unless the king desired her and she was summoned by name.

But when it came the turn of Esther, the daughter of Avihail, the uncle of Mordechai, who had taken her for a daughter, to go in to the king, she requested nothing other than what Hegai the king's chamberlain, keeper of the women, advised — and

Esther found favor in the eyes of all who looked upon her.

Esther was taken to the king Ahashverosh in his royal house in the 10th month, that is Teveth, in year 7 of his reign. The king loved Esther more than all the women, and she found grace and favor in his eyes more than all the virgins, and he placed the royal crown on her head, and made her queen in Vashti's place. Then the king made a great feast for all his princes and his servants, the feast of Esther, and he granted the provinces a remission in taxes and gave out gifts from the king's hand. And when the virgins were gathered together again, and as Mordechai sat in the king's gate: Esther had not yet revealed her kindred or her people, as Mordechai had instructed her, for Esther did as Mordechai instructed her, just as she had growing up.

In those days, while Mordechai was sitting in the king's gate, two of the king's chamberlains, Bigtan and Teresh, from those who kept the door, were angered and sought to lay hands on the king Ahashverosh. The matter became known to Mordechai, who told it to Esther the queen, and Esther reported it to the king in Mordechai's name. The matter was investigated and it was found to be true, and they were both hanged from the gallows, and it was written in the book of chronicles in the presence of the king.

# 2

# POLITICAL FAVOR

THREE YEARS AND MORE HAVE ELAPSED since the king's humiliation and his angry banishment of the queen,[1] and Ahashverosh begins to remember Vashti with longing. The immutability of Persian law and his own pride standing in the way of any reconciliation, Ahashverosh accepts the urgings of his attendants to search for "someone better than she." It goes without saying that such a one should be more concerned with the king's wishes and less with her own than had been her predecessor, so there is no point in advertising. It is not ambitious volunteers whom Ahashverosh seeks. Instead, the order goes out for the king's officers to conscript the most attractive virgins from every corner of the empire, so that the king may have a taste of each in turn until he finds one to his liking.

Among his other failings of character, it transpires that Ahashverosh now prefers his women powerless, a fact that in context comes as little surprise. Nothing offends the spirit so much as sexual cravings, which in and of themselves constitute overwhelming evidence of need, lack of control and powerlessness. Because sex provides proof of such manifest need, sexual relationships naturally paint every individual at his most vulnerable. This is why the longings of love are so easily transformed into rage, which arises in the effort to reassert the control lost when desire is confronted with rejection.

Ahashverosh has already suffered the consequences of allowing a woman to assert her own will in a relationship, and it is likely that fear of repeating the mistake—perhaps even a fear of women—has been responsible for the lengthy delay before he is prepared to return to the field. When finally the king does decide to reenter the arena, he makes sure that the game is rigged so that, as with his six-month winefest for winning the favor of the nobles, he believes he cannot lose. The virgins are not asked whether they wish to love him. They are merely to submit, each inexperienced girl alone facing the might of the empire, giving up her hopes and dreams and her own loved ones, and daring not object for fear for her life. Moreover, her submission on the single night of her exposure to him is guaranteed, for if she in any way incurs his displeasure, she is doomed to spend the rest of her days in childless imprisonment or worse. As for Ahashverosh himself, he is as protected from rejection as no man has ever been: He has never seen her before and will never see her again unless he wills it, and there is no one who will ever find out what takes place between them on that night. Nor must he fear that another in the kingdom will be told in the dead of some night, years hence, that he was a better man than the king, for she will have no other man. In such a relationship, the person of Ahashverosh is elevated to absolute mastery, while hers is essentially annihilated. It is the perfected institutionalization of rape, in which the king's will is the only will, his power the only power. Whether or not others have succeeded in implementing Memuchan's decree in their own families,

Ahashverosh, at least, has hit upon a way in which he may completely
"rule in his own house."

Into the king's dragnet falls a Jew named Mordechai, and his
orphaned cousin Hadassa, whom he has raised since childhood. We
know next to nothing about Mordechai—only that he is a Jew, and
therefore "exiled from Jerusalem among those expelled with Jechonia,
king of Judah, who had been exiled by Nebuchadnezzar, king of
Babylonia" (2:6)—and that is all. The narrative is unconcerned with
Mordechai's personality or personal biography, and concentrates
only on this, the central point: That being a Jew, he has been
stripped of his own nation and capital city, and has lost his own king
and any capacity to wield power in his own defense. That is, his
position with respect to the king and the empire is essentially no
different from that of the virgins. The Jews, like the virgins, have
been forced to give up everything of independent value to them and
are, it seems, powerless before the will of the state and its ruler.[2] Only
one echo of a fact escapes the anonymity in which Mordechai is
cloaked: The fact that this Jew lives not in "the town of Susa" where
the Jewish quarter was located, (3:15, 8:15) but in the midst of "Susa
the capital," (2:5) the fortress city which was the center of Persian
power, and the focus of every effort to control it, direct it or wield it.

On the surface, it appears that Mordechai's dealings with the
authorities are straightforward: Persia accepts only submission, and
submit to its will he does. When confronted with the demand that he
deliver the girl to be deflowered and tossed into the harem, he acquiesces,
understanding that whatever might be the terrors and degradation of
the night with the king and its aftermath, they cannot justify drawing
his anger and courting death. Thereafter, he instructs that she not
make known her people and her kindred, (2:10) although he knows
that to hide her identity as a Jew will guarantee that she will have to
make sacrifices in what religious observance she has been raised with.
What is more, although he has raised her with the Jewish name of

Hadassa, he counsels her to go by a Persian one in the court: Esther, meaning "star."[3] And since Esther "did as Mordechai instructed her, just as she had growing up," (2:20) it appears that passivity is her own strategy as well: That it is her complete submissiveness, along with the fact that she is "beautiful and fair to look upon," (2:7) which makes her the favorite first of Hegai, the eunuch in charge of the women, and then of the king himself. In Esther, the king had finally found a dispirited poppet who could be the answer to his dreams of domination.

Yet an incident related immediately after the account of Esther's bid for the throne makes it clear that this view of Mordechai's relationship with Persia is mistaken, and that the lessons Esther learned from her cousin were in fact of a substantially different nature. The narrative relates that by the time of the festivities surrounding the coronation of the new queen, and probably long before then, Mordechai had fallen into the habit of "sitting in the king's gate" (2:19)—the receiving area in which the supplicants of the empire waited for an audience with the king or tried to obtain one when they had business. In the absence of any sort of legislature or assembly, all of the most important politics of the empire were of necessity conducted there. Of course, those who make it their business to "sit" in the king's gate are no more inert than those today who have a "seat" in parliament, and the obvious inference is that Mordechai was by this time a known figure, deeply involved in the intrigues of the court. Thus when a conspiracy is hatched to assassinate the king involving members of his own bodyguard, Mordechai is sufficiently trusted, or else sufficiently skillful at bartering rumors and bribes, to be able to obtain reliable information concerning the plot, including the identities of the conspirators. (His talents in this regard appear again later when he passes Esther inside information from a supposedly private conversation between the king and his vizier. (4:7)) Once in possession of this intelligence, Mordechai tips off Esther who goes straight to the king, thereby setting off an investigation which results in the conviction and hanging of two members of the guard. (2:21–23)

Mordechai therefore purposely places himself in a position in which he can be privy to sensitive information, and then, on his own initiative, risks himself in order to take sides and influence the political struggles of the empire. Now, none of this is in any sense submissive. Instead, it reminds us that there are in fact three possible courses of action in the face of a regime such as that of Ahashverosh: Resistance, submission, and active support of the despot. From the role Mordechai plays in foiling the conspiracy, it is difficult to avoid the conclusion that he prefers not the second course, but the third.

Incongruous though this seems at first blush, Mordechai's reasoning is sensible. Ahashverosh's rule may be egregious in many respects, but it is for the time being not overtly hostile to the Jews. This is not to say that Persia is clean of anti-Semitism; just the opposite is true. And it is precisely *because* of this widespread antagonism towards the Jews that Mordechai is willing to accept Ahashverosh's relatively benign authoritarianism as the best of the available evils. There is no reason to think that any regime that might follow the overthrow of the king would be any better, either for the Jews or for anyone else, and there is every reason to believe it could be worse, particularly as Mordechai is familiar with the actual conspirators. Where the only alternative to bad government is something worse, there exists no reason to choose resistance. There is no value in risking death where nothing will be gained by it.

Submission is the easiest option. Men tend to abdicate from making decisions, from taking actions, from bothering and troubling. To become an implement in the hands of others, to let the light of the spirit go out, this is an option that Mordechai could have exercised from the very beginning—not seeking to disguise Esther's lineage, not coming every day to inquire after her well-being since all was lost, not making his presence felt in the court day in and day out, and certainly not coming to the rescue of the tyrant who had stolen his adopted daughter from him. Such is the course taken by most men at most times, beating the path of least resistance on the assumption that this way will draw the least attention and result in the least trouble.

But much as men wish to misunderstand this point, the truth is that in politics at least, the path of least resistance is never likely to be the path of least trouble. Even under the most serene circumstances, there is never any certainty that the menace which has been accommodated by submission today will not become something even worse on the morrow; and one may cast an eye at history and conclude that the eventual appearance of this something worse is even probable—and how much the more so in a viper's nest such as the court of Susa. Mordechai understands that with Esther in the clutches of Ahashverosh, and with himself and the entire Jewish people similarly powerless before the king, to follow his every order in passive submission is simply to wait for the fall of an axe that must come sooner or later.

The only recourse is to attempt to accumulate some measure of power that can be used for defense when the necessity arises. To the Jews of the quarter and many others, such an enterprise must have seemed chimerical: With their people scattered across the face of the earth, the idea of mounting a defense against anything must have appeared preposterous. Mordechai, however, lived in another world. In the political thicket of the capital, power might be elusive, but it was there to be had so long as one were willing to learn its rules and play its game: In Susa, even the weak could become powerful if they secured the king's willingness to use his authority in their favor—as politicians say, to "gain favor" with him, or to "gain influence" with him.

Ironically, there is virtually no way that this can be accomplished through passive submission to the king's commands. Countless are those whose flaccid spirits crave the rush of power in their chest, even if it be someone else's power, so that a man like Ahashverosh is invariably surrounded by a thousand flatterers seeking to serve, and whose sole virtue is that they part like warm butter before the knife of his will. But these the ruler can always replace with others just like them, so he values them little and develops no special interest in retaining them. As soon as they fail in something, or begin expecting substantial returns for their services, they become more trouble than they are worth, and the king quickly disposes of them.

Of immense value to the king, on the other hand, are those who are not submissive, but who initiate action that his will be done. To understand the difference, one need only consider the assassination attempt which Mordechai succeeds in aborting. Mordechai receives no instructions from the king. He is independently alert to the king's interest, and is willing to employ his judgment and talents in the king's service unbeknown to Ahashverosh himself—in a situation fraught with risk, in which assisting him means siding against would-be killers who may rule the empire by morning, and in which only independent and immediate action can be of any use. No number of obedient sycophants could have sufficed to save the king under such circumstances.

Passive obedience offers the king the use of another body; Mordechai's activism offers him the use of a mind. The king has millions of bodies at his command, as many as he needs for virtually any task. He lacks not body, nor spirit, but mind: The king's own consciousness, even if he were the wisest of men, is incapable of knowing all that must be known for effective rule, of paying attention to all that must be attended to, of deciding all that must be decided, of giving all the orders that must be given, of supervising that all these orders are done. And the question of whose mind is to watch over the king's interest in those times, places and situations in which he himself is unable to know, decide and issue commands, hounds every ruler from the first moment of his reign. What he needs is men who will be "second to the king" (10:3), acting in his stead but for his benefit: Men who, if forgotten for an hour or a year, will have done all that he would have willed from them and more. By watching to see who is actively taking initiative to see that his will is done, the king can learn whose interests he may profitably consider to be his own, and he comes to rely on such individuals as a matter of course. It is these whom the king truly appreciates, and it is these who would truly harm him if they withdrew from his service. For both these reasons it is to them that he may be willing to grant substantial favors and real influence.

Thus while there is certainly no love lost between Mordechai the Jew and the despot whom he may never even have met, he acts to save the king's life, endangering himself to demonstrate that when the worst has come to pass, there is at least one individual upon whom the king can truly rely. Mordechai cannot know for certain that something will come of this, but under the circumstances only such efforts to gain power through the favor of the king offer a chance of success.

Let us consider two biblical precedents for Mordechai's approach to building up Jewish power through the painstaking work of accumulating political favor, precedents to which we will have cause to return at different junctures in the narrative: Joseph, who had risen to be the vizier of the Egyptian Pharaoh a thousand years before; and Daniel, who, according to the account in the book of Daniel, had been slated to reach a similar position in the Persian court under Darius, several decades before the story of Esther takes place.[4]

Joseph had begun his political career in the society of his eleven brothers as an intelligence gatherer for his father Jacob, whose control over his independent and sometimes violent sons had been slipping with age. Scenes immediately preceding Joseph's appearance in the narrative suggest a deterioration into anarchy, with two of the older brothers massacring the inhabitants of an entire town against their father's objections, and another sleeping with one of his father's wives.[5] Lest the point be missed, the rabbis elaborated on the situation even further, suspecting the brothers not only of sexual misconduct, but of tormenting the younger brothers by referring to them as slaves, and of perpetrating unspeakable cruelties against the animals in their care.[6] In this context, it is apparent that Joseph's struggle against his brothers is from the start an attempt to reassert discipline on behalf of his father: "The lad was with the sons of Bilha and the sons of Zilpa, his father's wives, and Joseph brought his father their evil report."[7] The natural consequence is that he wins his father's favor, as expressed in the infamous gift of the striped coat: "Now Israel loved Joseph more than all his children because he ministered to him in his old age, and he made him a striped coat."[8] By demonstrating that his own will can be relied upon as a second to his father's, Joseph wins increasing influence and authority—and the hatred of his rivals among the brothers, who eventually decide to destroy him by selling him into slavery.

But far from being destroyed by being enslaved in Egypt, Joseph flourishes in an environment in which he can apply his uncanny skills. He throws himself into active pursuit of the interests of a series of masters, each of whom responds just as his father Jacob had, despite the fact that he is a slave and a foreigner, the epitome of powerlessness. Thus with regard to Potiphar, captain of Pharaoh's guard, who buys Joseph from the traders, we are told: "His master saw that the Eternal was with him and that the Eternal made all that he did prosper in his hand. And Joseph found favor in his eyes and served him, and he made him overseer of his house, and all that he had he put in his charge."[9] Later, Joseph similarly ingratiates himself with the keeper of the prison where he is sent as a ward, and ultimately he makes the same inroads with Pharaoh himself—

applying his cunning to reaching the high office of vizier, buying all the land in Egypt for the royal estate, and levying unprecedented taxes on the land for the benefit of the king.[10] And because of the investment he has made at winning favor in the Egyptian court, Joseph is able to use his authority to assist the Jews, feeding them and sheltering them at Pharaoh's expense during the years of famine which could easily have destroyed them all.[11]

Daniel, too, is well equipped with the kinds of traits which might make him a favorite of the Babylonian and Persian kings who are his masters. Like Esther and Joseph, he is attractive in appearance; he can interpret dreams after the fashion of the idolaters as Joseph can; and he has various other skills and knowledge as well.[12] But none of these could propel him to the top of Persian politics unless he shared with Joseph an understanding of what it means to be "second to the king," applying these exceptional talents to protecting the king's interest, which he in fact does: "As for me, in the first year of Darius of Media, I stood up to support him and to strengthen him."[13] When Darius promotes him to prominence, it is to a panel of triumvirs intended to watch over (and spy on) the empire's officials, "so that the king should have no loss."[14] Obviously, such a position is one of great trust, reserved only for those known to be able to pursue the king's interest with selflessness and enthusiasm. And Darius is not disappointed. Daniel quickly "became distinguished above the triumvirs and governors because of the exceptional spirit that was in him," and so thoroughly does he win Darius' trust, that he decides to make him vizier. Moreover, Daniel's service to Darius succeeds in turning the Persian king to a pro-Jewish course which results in his issuing an edict granting official protection to the Jewish faith.[15]

Joseph stands as the prototype of the Jewish second to the king, whose model clearly informs the careers of Daniel, Mordechai, Esther and others in imperial Persia centuries later.[16] But it is Esther, once she has been stolen out of her family and deposited in Ahashverosh's house of women, who proves to be the most gifted subsequent practitioner of Joseph's art. With her arrival in the precincts of the palace, the narrative relates that she immediately begins to gain the favor of those around her, beginning with Hegai, the keeper of the virgins. According to the literal meaning of the Hebrew, "Esther made good in his eyes," (2:9) as a result of which he is kind to her, advances her in the sequence of maidens who will come in to the king, and gives her the best of the facilities available. Later, as she gains in confidence, we are told that she "found favor in the eyes of all who looked upon her." (2:15) And finally, as Joseph was loved more than all his brothers, "the king loved Esther more than all the women, and she found grace and favor in his eyes more than all the virgins, and he placed the royal crown on her head, and made her queen in Vashti's place." (2:17)

Concerning Esther's personality and motives prior to ascending to the throne, the narrative is sparse. But in the one place where it bothers to explain why everyone is so taken by Esther, it is clear that it is not beauty which is driving her success, but an understanding of the workings of political favor much like that which dictates Mordechai's moves in the court. The scene concerns Hegai, the keeper of the women, whose responsibility it is to ensure that the girls brought in to the king night after night are at the pinnacle of their attractiveness. In order to bolster their confidence and allow each some measure of personality, the girls are permitted to take with them whatever accouterments and accessories may catch their fancy for their one night with the king: Jewelry, flowers, musical instruments, food, gifts. Esther's response is captured in a single, essential verse: "When it came the turn of Esther ... to go in to the king, she requested nothing other than what Hegai the king's chamberlain, keeper of the women, advised—and Esther found favor in the eyes of all who looked upon her." (2:15)

There can be no appreciating this statement without considering Hegai himself, a man whose life's work is catering to the sexual caprice of the king. The significance of this fact can be understood by recalling that Pharaoh, irritated at his wine steward and baker, had thrown both into prison and then ordered the baker hanged.[17] Hegai may very well have had a particular affection for some girls over others, but it is a mistake to think that such considerations would have altered his professional behavior where his livelihood and his life itself were at stake: Hegai's only real concern is to please the king with a suitable bride as quickly as possible, and so avert the imminent danger that Ahashverosh will become impatient with his work, or otherwise offended by it, and fly into a rage. His rapidly advancing Esther after being impressed with her is therefore not a gesture to her, but a career move of his own: The sooner the king has found his queen, the better. In this regard there is a tension between the girls' regaling themselves as they deem fit when going in to the king—which may have been the custom in the house of women well before his time—and his own interest in putting on the best possible show.

In her dealings with Hegai, Esther succeeds because she is her cousin's cousin. Rather than doing what the others do, Esther makes it clear to Hegai that she considers him to be the expert, and that his interest is identical with hers. Far from being passive, she makes it her business to understand what it is he wants, and seeks ways to advance his will with the active support of her own. This is the meaning of "she requested nothing other than what Hegai ... advised—and Esther found favor in the eyes of all who looked upon her." Esther finds favor with all who have power over her, just as Joseph had in Egypt, by convincing them that in all her doings, she seeks their interest. The rabbis of the Talmud used different metaphors for explaining this, with R. Judah comparing Esther to a sculpture which a thousand people can look upon, each seeing something that he personally admires.[18] Similarly, while the narrative suggests that a foreign wife who raised one's children in an alien tongue is a particular sign of dishonor and lack of control, R. Eleazar suspected that Esther put others at ease to such a degree that every man mistook her for a member of his own people.[19] R. Joshua ben Korha takes the argument to the extreme, claiming that Esther was not really physically beautiful at all—and that the attraction to her was exclusively the result of this appeal.[20]

When Esther finally comes to the king, it is this ability which turns the trick and makes her queen. By this point, Ahashverosh has had his fill of submissive girls who receive him as the trauma that he is, and of more assertive ones who remind him of Vashti by insisting on doing things their own way. When Esther comes to him, she looks first for what he desires, and makes sure he obtains all he wishes and more. And it is difficult to escape the conclusion of some of the rabbis that on this first night, this concern finds its expression in rather sensual terms: "If he wanted to find in her the taste of a virgin, he found it; if the taste of a married woman, he found it."[21]

But it is equally clear that Ahashverosh's yearning to replace Vashti cannot have been driven principally by his sexual appetite: Had his melancholia been sexual, his harem should have sufficed to treat it. His problem is, not surprisingly, one of the spirit, one of lack of control. For despite his abusive behavior toward her, Vashti had, it seems, offered the king a certain security which his other "vessels" and playthings had not been able to replace. Evidently a strong woman, the queen had been not only something to show off and to relieve his hungers. During those times when she was not resisting him, Vashti had apparently been a personality capable of increasing the king's sense of self-worth through the reassurance that one such as she could love him, of soothing the pangs of his spirit by offering him stability— crucial functions of love which are too often believed to be appropriate only to a mother figure. And it is here, more even than in the sexual, that Esther's personality truly shines. She understands that in the relations between man and woman, no less than in politics, the limp submission of doing what one is told, while superficially appearing to grant power, in reality grants very little. The feeling of power over others is greatest when one feels control over something of independent worth, something which might have resisted fiercely if it had so desired, but which *chooses* to be of service. Independent action rather than submission is thus the turnkey to love, just as it is to political favor. By giving Ahashverosh her initiative and the active use of her strength in pursuit of his interest, Esther bestows on the king a gift of power—precisely that for which he has so desperately longed, and for which he is immediately willing to make her queen.

Of course, in choosing against resistance and submission, and in favor of active support of the despot, both Esther and Mordechai open themselves to the charge that they have been blinded by their concern with ends; that they have corrupted themselves, prostituted themselves; that all this truck with tyrants constitutes a willful collaboration with evil, and that no good man should be involved in such endeavors, much less a good Jew. To be sure, Esther's concerted effort to actually become queen by means of her bedroom manner ranks rather high on the scale of collaboration, and Mordechai's saving the life of this Ahashverosh is only somewhat more tolerable. For if the king is such a villain, who would want to help him in achieving his desires? If this is the meaning of political favor, then perhaps such favor is immoral, a descent into filth and degradation? As the great medieval exegete Rashi suggests, Mordechai's entry into the world of government and political favor may of necessity have entailed a departure from all that is absolute and true.[22] If this is what Esther and Mordechai must do in order to succeed, would it not be better to refuse, to abstain, to die rather than play according to rules dictated by impure men?

Since politics is the pursuit of the possible in the world, impure and corrupt though it is, to answer this question is to pass judgment on politics itself. And later on in the tale, once Mordechai and Esther have achieved a degree of political success and find themselves forced to determine which Persians should live and which should die, the question of the legitimacy of political means for the Jews, and for all moral men, is to return again in force.[23]

# ESTHER THREE

[3:1 – 3:15]

After these things the king Ahashverosh promoted Haman, the son of Hamedata the Agagite, and advanced him, and set his seat above all the princes who were around him. And all the king's servants who were in the king's gate bowed and prostrated themselves before Haman, for the king had so ordained concerning him, but Mordechai did not bow nor prostrate himself.

The king's servants who were in the king's gate said to Mordechai: "Why do you violate the king's commandment?"

It came to pass that when they spoke to him day in and day out and he did not listen to them, they told Haman, to see whether Mordechai's words would stand, for he had told them that he was a Jew. When Haman saw that Mordechai did not bow nor prostrate himself, Haman was filled with rage.

But it was disdainful in his eyes to lay hands on Mordechai alone, for they had revealed to him Mordechai's people, so that Haman sought to annihilate all the Jews throughout the entire kingdom of Ahashverosh, the people of Mordechai.

In the 1st month, the month of Nisan, in the year 12 of the king Ahashverosh, they cast the pur, that is the lot, before Haman, testing day by day and month by month, until they reached the 12th month, the month of Adar.

Then Haman said to the king Ahashverosh: "There is a certain people scattered and dispersed among the people in all the provinces of your kingdom, and their laws are different from those of other peoples, and the king's laws they do not keep, so that it is of no benefit for the king to tolerate them. If it please the king, let it be written that they be destroyed, and I will weigh out ten thousand talents of silver into the hands of those who have charge of the business, to bring it into the king's treasuries."

The king took his ring from his hand and gave it to Haman, the son of Hamedata the Agagite, the persecutor of the Jews. And the king said to Haman: "The silver is given to you, and the people, to do with them as you see fit."

The king's scribes were called on the 13th day of the 1st month, and it was written according to all that Haman had commanded, to the king's satraps, and to the governors who were over every province, and to the princes of every people, to every province in its own script and to every people in their own tongue, in the name of the king Ahashverosh and sealed with the king's ring. And the letters were sent by courier to all the king's provinces, instructing to annihilate, to kill and to destroy all the Jews, the young and the elderly, children and women, in one day — on the 13th day of the 12th month, the month of Adar — and to take their property for plunder. Copies of the document to be given out as law in every province were distributed to all the peoples that they might prepare themselves for that day. The couriers went out in haste at the king's behest, and the decree was given out in Susa the capital. And the king and Haman sat down to their drink, but the town of Susa was left in turmoil.

# 3

# THE ENEMY

SINCE MEN ARE FREE, POLITICS CAN never deal in certainties, but only in probabilities—so that while everything may depend on the political move of a righteous man, even his best calculations cannot prevent the worst if someone else has prepared better and struck with greater skill. And so it is in Esther: Mordechai's interference in the attempt on the king's life—intended to gain him favor with the king and his advisers—instead plays into the hands of another, who has for years been moving, probing, pressing for just such an opportunity. And in providing him with this opportunity, Mordechai also ensures the ruin of his own hopes of gaining influence with the king, instead bringing himself into open confrontation with Ahashverosh's court.

The investigation of Ahashverosh's closest servants reveals that Mordechai's tip had been correct. Two of them had indeed conspired to murder the king, and the results of the inquiry bring about their discreditation and subsequent execution. Others among his officials are exonerated, but not without damaging the king's trust in them and their own capacity to perform their duties. Additional conspiracies are considered possible, but the king's advisers and the princes of the empire disagree as to where the threat may lie, and few of them are themselves above suspicion. Thus while the immediate danger may have passed, it is clear that the effects of the attempted coup cannot so quickly be repaired. Like Vashti's insubordination, the treachery of his trusted officers leaves Ahashverosh exposed, before the kingdom and in his own eyes: While he presumes to possess the power to rule the known world, it becomes apparent that he cannot even tell what is happening in the palace at Susa. And just as Vashti's rebellion leads him to reassert himself by deposing and banishing her, so too does the rebellion of the king's servants lead him to take drastic action to grind them all under heel. He responds to the chaos with the imposition of a figure he believes will be able to restore order, and whom he intends to inspire awe in other would-be conspirators: Haman the Agagite, before whom, Ahashverosh decrees, the entire political leadership of the empire is expected to pay obeisance.

The appointment and the heavy-handedness with which it is abruptly imposed cannot have been popular. The many advisers of the court and the princes and governors of the empire, each immersed in his own efforts to win the support of the king and gain influence over his government, suddenly learn they have to humble themselves before the new vizier—someone with whom they are certainly familiar, but whose upstart position in the court is evident from that fact that he had not even been worthy of mentioning as one of the king's advisers at the party a few years earlier. Mordechai himself considers the appointment and the way it has been carried out to be an outrage, and cannot reconcile himself to it. When confronted with the demand to prostrate himself before the vizier, he refuses to obey, defiantly declaring himself to be a Jew when asked for an explanation. Haman, enraged in turn, moves to eliminate this first threat to his authority—by ordering the massacre, eleven months hence, of every Jew in the empire.

Why does Mordechai refuse to obey the decree of the king? Nothing in Jewish law or custom forbids a Jew to bow before a ruler, and there is every reason to presume that when in the presence of Ahashverosh in earlier years, Mordechai had indeed bowed to him, as had everyone else in the empire. Indeed, Esther herself goes so far as to fall to the floor before the king in supplication later on in the story. (8:3) What is the difference between bowing to Ahashverosh, which is done without hesitation, and bowing to the vizier, for which it is worth endangering everything of value? The meaning of the book of Esther turns on there being a compelling answer to this question. For without such a reason it can be sensibly claimed that the treatment of Mordechai as a hero for the later salvation of the Jews is exaggerated and even absurd—since it is his own stubbornness which draws Haman's ire in the first place, making an enemy of him and bringing on the decree of annihilation. Rather than being the savior of the Jews, Mordechai should in this case be the culprit by whose intransigence the Jews are nearly annihilated root and branch.

Mordechai's public resistance to Haman's authority strikes a dissonant chord in another way: It contradicts everything that he has come to stand for throughout the first seven years of Ahashverosh's reign. Until this point, he hides his identity as a Jew and advises Esther to do the same, he seeks to be accepted at the king's gate and to be taken into the confidence of the king's advisers, and he goes out of his way to make himself useful to the king, even saving his life. As for acts of Jewish identification on his part, whether in public or in private, we hear nothing. Neither Esther's intermarriage nor anything else is able to inspire him to leave the path of accommodation and resist the government, and certainly not to violate the king's laws and embark on an open confrontation with his officials. Suddenly, we are told that he disdains to offer respect to the new vizier, and refuses to assist in the consolidation of his rule by contributing to the public's acceptance of him. He challenges the king as well, in effect denying that Ahashverosh has the authority to elevate Haman in such a way. Most important, Mordechai determines that if this battle is to be fought, he must fight it as a Jew, and he proceeds to announce what has not been known to many of the courtiers until now: That he is a Jew, and that this, somehow, is the reason for his collision with the vizier.

On the surface, it is as though Mordechai has recanted everything he has ever believed about his relationship with the Persian state. But Mordechai has not changed: It is Persia that has changed. To make sense of the revolution in Mordechai's behavior we must first understand the revolution that has taken place in the king's government, and the meaning of the coming to power of this vizier, this Agagite.

# 4

# THE TRUE STATE

HAMAN'S INSTALLATION HERALDS a dramatic shift in the nature of government in Persia. What had only recently been a state whose actions were driven by the hazardous buffoonery of the king's need to feel powerful, now embarks on a purposive drive to impose total political rule through terror and violence; an unpleasant but tolerable regime becomes one of injustice and idolatry. How does Mordechai come to believe that such a sea change in the motives of the state has come about?

While the narrative is once again sparse, we know several important facts about Haman's meteoric rise in the Persian court:

(i) Ahashverosh promotes Haman "after these things" (3:1)—that is, as an immediate result of the attack on his life in the previous episode;

(ii) The king takes the unprecedented step of setting Haman "above all the princes who were around him," (3:1) when prior to this we hear of the prominence and importance of "the seven princes of Persia and Media, who saw the king's face, and who sat first in the kingdom" (1:14);

(iii) The king commands "all the king's servants who were in the king's gate" (3:2) to prostrate themselves before Haman—in effect ordering the entire political leadership of the empire to humble itself before him.

The force of these innovations seems clear enough. Until this time, the narrative describes Ahashverosh's government as being open to influence from numerous directions, and Ahashverosh himself as respecting and relying on a large cast of nobles and staff to provide him with sound advice and direction. This is particularly evident in that Memuchan, the least of the seven princes present at the king's table, is permitted to speak before the others and to advise the king on a matter as personal as the fate of his queen; as well as from the fact that the search to find a new royal consort is instituted at the urging of an anonymous clutch of assistants referred to only as "the king's young men." (2:2) One must suspect that these two examples bespeak a far larger group of individuals who have the king's ear in the early stages of the tale, and this should not be surprising. The ruler of even the smallest country, and certainly of an empire, must make educated decisions on a vast range of subjects: On war and foreign relations, financial policy and taxes, religion and education, law, internal government and the maintenance of the power of the state, as well as on a host of local issues affecting the appeasement and functioning of every individual province, not to mention the management of the king's personal properties and the administration of his own royal person. Issues as sensitive as the king's personal security and his search for a wife are matters that must be delegated to experts whose opinions he is likely to treat as decisive. On every subject, the king must have trusted opinions, preferably several, to enable him to hear out the different aspects of an issue and make the best possible decision.

Indeed, the narrative goes out of its way in the first two chapters to stress that prior to Haman's elevation, it had been the king's habit to seek advice from *all* whom he believed to have an understanding of law and justice (1:13)—and to list by name no fewer than *eighteen* of Ahashverosh's advisers and servants who had a measure of influence on his decisions: Seven advisers on law and policy, seven administrators of the court (whom we know to play a pivotal role in policy as well from Harvona's crucial interjection at the climax of the story), two security men and two royal matchmakers. And all of these in addition to the throng of courtesans and politicos such as Mordechai who shift about the king's gate looking for some service to render.

In this maelstrom of voices competing for favor, trust, attention and control, the elevation of Haman constitutes not merely the promotion of one voice at the expense of the competition, as usually happens when one adviser proves himself to be more able than others. After the attempt on his life, Ahashverosh is rather paranoid—and in particular he becomes frightened of the tumult and confusion which is the political storm constantly taking place around him. He suddenly realizes that he does not really understand the aims of many of those pushing to be close to him, princes, advisers, lawyers, officers and servants. While most may be innocent of criminal intent, they all look to him much as had the two security men before their betrayal: Constantly maneuvering and plotting, shifting and challenging and pressing their points of view. Who knows which are benign and which lethal? Who could know?

Terrified of the implications of this perpetual battle for power, with him at the center, Ahashverosh's instinct is identical to that of countless other utopians and totalitarians: He determines to end history. By positioning Haman above all else, Ahashverosh seeks to terminate the politics of the court, rendering all his servants silent and harmless by making them answerable to a single enforcer whose capacity to terrorize will be unquestioned.[1] The fact that the court is prostrating itself before a relative newcomer is all the better for humiliating the rest of the courtesans and emphasizing the power of the king to do as he pleases. This was a point the rabbis stressed by asserting that the vizier had previously been a barber[2]—lowly and servile, but with the unquestioned capacity to slit the throats of the mighty; the same idea could be expressed by assuming that Haman had been a brutally successful provincial governor, brought in to do the same work in the court. In either case, it is clear that Haman, though also a man of overwhelming spirit, brings to the service of the king a quality he lacks—the methodical purposiveness and direction of the razor, which will cut all that is uneven down to the stubble. Whether one was a courtier of long standing or a commoner, the new rule was intended to crush all aspiration and place all in order, so that henceforth Ahashverosh would have to hear only one, trusted voice: Haman's. And the narrative reflects this new reality by literally silencing everyone else. After the vizier's installation, no opinion is recorded in the palace other than those expressed by Haman, and none of the king's other advisers and servants is even worth mentioning by name. Moreover, from his subsequent acquiescence in Haman's plot to murder the Jews, it is clear that the king is deadly serious in his intention to distance himself from all advisers, and listen only to the one. As Ahashverosh is in love, so he is in politics: Just as he had extinguished the will of his queen and instituted in her place a system of dealing with women only through silent compulsion, so too would he now extinguish the will of his servants and institute in their place a system of dealing with the empire only through silent compulsion.

Yet stunning as may have been the king's decision to elevate
Haman above all his advisers—and his subsequent decision to remove the signet ring from his own hand and place it in Haman's
keeping, symbolically delegating to him all of his authority (3:10)—it
remains unclear why all this should have been so difficult for
Mordechai to accept. For what possible difference could it make
whether absolute authority was exercised by Ahashverosh or by his
vizier?

The Talmud touches on the question of what Mordechai believed to be fundamentally wrong with the new arrangement when it
asks what arguments he must have made to rally gentile opposition
to Haman's installation and to his decree against the Jews, which
follows no more than a few weeks later. According to Rav, Mordechai
argues that: "Haman has raised himself above Ahashverosh."[3] On
this reading, Mordechai attributes criminality to Haman's behavior
from the outset—claiming that through his machinations he has
succeeded in usurping the authority of the king. This may well have
been an argument that could have stirred up the Persians against the
new vizier, but it suffers as a motive for Mordechai himself, not least
because it is false. At no point in the narrative does Ahashverosh
actually lose control over Haman, although he does fear this possibility. The vizier never makes a move without the king's permission
from the day he takes office to the very end. What is more, this line of
argument fails to resolve the central question of Mordechai's motive
for resisting Haman. For if the vizier were merely taking the king's
place as the absolute authority in the realm, why should Mordechai
have treated him any differently from Ahashverosh, or any other
eastern despot?

A second opinion cited in the Talmud, however, cuts deeper into
the matter. According to Shmuel, Mordechai's problem with the
installation of the vizier is that: "The king below has prevailed over
the king above."[4] That is, that Ahashverosh himself has set the state

on a new and evil course, arrogating to himself authority which rightly belongs only to God.

But what does this mean? What authority does God claim over non-Jewish states, over any state? And what does it mean for a king such as Ahashverosh to prevail over God?

The point of departure here is that God concerns himself with the peoples of all nations, as he tells Jonah of the pagan city of Ninveh: "Should I not be concerned for Ninveh, for this great city, in which there are more than one hundred twenty thousand people, who do not know their right hand from their left, as well as much livestock?"[5] Although God is sometimes forced to repay wrongdoing with destruction, his essential position is one of concern for the men of all nations, whose well-being he desires and demands of those who can affect it. Foremost among these, of course, are the rulers of nations, in whose hands are placed the lives of so many others. When these rulers earnestly pursue the good of their people, God and his servants stand up to strengthen them, as Daniel "stood up to strengthen" Darius—the ruler who seeks the good of his subjects does God's will. As Jeremiah said of Josiah, king of Judah: "Did he not ... do justice and righteousness? Then it was well with him. He judged the cause of the poor and the needy. Then it was well. Is this not to know me? says the Eternal."[6] Thus all nations should be ruled for their well-being: The ruler who strives for this serves God himself, even if he is an idolater such as Darius. The ruler who does not rebels against God, raising his arbitrary desires above those of the King above.

All this is common to the entire Jewish tradition, as far back as the destruction of Sodom for its cruelty and oppression, at the beginning of the books of Moses.[7] What is new in the book of Esther is that it was composed in a later age, during roughly the period when philosophers were seeking structural theories for how to produce the "best regime"— attempting to assess, for instance, whether one produces a better state by structuring it as a monarchy so that ultimate authority is in the hands of one man, or as a democracy in which authority is given to the many (having experienced both, they advocated monarchy). Esther, too, speaks to its time by bringing the search for structural explanations to the classic Jewish problem of the difference between good and evil rulership. It claims that what causes the state, never too highly regarded in the biblical tradition, to be tolerable is its openness to competing views—as represented by the eighteen advisers surrounding Ahashverosh at the beginning of the tale. What makes the state bestial is the inclination of the powerful to shut out competing voices which should be heard if one is to make a rational judgment. In this case the government becomes nothing better than a clique of arrogant men sitting down to revel in their power, while the people suffer from their decisions: "The king and Haman sat down to their drink, but the town of Susa was left in turmoil." (3:15)

Let us consider more closely how this theory works to explain the difference between the good state and that which "prevails over the king above."

It was Plato who first spoke of the state as a ship, and this metaphor is instructive. For it makes no difference who is captain or how he has attained this position. If he is a poor navigator, the ship sinks.[8] Of course, this is true with regard to the individual, as well: If he is a poor navigator, he will just as surely bring about his own personal ruin. But unlike the individual, the decisions of the state affect the lives and deaths of millions, and so it is all the more important that the state, which has no mind or will of its own, be piloted by the best possible reasoning: The ruler must issue laws and judgments and decisions in response to every situation and question that arises—and all these must be correct. Thus while the state rules, its purpose is to rule truly, and the true state is that whose ruler understands the reality of what is taking place in his state, and what must be done, and uses his power to implement this truth.

The Greek affinity for monarchies was based on the belief in the possibility of a virtuous and scholarly king, who, by virtue of being a philosopher as well as a ruler, would be able provide the state with the wisdom necessary to flourish. But the philosopher-king was a type which the Bible, for all its idealism, would have considered rather unlikely. Instead, the biblical tradition held rulers in general—and there is no reason to think that this assessment should be restricted only to monarchy—to be much like Ahashverosh: A great deal of spirit and very little brain. The ruler, like the state itself, was a thing of immense power, "an axe in the hand of the wielder"; but left to his own devices, he would always be short of knowledge, and lacking as well in reason to weigh this knowledge. The ruler was thus expected to be capricious and deadly, although subject to substantial improvement if *advised* by men able to direct him properly—"the wrath of a king is angels of death, but a wise man will placate it."[9]

On the face of it, it may seem that all one needs in order to establish just rule is a king willing to be told what to do, and a single, highly competent adviser who is capable of unambiguously discerning the true goals of the state. But the Jewish tradition discounts this possibility as well, because it is more or less impossible to find such an adviser: According to a theory of R. Johanan, at least, each person grasps reality from a different perspective, so that no one man can ever understand the whole truth of any matter by himself: "Every word that went forth from the Eternal was fragmented into seventy languages."[10] Thus not even something as unequivocal as a communication from heaven can help being fragmented into scores of different perspectives when perceived by different men, each with his own "language" for interpreting the world.

One need only recall the story of the tower of Babel—on which the theory of the "seventy languages" is apparently based—to recognize the far-reaching political implications of R. Johanan's theory. According to the books of Moses, the earliest men did have a simple and unambiguous understanding of what was good policy for their state, such as every government desires: Their goal was to erect an all-encompassing metropolis in Mesopotamia for the entire human race, centered around a tower reaching to heaven, and this project was considered feasible because all men were united in supporting it—being "of one language and unified words." The implication in the narrative is that man would have succeeded had God not "scattered" the builders, saying: "Let us go down and confound their language, that each will not be able to understand what the other is saying. So the Eternal scattered them from there across the face of the land, and they ceased to build the city."[11] In the view of R. Johanan, the reason that the Mesopotamians ceased to construct their united city was not that they simply could not understand the literal languages being spoken; they could have used interpreters. Rather, the account of the tower depicts the creation of different worldviews, each dictating its own understanding of reality—each man with his own "language" so that he has difficulty in appreciating the views and interests of his neighbor. What prevents men from unified political action is therefore the existence of the "seventy" perspectives, which ensure that every proposal seeming good to some will be unacceptable to others.[12]

In the book of Esther, however, the aim is assumed to be for the ruler to recognize the existence of the different perspectives, and to approximate the true state by seeking out men who may, each in his own area, provide him with a part of the true picture. That these perspectives will contradict one another is obvious, as the rabbis envisioned God informing Ahashverosh, who wished for all his citizens to be silent and simply to love him: "Two men seek the hand of the same woman. Can she marry both of them? ... So two ships lie in the same harbor, one waiting for a north wind, the other for a south wind. Can the same wind carry them both together?"[13] And precisely because the differing political perspectives contradict, one adviser may never suffice the king in practice: Each lobbyist fighting to advance his own sectarian interest is also the bearer of information as to what is happening in the empire and advice as to what should be done. And while all these minor truths and half-truths clamoring and pecking at the others may be a nuisance and a menace to the king, each constitutes a small part of the answer as to what must be done in the empire—and it is the role of the ruler, if he is to try to understand the condition of his state and its needs, to *hear* these and attempt to weigh each against the other.[14]

The narrative in Esther considers Ahashverosh to be implicitly guided by this ideal, although it presents the argument in reverse. It claims that for all his detestable personal traits, the actual evil which Ahashverosh can do is kept reasonably in check so long as he is surrounded day and night by a variety of advisers representing various perspectives which he has no choice but to take into account—if only because he wishes to impress them all so that he may harvest their appreciation.[15] The main exposition of this point is the episode of Vashti's banishment. The king has been driven onto a towering spire of rage as a result of being publicly embarrassed by a member of his court. And yet for all this, Ahashverosh actually succeeds in abusing his power to a rather inconsequential degree. After all, what really happens? The queen is tossed out of court, and a foolish but on the whole benign edict is issued informing Persia that wives should obey their husbands.[16] A real catastrophe—such as a decree of death for wives who disobey their husbands—is avoided, and the reason for this is clear: "The king consulted with his advisers, who understood the precedents, for such was the king's habit before all who knew law and judgment." (1:13) In the worst case, the decision as to what is to be done is made while the drunken and outraged king is surrounded by advisers and servants—standing symbolically before the watching eyes of the entire empire, whose reactions must be taken into account. Almost always, one of these advisers is clever enough to help him down without damaging himself or the empire irreparably—and if this one were to stray much too far from a tolerable solution to the crisis, his proposals would for the most part be blocked by those of the others.[17]

This system is very far from the ideal of the true state, being in fact no more than its mediocre shadow. But it nonetheless stands in stark contrast with the rule of Ahashverosh through Haman, whose "advice" represents not even such a mediocre approximation of the truth, but a scant one-seventieth of the truth—in most cases necessarily a lie. Ahashverosh now rules a state which cannot even hope to approximate true policy, since it is structurally prevented from doing so: There is now only one person whom Ahashverosh must try to impress, whose appreciation he must concern himself over. For this reason, the most fateful decisions will now be made in private, without consulting anyone else or taking any other interest into account. Ahashverosh, out of fear and laziness, assumes for himself the prerogative to rule the state not in accord with what is truly for its benefit. Rather than being the captain whose role is to pilot his ship among the shoals of reality, he chooses to steer by some other method with the purpose of achieving some other goal. And in so doing he sets his own will with regard to the government of the state above that of God: "The king below has prevailed over the king above."

And the evil when such a deed is done does not remain abstract. When, under the reign of Haman's advice, offense is once again taken because of the rebellious behavior of a member of the court, the result is radically different from the last time. This time, it is not Memuchan, implicitly balanced by the potential reactions of the other princes and the rest of the servants and the throng, who provides the reasoning to instruct the king's appetite for rule. This time, the machinery of the state accepts the perspective of one man, unbalanced and untempered, and the result is an unbalanced and untempered eruption of evil: "Then Haman said to the king Ahashverosh: 'There is a certain people ... and their laws are different from those of other peoples, and the king's laws they do not keep, so that it is of no benefit for the king to tolerate them. If it please the king, let it be written that they be destroyed....' The king took his ring from his hand and gave it to Haman, the son of Hamedata the Agagite, the persecutor of the Jews. And the king said to Haman: '... Do with them as you see fit.'" (3:8–11)

# 5

# IDOLATRY

YET BENEATH THE POLITICAL MOTIVES for Mordechai's refusal to prostrate himself lies something more. After all, the refusal to bow is a traditionally Jewish expression of religious faith: Jews do not refuse to bow before kings or their viziers. Jews refuse to bow before *idols*. Are we then to understand that Mordechai believed the vizier somehow to be an idol, that he had made of himself a god?

When the rabbis retold the story of Mordechai's refusal, they understood that such was indeed the case, writing, for example, that the new vizier had affixed an idol to his tunic: "Was Mordechai just looking for quarrels, or just being generally disobedient to the king's commands? The fact is that when Ahashverosh ordered that all should bow down to Haman, the latter affixed an idolatrous image on his breast for the purpose of making all bow down to the idol."[1] The Talmud also cites the opinion of R. Huna, who was even more direct: "What had Mordechai seen that he picked a quarrel with Haman? It was for this reason, that he had made himself an object of worship."[2] The argument is that Mordechai's assault on the installation of the new vizier is not only a reaction to a current political event. In taking up this political cause, Mordechai the Jew joins in a far broader Jewish war, already in progress a thousand years and more; and Haman, while certainly the purveyor of an immediate political evil, is also the latest champion of that same philosophical and religious horror which Judaism had come into existence to fight in the time of Abraham. If we are to fully appreciate the Jews' war against the vizier, a war which opens with a man who will not bend, and closes with the deaths of a substantial part of the fighting power of Persia,[3] we must understand the idolatry against which the war was fought.

Judaism and idolatry are antinomies, for Judaism is the rejection of the servitude to idols and false-gods. Thus R. Johanan argued: "Anyone who repudiates idolatry is called a Jew."[4] And historically, at least, this was the case: Judaism arose from within the blast-furnace of Mesopotamian and Egyptian idol worship in the time of Abraham as a reaction against what was then considered civilization. But R. Johanan was not only referring to the distant past. The rabbis considered the battle of Abraham against all of Mesopotamian thought to be that of Mordechai in Persia as well: "Why is he called a Jew [man of Judah], surely he was a Benjaminite? Because he declared the unity of God's name before all mankind, as it is written, 'But Mordechai did not bow nor prostrate himself.'"[5] Thus the opposition to Haman was itself understood by the rabbis to be tantamount to "declaring the unity of God's name," the central tenet of Jewish belief.

We usually understand by idolatry the making of figures, from clay or metal, wood or stone, which represented gods—or which were themselves considered gods—whose pleasure and grace were thought necessary to obtain human good: Sustenance, fertility, victory, peace. Frequently, there were men who claimed to have the ability to provide these commodities, and these too were referred to as gods; everywhere in the ancient world there were men who were idols just as surely as there were statues that were idols. In both cases, good for mankind was to be achieved by appeasing these gods, whereas suffering and evil were the result of incurring their displeasure. Of course, as each people, each community generated its own idols in accord with local ideas, there was a virtually unlimited range of theories as to what were the appropriate gods for human worship, and which among human behaviors were pleasing and displeasing to these deities. So it was that some gods would exercise their influence in return for food and wine, others enjoyed parties and entertainment, and yet others appreciated the sacrifice of produce and beasts. Many appreciated sex in the form of orgies, homosexuality and bestiality. And there were those whose pleasures centered on human blood, consuming the hearts extracted from living men, consuming children burned to the beating of drums.

Since the evil in idolatry was so great, it is difficult to understand why men found it good. But idolatry was actually the result of a positive human desire to ascertain the causes of suffering and ameliorate them. Before idolatry there was only helplessness—the belief of an infant who falls but knows neither the reasons for his hurt, nor any way of preventing his suffering from recurring. Idolatry was the first intellectual endeavor of man as he rose above the immediate and visible in the search for effective means of treating his afflictions. As Rava ben R. Isaac related of a certain idolatrous temple, its intention was for good, although the results were heinous: "Whenever the world is in need of rain, the idol appears to its priests in a dream, saying: 'Kill me a man and I will send rain.' They kill a man for it, and rain really does come."[6]

The point is that idolatry was not a perfect falsehood, such as one would have if these murders were committed and the rains then did not come. On the contrary, the obstinate persistence of idolatry derived precisely from the element of truth that was in it: They would kill a human being and the rain would in fact come. And from the perspective of the idolater, the relation between the two events appeared effective, undeniable and true. The flaw lies not in the idolater's willingness to accept falsehood, but in his unwillingness to consider causes and effects ("truths") other than the most local ones visible to him within his own perspective. The idolatrous farmer believes that his need for rain can be alleviated through murder, because no other *causes* for rain are considered beyond the most local one—his own actions and those of his priest; likewise, the idolatrous farmer believes that his need for rain can justify murder, because no other *effects* of murder are considered beyond the most local one— his own betterment and that of his priest. Idolatry is thus in its core an arrogance: The belief that the local truth of one's own perspective comprises truth as a whole—that one-seventieth of the truth is the truth itself, when this one-seventieth amounts to a barren lie.

The example provided by Rava ben R. Isaac also touches on that other immense flaw which proved to inhere in idolatry: So dark were the demands for the destruction of property, sex crimes, mutilation and murder made by the false-gods, that their overall effect was not to ameliorate human suffering, but to embitter life even beyond what it might have been without them. Often enough, what they de- manded in exchange for empty promises of well-being was the release of the most vile of human inclinations, to the pleasure of some among men and the ruin of society as a whole. And it was just this disregard for idolatry's other, overall effects which transformed it into a menace to the well-being of all its practitioners and their environs. As the rabbis argued, the ultimate end of every idol was that it came to life in order to spit in its master's face.[7]

Both in thought and in action, the system of the idolaters was what we refer to in today's terms as moral relativism: The belief that in every place and time, human suffering is governed by *local* truths relevant to each place and each people, and ultimately emanating from the perspective and will of local, individual men.[8] Judaism came into being as the categorical denial of the effectiveness of such local prescriptions, as well as of the desirability and permissibility of acting on the basis of such claims. Instead, it insisted that the appearance of evil is governed by *universal* principles determined by the nature of mankind and creation, as established by the Eternal, God of Israel, whose decalogue opens with a comprehensive rejection of the relativistic epistemology of idolatry:

(i) I am the Eternal your God;

(ii) You will have no other gods beside me;

(iii) I, the Eternal your God, am a zealous God, returning the errors of the fathers upon the children to the third and fourth generation of those who hate me,

(iv) but showing mercy to thousands of generations of those who love me and keep my commandments;

(v) I am the Eternal your God who brought you out of Egypt, out of the land of bondage;

(vi) You will not make yourself a carved idol;

(vii) You will not bow down to them and serve them.[9]

These first claims serve as the substructure on which were built the first universal laws of morality: (i) That righteousness consists first of seeking the good of man—respecting his life, his family, his property, his dignity, his right to respite, his right to privacy, his right to justice, these being the remaining seven of the ten commandments; and (ii) that evil is caused by men who ignore these universal principles, instead doing what appears right in their own eyes according to their own local perspective.

It is therefore no surprise that the pagan gods and their human beneficiaries saw every Jewish demand as either theft or warfare: Jewish insistence on the existence of absolute rights as a theft of their own prerogatives, and Jewish resistance to the implementation of idolatry as nothing short of a slave rebellion by those who refused to understand that they were rightly the slaves of some god-king or other. This is why it is the collision between Moses and his Eternal God and the will of Pharaoh which serves as the archetype for the war which the emergence of Judaism brings into history. Moses comes to Pharaoh—a full-fledged pagan deity in his own right, whose will is truth for an entire civilization—and *orders* him, in the name of absolute right, to cease the merciless servitude of the Jews:

> Afterwards Moses and Aaron went in and told Pharaoh: "So says the Eternal, God of Israel: Let my people go that they may celebrate me in the desert."
>
> Pharaoh said: "Who is the Eternal that I should obey his voice to let Israel go? I know not the Eternal, nor will I let Israel go."[10]

Pharaoh had in the name of his own divine will pursued every evil against the Jews, up to and including the slaughter of their children, all of whom he understood to be his possessions. And the response of the Jews is that of absolute right settling accounts: Egypt is torn asunder by a relentless war of wonders that destroys its water supply, its livestock, its grain and finally slaughters its children before return- ing to conventional war and eliminating Pharaoh's armed forces. And while the ferocity of the attack can be missed amid its super- natural effects, this was understood by ancient Jews to be the only method of doing business with idolatry: The Eternal, the Jewish God, promised to return evil until the third and fourth generation— that is, against all living members of any society which lived by villainy.

Nor is the Jewish war against idolatry limited to periodic resistance against king-idols and their states. From the time of Abraham,
the Jews claimed the right to establish a society on earth free from the
pollution of idolatry. And while it may have been impractical for the
Jews, "the fewest of peoples,"[11] to wage war against the pagan empires
of Egypt and Mesopotamia, they did claim for themselves a small
patch of land along the trade route between the two superpowers, in
which they were able to serve as a bone in the throat of the entire
idolatrous world. In the land of the Jews, idolatry—the belief in the
absence of absolute right and wrong, and thus the source of evil—is
to be driven from the land. No prisoners are to be taken, no inquiry
is to be made into their ways, no treaties are to be signed with them.
And the reason for this is explicit: "For every horror which the
Eternal hates have they done for their gods. Even their sons and their
daughters have they burned in fire for their gods."[12]

There is little in our own experience which can approach the
circumstances being described here, or the war that the Jews are
expected to wage against idolatry. Certainly, even contemporary
democracies engage in "unconditional" warfare; the nuclear target-
ing doctrine of "countervalue" warfare also aimed to destroy the
largest possible civilian population, naturally including children and
the aged, all in the hope of ending war more quickly.[13] But the
purpose of the wars of Judaism against idolatry was not to protect
Jewish lives by ending the war more rapidly. It was to protect the
Jewish people, and ultimately all of mankind, from infection by an
idea—an idea which, once accepted, duped men and drugged them
into moral insensibility, justifying in their minds every conceivable
darkness. Idolatry was amnesia, and against it Judaism strove to
make men remember: That murder was evil, that perversion was evil,
that right was a tree of life to those who embrace it, that wrong
would bring certain ruin. Idolatry would teach the Jews to forget,
and to forget meant their end as Jews, as individuals and as a people.

And in the theology of Judaism, in which the human race could be elevated above the morass of endless depravity only if some would take it upon themselves to believe in this elevation and fight for it, the end of the Jews and their mission was the end of the world. Hence the famous dictum of Resh Lakish: "The Holy One, may he be blessed, spoke to the works of creation, saying to them: If Israel accepts the Tora, you will exist, but if not I will return you to chaos and void."[14]

As the Jews entered the land that would be their own in the time of Joshua, the eradication of the amnesia of idolatry was therefore considered the bedrock upon which civilization and civil life itself were to be based—and every human urge was suspected of being a threat to the memory which the Jews were to fix in their heads. For this reason, the Jews were forbidden to allow the children of the idolaters to remain among them, lest they come to love them and become influenced by them; they were forbidden to make any use whatever of religious treasures, lest they come to use them as the idolaters had; they were told not even to inquire as to the nature of the idolatry once it was destroyed. The war of the Jews against idolatry was total, a war of national survival that was, at its heart, a war to uproot the disease of moral relativity from the world. No wonder then, that when in a later age the rabbis sought to explain what it was that had made Abraham worthy of being the first Jew, they hypothesized that as a boy he had smashed the idols that his father had made. For them the essence of Judaism is what Nietzsche, in a later time, called "philosophy with a hammer"—the smashing of the idols.[15]

It is within this context that Mordechai's war against Haman and his followers can be understood. So long as Ahashverosh took decisions through broad consultation with a range of advisers, there was every reason to hope that the laws and actions of the Persian state would tend towards at least the roughest approximation of a just settlement among the competing perspectives, interests and truths in the empire. Haman's installation, however, eliminating as it did the action of interests other than his own, in principle suppressed the search for a greater truth on the part of the state; henceforth it would become that defined by the perspective and desires of a single man, Haman. Since it would be his desires rather than truth which would now determine right and wrong for much of mankind, his elevation transformed him (and Ahashverosh, as well) into a usurping god, a pretender to knowledge and power he did not have, an idol. To serve his whim would be as service to the Canaanite gods, for whom men had murdered their children. In principle—and, as it quickly became clear, in practice as well.

# 6

# DISOBEDIENCE

MOST OF THE EARLY LEADERS among the Jews were individuals whose confrontation with idolatry began from a position of weakness: The false-gods wielded state authority and with it commanded armies and police, gave orders and were obeyed. And where there was no hope of military resistance, the role of the Jew was to fight by other means. The biblical account of the Jewish nation therefore closes with the repeated disobedience of Mordechai and Esther, through which the Jews are saved from annihilation—much as it begins with the disobedience of Shifra, Pua and Jocheved, through which the Jews were saved from enslavement to Pharaoh. In between, the narrative depicts over a thousand years of nearly continual willingness to abrogate law and state authority in order to do what is right.

Remarkably, this message of Jewish resistance to state idolatry and injustice has been consistently misread or ignored by those—both foes of religion and its "friends"—who have sought to characterize the Bible as a book of submission. Such interpretations invariably point to Abraham's willingness to sacrifice his son Isaac at God's command.[1] But this reading distorts the plain import of the text, which is that Abraham was willing to sacrifice that which was most precious to him, the son for whom he had waited all his life, in the service of a higher cause. The call for submission to God does not in any way connote a call to submit to *human* authority; indeed, it is the exact opposite. For God's will in the Bible can be considered equivalent to what today is referred to in secular terms as the higher law or universal justice. To equate obedience to the dictates of justice with obedience to injustice is to miss the point of the entire Bible, which is that the individual must obey only the dictates of moral truth, even (and especially) when these violate the dictates of the state.

In all of antiquity, the Bible is the only document that consistently advances the fundamental ideas which are today known as "civil disobedience," unequivocally articulating the familiar principles which were then alien to virtually the entire world: That there is an absolute of right and wrong that transcends the decrees of the state; that the state has no right to rule if it rules unjustly; that conscience and not the state must be the ultimate arbiter of the actions of every man; that individual disobedience is justified and obligatory in the face of state injustice; and that resistance and even the overthrow of the state is justified and obligatory in cases of unbearable tyranny. Indeed, the biblical narrative consists in large part of explicit indictments of both Jewish and non-Jewish governments for the injustice of their laws and the unjust behavior of their rulers—accounts in which those who act independently and offer resistance are invariably the heroes. By looking at this tradition more carefully, we may more fully understand what is meant by the decision of Mordechai the Jew to continue after the way of his people—the people of the book, and therefore the people of disobedience.

The biblical account of the emergence of the Jews begins with a refugee problem: The flight of Abraham, the first Jew, from the Mesopotamian city of Ur, in the very heart of the civilized world—a flight which ends with Abraham's determination to make his life anew, at the age of seventy-five, as a herder of goats and sheep on a patch of land he finds along the trade route to Egypt, the underdeveloped and culturally irrelevant wilderness of Canaan. The narrative itself tells little about the reasons for Abraham's escape from the civilization of the Euphrates River basin.* Yet it is clear from his turbulent stay in Egypt, which ends in a hasty retreat, that there is no love lost between the Hebrew patriarch and the great Nile civilization, either. It is therefore no sudden distaste for the particular fads of Mesopotamian culture, no warrant for his arrest in the hands of the Mesopotamian police, which drives him to break with the world he had known his entire life. Instead, he cashiers the glory of the world-empires of his day because he believes that in this way he and his descendants, and the rest of the world as well, will be blessed.[2] He had come to the conclusion, after years of bitter turmoil, that in Mesopotamia and Egypt, nothing resembling the blessing he wished

---

* In considering the reasons for Abraham's departure from Mesopotamia, one frequently meets with the response that he left "because God commanded it." Yet this only raises the parallel question of what it was that moved God to concern himself with Abraham's place of domicile. And unless one is to claim that God's commands as recorded in the Bible are arbitrary and without reason, there is no choice but to return to the circumstances surrounding them in order to discern their motive: What are the *reasons* for Abraham's escape from Mesopotamia; what are the *reasons* for God's instruction to Moses to smear the blood of a sheep on the doorposts on the night of the Jews' departure from Egypt; and so forth.

for his children could be found. And one need only consider the civilizations from which Abraham escaped in order to begin to understand that he was right.

For more than a thousand years before Abraham, the Nile and Euphrates rivers had given rise to the most advanced cultures mankind had known. The unparalleled might of these two rivers had been harnessed for massive irrigation projects and a flourishing water-borne trade, allowing the rise of the Sumerian empire and its successors in Mesopotamia, and of Egypt of the Pharaohs. Both empires, like those of China, India and Persia, engaged in public works on an unprecedented scale to increase the land available for farming, engaging their entire populations as slaves for periods of weeks or months when important projects were under way. The enforced management of millions of people was a form of taxation, and necessitated the establishment of a huge bureaucracy capable of keeping records of the entire population and its contributions to the public weal. Needless to say, it also enabled the spectacular enrichment of the king and his family, as well as requiring the creation of a colossal military apparatus capable of enforcing the labor tax and defending the developed areas against nomadic peoples, who coveted the wealth and power that had been amassed in the river valleys.

The social consequences of such wholesale organization of men were of the first degree. In order to bring an entire empire into the service of building mammoth physical structures such as the pyramids in Egypt and the Chinese Great Wall, every source of fear and authority that could be devised had to be brought to bear in securing beast-like submission—even where, as with these undertakings, this submission would mean the inevitable ruin of a certain portion of the race. To coerce the bodies of every person capable of physical labor, the king would employ a vast police apparatus, relying for information on the bureaucracy which tracked his legions of internal informers. While these tentacles of the state coerced the body, man's mind too was brought under heel by a religious system which ordained that the will of the gods was identical to the will of the ruler: The king was himself a descendant of the gods and their principal servant, wherever he was not himself an essential deity in the pantheon. Law issued by the ruler was therefore a reflection of the unchallengeable law of the universe, and had to be obeyed on pain of earthly hell, which was a down payment for what was coming after death. Direct evidence of the divine powers of the state was provided by the official priesthood, which generally maintained a monopoly on all science, astronomy, engineering and math. Besides the intimidation inherent in this complete control of wisdom and knowledge, these skills were applied to the erection of gargantuan towers and astronomical observatories, connecting the state to the heavens in a way that was obvious to any with eyes to see. The priesthood itself was on the payroll of the state, thus ensuring that it played its role. Under such systems, religion was nothing more or less than the cosmic ideology of the government, the intellectual and spiritual mortar which fused the masses into a single tool in the hand of the state by reassuring that obedience meant salvation, and disobedience rightful and inevitable agony.[3]

It follows, of course, that there was not much discussion of a right to disobedience in the ancient world. Neither in Egypt, nor in Mesopotamia, nor anywhere else did mankind bother to struggle, as later thinkers did, with questions of what limits there might be to what the state may require of men. And the notion that there might be a right of the individual to dissent against unjust government was without foundation in the thought of any people. Of course, this does not mean there were no lawbreakers. In every civilization there have always been rogues and thieves willing to break the law for personal gain. Likewise, every tyranny of the ancient world sired its fair share of putsches and assassinations, usually the brainchild of a would-be usurper whose principal concern was to bring the machinery of absolute rule under his own control. And while a successful usurpation of power might be rationalized as being proof that the new rulers had the support of heaven—and could therefore claim absolute obedience as had their deposed predecessors—under no philosophical, moral, ideological or religious system were such actions considered legitimate *in principle*.

This is the world from which Abraham found no choice but to become a refugee. He turned his back on the slave labor and terror gods of Mesopotamia, staking his claim to an undeveloped patch of hill-ground in Canaan where he could shake off the yoke of the state. Unlike the heroes of other ancient narratives, the figures of the books of Moses are therefore neither royalty nor nobility; nor, after the fashion of modern literature, are they democratic figures near the bottom of the social structure. Instead, Abraham and all his descendants are shepherds, nomads who view civilization from the outside, looking down from the hills at the doings of society and state as they chart their own independent course through the wilderness. The splendor and lies of urban life are of little worth to them; even less so the beast-life of the farmers in the valleys, living out their days in toil that these lies may be fed. For in Canaan, Abraham and his people have found what is more precious to them than all else, political and ideological independence: Political independence in that they live as nomads, ungoverned, their labor and their property and their actions unregulated and untaxed by anyone other than themselves; ideological independence in that their vantage point and the freedom and dignity of their work allow them to gaze long and deep into the sky, focusing on what truly matters—the proximity of all men to danger, error and death, and the consequent responsibility they must take for discovering the true course and acting on it.

The degree to which the Bible values conscience as the core of such political and moral independence is dramatized perhaps most forcefully by the fact that the biblical heroes do not, as should be expected, tend to submit passively even to the will of God: Abraham, the first Jew and the prototype of subsequent Jewish values, is depicted as a man with the conscience and strength to challenge God himself. When God intends to destroy every man in Sodom, Abraham argues: "Will not the judge of all the earth do justice?"⁴—and God himself gives in. Moses, the archetype of a Jewish national and religious leader, argues with God and alters the course of his judgments.⁵ Indeed, in case the message is somehow to be missed, the books of Moses inform us that the very name of the Jewish people, Israel, is derived from this most crucial of qualities, the ability to struggle with the world as it has been decreed: "Your name will no longer be Jacob, but Israel, for you have struggled with God and with men and have prevailed"—Israel meaning "will struggle with God."⁶ What in other cultures would have been sacrilege is thus elevated into a national symbol and the crux of Jewish belief: The refusal of the shepherd to accept the order of the universe as it has been decreed, and the demand of his conscience to know why it cannot be improved.

It can come as no surprise that a people whose tradition so strongly emphasizes the need to contend even with God in matters of justice, gave rise to a long history of men and women unwilling to be intimidated by the pretenses of human institutions. Indeed, the tone with respect to earthly rulers is set in the first scriptural reference to them, the description of the Mesopotamian ruler Nimrod: "He began to be mighty on the earth. He was a mighty hunter before the Eternal..."⁷—that is, a man of spirit, power and violence. The narrative then presents the results of the accumulation of vast powers in the hands of the Mesopotamians and their empire: "They said: Come, let us build a city, and a tower reaching to the sky, and we will make a name for ourselves, lest we be dispersed across the earth."⁸ From the perspective of the shepherd, the establishment of the great and tyrannical world-empires is in its essence vanity, consisting of the pursuit of glory and power to no productive end; other than the erection of huge monuments of ego and stone at incredible expense, there seems to be little good in it. In the end God is depicted as dividing them into disparate nations and scattering them abroad. The fate of all states built on the search for fame and power is understood to be dissension and dissolution.

This suspicion of states and rulers is a common thread running through the entire Bible, beginning with the stories of the patriarchs. Indeed, with uncanny consistency, each new figure in the narrative is almost immediately introduced to readers in terms of his resistance to the state. Thus, other than his actual arrival in Canaan, the first event we learn of in Abraham's life is his resistance to the will of the Egyptian Pharaoh, who he has reason to fear will murder him to take his wife.[9] A similar account introduces Isaac as well, and later, when he finds his father's wells being destroyed by a Canaanite king, we are told that he resists the rulers by redigging one well after another.[10] Likewise, when Jacob and his sons travel back to Canaan, the first event of interest to the narrative is his peaceable purchase of a plot of land on which to encamp, only to have his daughter Dina raped by the local prince—for which Jacob's sons Shimon and Levi then destroy the inhabitants of the town.[11] Perhaps most tellingly, it is as a result of the Hebrew shepherds' greatest misdeed, the plot to murder their brother Joseph, that they receive the ultimate punishment: They are forced to give up their nomadic life and come under the totalitarian rule of the Egyptian Pharaoh.

The story of the Jews in Egypt is itself nothing short of a chronicle of resistance to oppressive government. Like the other tales of the books of Moses, this one opens immediately with an act of resistance to the state: The Egyptians have come to fear the strength of the foreign Jewish population, and Pharaoh determines to submit the Jews to slavery—the making of bricks with which he can build his edifices—in order to strip them of the capacity to resist him.

Having done so, he then summons the Jewish midwives and orders them to kill every male child born among the Jews, the intention being to absorb the women into the Egyptian population and so eliminate the Jews as a people. But the midwives, Shifra and Pua, refuse the command:

> But the midwives feared God and did not do as the king of Egypt commanded, keeping the children alive.
>
> And the king of Egypt called in the midwives and said to them: "Why have you done this thing, keeping the children alive?"
>
> And the midwives said to Pharaoh: "Because the Hebrew women are not like the Egyptian women, but vigorous, and they give birth before the midwives can arrive."[12]

Seeing that the midwives will not cooperate, Pharaoh seeks a different method of enforcement, ordering that his entire people participate in slaughtering any Jewish boy that should be born. It is Jocheved, a woman from the tribe of Levi, who decides she must resist the law, giving birth in secret and hiding her son for a full three months as the killing of the other Jewish babies takes place all around her. When finally she cannot hide the child any longer, she sets him adrift on the Nile, hoping for a miracle. And she receives one: For Pharaoh's daughter, finding the ark and pulling the screaming baby from the water, immediately understands what has happened, and decides that she, too, will risk her life for the child by violating her own father's decree—in so doing, according to the rabbis, becoming a Jew because she renounces her servitude to the idol in order to do what is right.[13] Jocheved's young daughter Miriam is also implicated: Standing by the river and watching the entire scene, she asks Pharaoh's daughter if she would like a Jewish wet nurse for the child. She brings Jocheved, who cares for the boy until he is weaned and adopted by Pharaoh's daughter as a son.[14]

It is by means of this incredible conspiracy that two Jewish women and an Egyptian princess together abrogate the Egyptian law and manage to save a single Jewish boy from the holocaust: Moses. Neither does the narrative leave any question as to what kind of an education the Levite child received from Pharaoh's daughter. Before we learn anything else about Moses as a grown man, we find that he, too, is unafraid to shatter the Egyptian law for the sake of what he believes to be right:

> It came to pass that when Moses was grown, he went out to his brothers and saw their suffering; and he saw an Egyptian man beating a Hebrew man, one of his brothers. He looked this way and that, and when he saw that there was no man, he slew the Egyptian and buried him in the sand.[15]

Although raised in Pharaoh's court, there is no question that Moses retains his shepherd's eye for resistance, and it is this, no less than his upbringing as a leader among the Egyptian nobility, that prepares him to become the first political and religious leader of the Jewish nation—and the one who will lead it to revolution.

Having fled Egypt for fear of the king's anger, Moses becomes a shepherd like his forefathers. It is while tending his flock in the wilderness that he has his first encounter with God, an encounter which sends him back to Egypt seeking an end to the enslavement of his people. The grueling rounds of Moses' confrontation with Pharaoh—each punctuated with the demand that the Egyptian king "let my people go, that they may serve God"—are the mold from which is cast the entire subsequent tradition of the Hebrew prophets and the unprecedented belief in their authority to castigate the holders of state power. Of course, the Jewish slaves are not necessarily built for such a bruising battle, and their leaders even blame Moses for the wrath Pharaoh visits upon them.[16] Nevertheless, Moses does not end up with sole responsibility for the revolution when it comes: Before the Jews gain their freedom from Egypt, on the night of the last plague, Moses requires that every one of them publicly return to his shepherd past—trampling on the Egyptian law by slaughtering a sheep, a god to the Egyptians, roasting and eating it "so that nothing remains of it in the morning," and then smearing its blood on the doorposts of the house for all to see. It is made clear, moreover, that only those who do so can expect salvation and freedom.[17] Thus disobedience, by which Moses came into the world, also becomes the act by which each Hebrew slave turns his back on the state of the oppressor and accepts the higher law which makes him a Jew.

This suspicion of ruling authority continues to pervade the thought of the Jews even once they have entered Canaan and have no choice but to wield political power themselves. The first effort on the part of the people to erect a centralized state fails because Gideon, whom they have chosen to be king, refuses to take part, declaring: "I will not rule over you, and my son will not rule over you. The Eternal will rule over you."[18] Only after further generations of civil war and humiliation on the battlefield does the determination of the Jews to establish a strong centralized state such as those of other nations reach an irresistible pitch, and even then the people find themselves opposed by the prophet Samuel, who objects to the state on account of the oppression that will inevitably follow from such an accumulation of power.[19]

Although the Jews ignore Samuel's warning, crowning Saul as the first king of a united Israel, the spirit of his critique is accepted nonetheless. From the outset, the Jewish tradition of opposition to government ties the king's hands, making absolute rule impossible. The books of Moses themselves had laid down laws specific to the Jewish king, limiting his right to amass wealth and luxury, and insisting that the duration of his rule was dependent on his adherence to God's law.[20] And in subsequent accounts, the narrative repeatedly emphasizes the Jews' rejection of the laws of their own kings when they deemed them unjust. In one famous scene Saul orders his men to fast in preparation for battle with the Philistines, and threatens death should anyone disobey. When his son Jonathan is found to have violated his decree, Saul orders that he be executed for transgressing the king's law. But the soldiers of Saul's army reject his authority to have such a thing done:

> Jonathan told him, saying: "I tasted some honey with the end of the staff that was in my hand; therefore I must die."
>
> Saul said: "So will God do and more. For you will surely die, Jonathan."
>
> And the people said to Saul: "Is Jonathan to die who has brought this great victory to Israel? Absolutely not. As God lives, no hair will fall from his head, for he has done God's work today." So the people rescued Jonathan, and he was not killed.[21]

And disobedience to unjust use of authority was not only a fact of Saul's relations with his people. It was an institution of Jewish life throughout the period of the Jewish kings—an institution called the prophet. The function of the prophet in ancient Israel was unparalleled in any other nation of the ancient world. While virtually every people had some kind of tradition that the authority of its king and state derive from the favor of one deity or another, nowhere else did there exist an entire class of individuals whose role it was to declare the message of the deity in opposition to the actions of the king, his servants and the official priesthood. Despite the establishment of a Jewish state, the prophets continued the heritage of moral resistance that had been bequeathed to the Jews by their forefathers, bringing their oratory and rage to bear on any act of state which in their view undermined the cause of justice.

In some cases, as in Nathan's famous accusation against King David—who had taken another man's wife and then arranged to have him die in battle—the intention was to shake up the ruler and bring his behavior back into line.[22] But on occasion the independent moral authority of the prophet was used for full-blown resistance amounting to revolution. When Saul's rule becomes intolerable, it is the prophet Samuel who declares David his successor, in effect setting out to overthrow the ruling line.[23] The prophet Elisha goes even further, pronouncing Jehu the new king during the villainous rule of Jehoram and his mother Jezebel, thereby touching off the execution of the royal family and the eradication of the entire priesthood of Ba'al from Israel.[24] And when the prophet Jeremiah believes that Jerusalem is about to be razed because of the suicidal policies of Zedekia's government, he goes so far as to call for the people to disobey the law and go over to the Babylonian enemy so that something may be saved.[25]

The biblical history of the Jewish nation closes with the exile of the Jews into Babylonia and then Persia, a turn of events which might have been expected to temper the Jewish enthusiasm for uneven fights with authority. Yet it is remarkable that the books which describe this period are as unabashed as their predecessors in advocating disobedience: In the book of Daniel, three Jewish leaders in the exile, Hanania, Mishael and Azaria, brazenly defy the law of Babylonia which requires them to prostrate themselves before a gold statue Nebuchadnezzar has erected.[26] Daniel himself later refuses a similar order to worship the Persian king Darius.[27] The book of Esther is even more aggressive, sanctioning not only the violation of unjust laws, but repeatedly establishing the effectiveness and importance of abrogating other laws in the pursuit of right, as called for by modern theories of civil disobedience.[28] It turns out that Mordechai's repeated refusals to bow before Haman (3:1–2, 5:9) are only the opening rounds in a campaign which includes an illicit court appearance by Mordechai in mourning attire, (4:1–2) his certainly illegal incitement of Esther to go before the king unsummoned despite the prohibition against approaching the king, (4:8) and Esther's two

separate decisions to break this law and come before the king to plead
for her people. (5:1–2, 8:3–4)

The theme of disobedience to the law of the state is especially
striking when argued against a background of God's apparent silence, which is assumed to be a point of departure in the book of
Esther.[29] It is one kind of act of faith to take on the power of the state
when one might hope for overt divine assistance to save the day in the
end; it is something else again to insist on provoking confrontation
with the state when such assistance is unlikely to come.[30] Faced with
the overwhelming power of the empire-idols which enslaved the
earth, one could easily have concluded, as the early Christian thinkers
did, that it is better to submit in this world and triumph in the next.[31]
Yet it is one of the great achievements of Mordechai's disobedience
that it was able to demand the continuation of Jewish activism into
an era in which man began to feel himself suspiciously alone as he
stood before the enemies of his truth. Even in the bitterest days of
Roman oppression, when Jerusalem lay in ruins and the land was
filled with the bodies of the fallen, the rabbis continued to preach
Mordechai's message of disobedience, arguing that power and rule
on earth, no matter how vast, cannot grant sovereignty, the right to
command—a right which ultimately rests only with the individual
(or the state) when guided by truth. Thus R. Simlai argued that it was
nothing less than independent sovereignty that was granted every
individual at Mt. Sinai, where "six hundred thousand ministering
angels descended and set two crowns on the head of every individual
of Israel, one for action and one for understanding."[32] Moreover,
they completely rejected the possibility that one had a right to use
this individual independence and sovereignty to withdraw from the
world as called for by non-Jewish philosophies of the time: "If
someone says: Why should I concern myself with the troubles of
society, bother with men's controversies, and listen to their voices?
Peace be unto you, my soul. Such a one is destroying the world."[33]

# 7

# JOSEPH

JUDAISM IS A REBELLION against the authority of the ruler to establish moral valuation according to the weight of his interests and the perversity of his whims. But the biblical texts are without delusions: The Jewish effort, during the period of the judges, to live without central government and with only God as king ended in misery and failure. Even Abraham, the shepherd-idealist, could not survive without to some degree learning to manipulate men, their states and their wars.[1] And while he withdrew from civilization to lead a purer, truer life, the fact is that in times of famine—and there was threat of starvation in Canaan in every generation from Abraham's arrival until the Jews finally resettled in Egypt—it was to the wealth and technology of Egypt that he and his followers turned time and again in order to survive. While the goal was ever to bring heaven to earth, it rapidly transpired that to do this one would of necessity have to deal with the ways in which things are done on earth—and this meant collaboration with the very state-idolatry which Judaism rejected.

The inevitable incursion of the state-idols into the idyll of the Jewish shepherds in Canaan is the subject of the Joseph tale in the books of Moses, which serves as a touchstone for all subsequent Jewish discussion on the topic. Three other books of the Bible— Daniel, Nehemia[2] and Esther—address themselves to the questions of Jewish power under foreign empires, all of them more or less explicit responses to the story of the descent of the Jews into Egypt at the hand of Joseph, and its consequences.

The patriarch Jacob has twelve sons, all of whom remain within the fold of his shepherds' faith and form, for the first time, a real Jewish society. Like every society, it has its own intricate politics, with no fewer than five of the brothers aspiring to inherit the leadership of the clan: Reuben, Shimon, Levi, Judah and Joseph. Of these, Joseph is the youngest, yet by the time he is seventeen, it becomes clear that he is possessed of very special traits. He has a particular talent for using the ways of worldly power—appearance, favor, influence—to gain what his status as the youngest and weakest cannot give him. The narrative speaks of how Joseph "shepherds his brothers," serves as his father's agent in his efforts to control them, and so wins the favor of his father, who "loved him more than all his other children" and gives him special gifts.[3] He is also physically attractive, which boosts the appreciation of those who appreciate him, as well as his own vanity.[4] Moreover, Joseph reports being visited by dreams in which he and his brothers are binding sheaves of grain, their sheaves prostrating themselves before his grain, and in which the stars and the heavenly bodies prostrate themselves before him. To these the brothers retort in hatred: "Would you indeed reign over us? Would you rule over us?"[5]

Joseph's dreams reflect what the brothers might otherwise have guessed: That Joseph sees them all not as shepherds, as nomadic and independent agents and therefore fundamentally as equals; but as *farmers*, members of a vast structure of earthly power in which their lives depend on the protection of rulers who provide sustenance and arms—a power structure in which it is his talents, and not theirs, which are essential. As it turns out later, there is no small measure of realism in this view, and the Jews, too, will have to come to terms with this fact. Moreover, Joseph's desire for control is in no small part a desire to impose truth and peace on the relations of disunity, violence and disrespect which have come to mar the life of the clan with the decline of their aging father's authority.[6] Unlike Jacob, however, the brothers are incapable of digesting these crucial aspects of Joseph's message. To them, their younger brother, with all his manipulations and his dreams of rule, is everything that their fathers rejected. He is like a Mesopotamian, an Egyptian. Even the interpreting of dreams itself is not a Jewish custom but a science of the Egyptians.[7] As R. Levi argues, when the brothers say, "Look, here comes the dreamer," what they are really driving at is: "Here comes the one who would ensnare them into serving foreign overlords."[8] It is therefore with no small pleasure that they take the first opportunity to tear the cloak of his authority off of Joseph, sell him to a caravan of traders, and send him where they believe he rightly belongs: Egypt.

In Egypt, Joseph does indeed thrive, rising rapidly in every task assigned him by Potiphar, the Egyptian officer who has purchased him. At first it seems as though all he must do to succeed is apply his formidable talents, and all will be well. But it soon turns out that this is not the case—that there is a fundamental contradiction between the ways of power and the purist ideals on which Joseph was raised. Such a crisis first appears in the Joseph story in the episode in which he is subjected to the advances of Potiphar's wife. When it becomes clear that she cannot be deterred, Joseph is faced with the decision of his life. Everything he has worked for and achieved stands to be destroyed if he refuses her, and yet to accept her is to sacrifice the most basic teachings from his father's house. As taught in a parable of the school of R. Ishmael, Joseph's father appears to him in the window over Potiphar's bed, saying: "Your brothers will have their names inscribed upon the stones of the priestly garments [in the future Jerusalem] and yours among theirs. Do you wish to have your name erased from among theirs in order to be called a patron of harlots?"9 More than this, to accept her means to allow the immediate exigencies of power to dictate right and wrong rather than an absolute standard, and therefore to become just as the Egyptians are, doing everything in the service of their empire-idol. This is the meaning of the dictum of R. Avin that Potiphar's wife had an idol over the bed to which she struggled to bring Joseph.10 In that moment, the quest for power itself stood to become the god in whose service he worked.

Potiphar's wife confronts Joseph with the dilemma faced by his great-grandfather Abraham: Succeed according to society's standards by adopting its values, or smash the idol and become a failure and a laughingstock. At this moment, Joseph evidences the exceptional strength that is in him, and succeeds in resisting.11 If the price of power is adultery, we believe him to be saying, this price is too high, and his career comes to a wretched close in an Egyptian dungeon. For long years he rots in the pit, his life ruined.

In later rabbinic literature, this painful triumph over the Egyptian temptress is understood as a representation of what Joseph had to endure throughout his entire subsequent life. Thus in one vivid dialogue, Joseph is depicted as trying to fend off Potiphar's wife, only to find that it is Egypt itself which seeks to seduce him:

She said to him: "Yield to me." He said: "No."

She said: "I will have you imprisoned." He said: "The Eternal frees the captives."12

She said: "I will bend your proud posture [with slavery]." He said: "The Eternal lifts up those who are bent down."[13]

She said: "I will blind your eyes [with idolatry]." He said: "The Eternal gives sight to the blind."[14]

She offered him a thousand talents of silver to yield to her, "to lie with her, to be near her."[15] But he would not listen to her: Neither "to lie with her"—in this world, nor "to be near her"—in the world to come.[16]

Since Joseph does succeed in remaining a Jew to the end of his days—and one whose children themselves stay Jews and become leaders in Israel—the rabbis recognize this first spiritual victory as being symbolic of his far greater achievement of wielding power in Egypt, and yet using it in the service of his people. It is thus the refusal of Potiphar's wife which, according to R. Johanan in the name of R. Meir, earns Joseph his place as a Jew: "From this was he worthy to be made a shepherd."[17]

Yet this sanguine assessment of Joseph's life was not accepted by the rabbis unanimously. Among the great commentators were those who claimed that Joseph's behavior in Egypt was flawed, criticizing his adoption of Egyptian customs ("Why did Joseph die before his brothers?... Rabi said: Because he embalmed his father");[18] his willingness to allow his servitude to Egypt to dishonor the Jewish patriarch who was his father ("In the opinion of the rabbis: Nearly five times did Judah say: 'Your servant, my father,' 'your servant, my father.' Yet he [Joseph] heard it and kept silent");[19] and the arrogance of rule that disfigured his character even as an adult ("R. Judah also said in the name of Rav...: Why did Joseph die before his brothers? Because he conducted himself with rulership").[20] They referred to Joseph as "bones," the symbol of living death in exile;[21] and as a cask of wine that had been emptied of its contents.[22] Even an ostensibly supportive commentator remarks that Joseph's great achievements as

a Jew take place in private.[23] And these unflattering statements come
on top of the criticism leveled against Joseph by the books of the
Bible dealing with Persia, all of which considered his performance in
Egypt to be in one way or another troubling.

The reason for the ambiguity in the tradition is that, despite
Joseph's survival as a Jew, it is far from clear what lessons he actually
draws from the years lost in Pharaoh's prison. For the truth is that the
story of Potiphar's wife, in which Joseph sacrifices all he has gained of
earthly power in order to triumph as a Jew, does not repeat itself. If
anything, the opposite seems to be the case: Never again does Joseph
refuse the order of a superior, and nothing he does for the rest of his life
works in contravention of his own increase in power—and that of the
god-king he serves. It is almost as though his encounter with Potiphar's
wife is also his *last* stand as a shepherd, and the lesson he draws from
the dungeon is that to be an idealist in Egypt is untenable.

It is true that Joseph's work in the service of Pharaoh ultimately
prepares Egypt to survive seven years of famine—apparently saving
the Jews and all of Egypt from starvation. But from the viewpoint of
the shepherd, there is a horrible sense in which everything is lost
here. For Joseph's life's work becomes the construction of the Egyptian house of bondage, an idol just such as Abraham had sacrificed
everything to reject. Dying in political triumph, ruler of the world as
he had dreamed as a boy, the narrative nevertheless posthumously
hands Joseph his punishment for having collaborated with idolatry:
It is two centuries and more before his final, Jewish wish is granted
and his bones are brought out of Egypt to be buried in Shechem in
the land of his fathers. In the meantime, the idol he has himself
assisted in building goes about flaying the flesh from the backs of his
children and their descendants—until Moses, raised amid the idolatry of the Egyptian court, follows in the steps of his forefather
Abraham, becoming a shepherd, returning to the Eternal, and destroying the work of Joseph's hands with a stick.

The bitter ironies of this tale are endemic to the thought of the earliest Jews: Yes, mankind might have perished but for the successes of this idol-state, and a Jew might save his people and save the world by building the greatest empire-idol of them all. The Joseph tale, for all its miserable ambiguity, makes clear that while the empire-idol is the source of spiritual death, it is also the fount of physical life—and hence its allure. Without Joseph's Egypt, there would have been no Jews. But what kind of salvation is it to return to the house of bondage, to serve it, to build it that others may serve it and so increase the suffering and idolatry in the world? Is this not evil itself?

The argument in this direction is so strong that the three later Persian political writings, all of which in principle defend Joseph's decision to go into the service of Egypt, are nevertheless at pains to reject various decisions Joseph makes in trying to come to terms with his servitude.

In Daniel, the argument against Joseph is that he erred in adopting Egyptian ways in order to gain favor and the power this entailed.[24] In this view, there is no need for the Jew to make even the smallest compromise on any of his principles, because political success depends directly on scrupulous observance of Jewish traditional ritual and faith. Thus keeping kosher miraculously makes Daniel and his fellows stronger and more handsome than those who eat the meat served by the Babylonian king, and their refusal to follow state laws which directly contradict Judaism is of no consequence: The death penalty miraculously fails to work when applied to Jews, and a swift demise awaits those who attempt to enforce it.[25] The secret to success is therefore piety in its most obvious form: Sacrifice nothing of the law, and salvation will come from heaven, without much waiting or speculation required to see it.

In Nehemia there is no miraculous reconciliation between Jewish piety and political interest, and so no criticism of Joseph for having compromised his outward Jewishness in order to gain power.

Rather, the criticism is that having gained power, Joseph failed to use it to do right. Thus Nehemia, in a position similar to Joseph's as a close adviser of the king of Persia, uses his influence to allow the Jews to return to the land of Israel and to rebuild their autonomy and military power in Jerusalem, whereas Joseph appeared loath to approach Pharaoh to ask for his people's freedom.[26]

Even more stunning is Nehemiah's rejection of the manner in which Joseph ruled in Egypt. Since Joseph always understands his role to be advancing the interest of his master, he has no compunction about taking advantage of the bitter years of famine to extort from the starving populace its land and livestock, and to reduce the Egyptian people themselves to slavery, all in exchange for grain which he had previously taken from them in taxes:

> So Joseph bought all the land of Egypt for Pharaoh, for every Egyptian sold his field, because the famine prevailed over them, and the land became Pharaoh's.... Then Joseph said to the people: "Behold, I have bought you and your land this day for Pharaoh. Here is grain for you, and you will sow the land. And it will be that at harvest times, you will give a fifth to Pharaoh, and four-fifths will be your own...." They said: "You have saved our lives...."[27]

Nehemia discovers that the analogous situation has been taking place in the land of Israel, with the Jewish landholders lending to the populace so that they may survive the famine and the king's taxes, then foreclosing on the land and driving the people into poverty and slavery. When he hears of it, however, he is outraged:

> I reprimanded the nobles and the rulers ... and I held a great assembly against them. I said to them: "We have redeemed our brethren, the Jews who were sold to the gentiles, as best we were able. Will you now sell your brethren, or have them sold to us? ... I likewise, and my brothers and my servants, have lent them

money and grain. I pray you, let us release this debt. Restore to them, I pray you, even today, their lands, their vineyards, their oliveyards and their houses, as well as the interest on the money, the grain, the wine and the oil, that you exact from them." They said: "We will restore them, we will require nothing of them. We will do as you say."[28]

Thus Nehemia avoids the utopianism of Daniel in which every political goal may in fact be achieved without compromising anything. But rejected as well is the premise of the Joseph story, in which the statesman is inevitably the servant of the state-idol and its values, the taskmaster in the construction of the house of bondage. In Nehemia, the Jew may use the politics of a foreign empire to achieve that which is right, provided he can rise above the politics of the king's interest and do his own will with the power he has attained.

But what if one is not already the king's adviser? What if one is far less powerful—as were Joseph and Daniel at the beginning? We know nothing of how Nehemia *rose* to power, and herein lies the greatest challenge. Is Joseph right in compromising so much to become Pharaoh's vizier? Is Daniel right in compromising nothing whatsoever to become Nebuchadnezzar's vizier? In the middle ground between them is the teaching of Esther.

Mordechai accepts Joseph's claim that if the Jews wish to survive the famine, they must have a friend in Egypt. This is precisely why he chooses not to live in the Jewish quarter, but in the fortress of Susa—the "Egypt" of the Esther story—downplaying his Jewish identity and spending his time in the pursuit of power in the court of Ahashverosh. He believes in doing the work of the world, and he does it according to its own rules. This is why the rabbis taught that "the descendants of Rachel are alike in the miracles they experience and in their greatness"—the descendants of Rachel being Joseph, Mordechai and Esther.[29] Both tales speak of sacrifice in terms of outward Jewishness in order to achieve greater ends; and in both cases, due to the talents of these figures, the result is indeed great political achievements.

Yet in refusing to bow, Mordechai too denies the necessary conclusion of the tale of Joseph in Egypt—that one either refuses to serve the king, or else becomes his servant entirely. For Mordechai, the elevation of the vizier to exclusive power represents a line beyond which one cannot continue serving the master without losing everything, a line beyond which no Jew and no man should go. True, the Jew can and must compromise, obey and bend to gain power for good; but in the end salvation can never come from gaining power, only by *expending* the power that has been gained to alter the course of events. If this is true, then the power to bring redemption can come only through rejecting Joseph's road as Mordechai does, and traversing the road of Moses and Abraham, the road of disobedience and war.

# 8

# AMALEK

BEYOND THE INSINUATION OF IDOLATRY, the narrative sends audiences familiar with the Bible a second, unmistakable signal that the introduction of Haman into the story is a red-flag event, a point of no return beyond which there is no choice but to drop all pretense of political nicety and fight. For Haman, we are told, is an Agagite. Writers have argued over whether Haman is supposed to be considered a literal descendant of Agag, king of the Amalekites, who had led them against the Jews in the period of the first kingdom five centuries before, or whether the reference is figurative. But in either case the association is clear and the narrative stresses it in various ways so that it cannot be dismissed. Mordechai is introduced as being a Benjaminite, the son of Kish, and therefore a relation of Saul, the son of Kish who became the first king of the Jews and united them in the war against Agag.[1] Moreover, the war against the

Amalekites itself goes back even further, dating from the first days of
the Jews in the desert, when Amalek harassed the recently freed slaves
without mercy. The result is that Haman is not merely "the enemy of
the Jews" because of his determination to murder them, nor is he
simply an anti-Semite, although this is also the case. Haman the
Agagite is heir to a conflict which has dogged the Jews from the day
they left Egypt and became a people.

The exodus of the Jews from Egypt is the central event around
which all of later biblical and Jewish history is built: To do God's will
a people must depart from "the house of bondage" where the Jew is
enslaved to the will of men, strike out into the wilderness of Sinai in
search of eternal truth and law, and only then proceed with freedom
and knowledge to the land of the promised redemption.

The message is one of eternal hope for the Jews as well as all
mankind, and yet it is hardly one of optimism. Having left Egypt amid
signs and wonders, the Jews find themselves very far from utopia. The
books of Moses relate that immediately upon arriving in the wilderness,
the entire project is threatened with ruin by two challenges that hound
the Jews throughout the years to come, and throughout the millennia
to come. The first is internal to the camp of the Jews—the loss of nerve
and embitterment against the physical hardship that must be endured:
The lack of water, and then the lack of food, and then the lack of water
again.[2] The second is external: The ambush by the Amalekite fighters
who fall on the Jews—untrained in bearing arms, burdened by their
women, their aged and their children, and exhausted from the desert—
slaughtering them without mercy.

In both cases, the narrative reports that the Jews are saved from
certain death by a miracle, and yet there is a difference. The hardship
that comes of physical duress—hunger and thirst and the loss of
material comforts such as fresh vegetables—is inevitable. Every great
struggle is fraught with difficulty; were it not, it would hardly be
worth remembering. But the difficulties imposed by the war waged

by Amalek are not inevitable. They are the choice of men, and the judgment of the biblical narrative against the men who chose to become such persecutors is harsh. The books of Moses promise an eternal war against Amalek until the very name of this people is obliterated from under heaven: "And the Eternal said to Moses: I will utterly blot out the remembrance of Amalek from under heaven … Because the Eternal has sworn by his throne that the Eternal will wage war with Amalek from one generation to the next."[3]

There is clearly something greater here than meets the eye. Most marauding desert tribes are in no sense eternal, nor do they boast either the merits or the demerits necessary for God to bother vowing to wage war against them. Moreover, while the Amalekites are certainly idolaters, the imperative to war against them is even more brutal than that against the Canaanite nations: The Canaanite idolatries are to be liquidated from the land of Israel so that they should not be a snare to the Jews, but those who flee the land will be spared. Here there is no mention of idols, no mention of snares, no mention of the land. Instead, Amalek is to be warred against "from one generation to the next," wherever they may be found "under heaven," until not only they but their memory as well are "blotted out." Who are these men?

A more direct expression of what is at stake is found in Deuteronomy, where the story of the Amalekite attack at Refidim is retold:

> Remember what Amalek did to you along the way, when you had come out of the land of Egypt. How he met you along the way, and attacked your rear and all those who were faltering behind, and you were faint and weary, and he feared not God. Therefore, when the Eternal has given you rest from all the enemies about you in the land which the Eternal your God has given you for an inheritance to possess it, you will blot out the memory of Amalek from under heaven. Forget not.[4]

Here the text enumerates three aspects of the events at Refidim to explain the relentless stance to be taken by the Jews against Amalek for all time: (i) Amalek attacked those who were worst off; (ii) Amalek attacked when it was clear that the Jews were powerless to fight; and (iii) Amalek feared not God.

Thus it is not merely the fact that Amalek made war against Israel which earned it the eternal enmity of the Jews. For there may be many reasons to kill when a force of hundreds of thousands is marching through the desert. Wars are fought against rival powers to eliminate them as a threat, or to despoil them, or to enhance one's own reputation. But in all of these cases, the Amalekites should have sought to engage the Jews as a military force—attacking the best men and the least tired in order to destroy them as a threat, or to take them and their possessions into captivity, or to gain in stature for having demolished a formidable power. But in none of these instances should they have wished to pursue the course they did, cutting down the women and children, the old and the lame when it was clear that there could be no benefit to this: Having drenched the sands of Sinai with the blood of Jewish children, they would be no closer to removing a threat, no closer to taking spoil, no closer to glory. What could possibly be the purpose of such a crime?

One answer of course could be that there is no purpose beyond the pleasure involved, beyond the sensation of unrefined liberty which is the spring of cruelty. There are those in the world who need no excuse to taste of this and so enjoy the anguish of the other.

But it seems there is a more compelling reason. The territory of the Amalekites was in the Negev, in the southern reaches of the land of Canaan. If the Jews were to make their way directly across the wilderness of Sinai, it would be the land of Amalek which they would enter first. The threat to Amalekite interests was overt, and the Amalekite response methodical: To kill the children in order to induce the Jewish political and military leadership to give up on the possibility of a more serious fight and back off. For when one attacks the parents or wife or children of a soldier, there is an attack on him as well, not on his body but on his spirit, his sense of rule and his confidence to fight. Damaged enough in early rounds of applied terror, even the most physically powerful opponent may be made to feel that control is lost and that further engagements will bring worse—even that capitulation and "peace" are preferable to further confrontation. The most basic method of terror war even today is just this: The use of applied cruelty against innocents, the more efficiently to forestall the need for direct military engagement.

And there is good reason to think that the Amalekite terror worked precisely as intended. For while the Jews manage to win by miracle in their first engagements with Amalek deep in Sinai, the price of battle is high: When twelve representatives of the Jewish leadership subsequently cross into Canaan to gain an understanding of the forces they will have to challenge, "whether they are strong or weak, few or many,"[5] the result is a complete collapse of nerve. Still feeling the lashes dealt them by a few detachments of Amalekite fighters far from Canaan, the extrapolation to full-scale war is for them simply inconceivable. They gape at the fortifications of Amalek in the south, of the Hittites, Jebusites and Emorites on the central mountain ridge, and of the Kenites in the plains and valleys, and the majority of them return with spirits crushed, unequivocally and absurdly reporting: "All the people that we saw in [the land] are men of great stature.... We were in our own sight as grasshoppers, and so we were in their sight."[6]

There are, it is true, a few men of unquenched spirit among the Jewish leaders—Caleb from the tribe of Judah and Joshua from the line of Joseph are singled out as the leaders of the opposition—who are adamant that the strength of the Canaanites is exaggerated, saying: "Let us go up and possess it, for we are certainly capable of it."[7] But their voices fail to carry the day, and the leadership, supported by most of the people, insists on withdrawal rather than war. And once this position is staked out, the incredible conclusions are quickly drawn. Judging themselves unable to enter the land, the Jews decide they have no other choice but to capitulate further and return to slavery in Egypt: "Why has the Eternal brought us to this land, to fall by the sword, and that our wives and children should be prey? Would it not be better for us to return to Egypt? ... Let us appoint a leader and return to Egypt."[8] The taste of blood offered the Jewish wives and children at the hand of Amalek has done its work: The Amalekites have gained themselves peace from the Jews for forty years and more—during which time they continue their abominations at leisure, while the Jews, restrained from returning to Egypt by Moses, wait out their qualms in a desert purgatory of their own devising.

In this dreadful episode lies the basis of the Jewish God's war against Amalek from generation to generation. Amalek's wrong is in its insistence on savaging those least capable of defending themselves—for the pleasure in it, or because it is the least strenuous method of asserting Amalekite control and bringing Jewish military power to its knees. An invalid or a child is for Amalek a tempting target, precisely because each is no threat to him at all—and once he is willing to ask what good may come of destroying these, he inevitably finds satisfactory answers. In so calculating, Amalek pursues his own ends, whatever these may be, without any threshold to stay his hand. Amalek concerns himself with no consequences other than those that a mismove in the shifting of earthly power can produce. In the language of the books of Moses, Amalek "fears not God"—and so brings himself into collision with the thought of the Jews, in which to "fear God" is considered a cornerstone of the entire structure of the law and of civilization itself, as the books of Moses demand: "And now, Israel, what does the Eternal your God require of you, other than to fear the Eternal your God...?"[9]

Yet contrary to what might be inferred, the difference between the man who fears God and the one who fears not is not necessarily emotional at all—that is, not necessarily a matter of being afraid; rather, what is of highest significance is that the man who fears God behaves differently towards his fellow man, as is evident from the other uses of this expression in the books of Moses: "You will not curse the deaf, nor place a stumbling block before the blind, and you will fear your God...."[10] And: "Love the stranger, for you were strangers in the land of Egypt. You will fear the Eternal your God...."[11] Similar verses associate the fear of God with respect for the aged, and with the refusal to engage in fraud, the abuse of one's bondsmen, or extortion from those who have taken on loans.[12] Each case is the same: One may easily harm another who is dependent and weak—the deaf, the aged, the farmer, the slave. A person who "fears God" will recognize a limiting line beyond which he may not cross; while one who "fears not God" will recognize no such line, as suggested by Abraham's infamous assessment to Avimelech: "Surely, there is no fear of God in this place, and they will kill me to have my wife."[13]

Yet there is much more profound disagreement here than a mere dispute over whether moral delimitations are recognizable in the nature of the world. What Amalek represents is the oldest position in moral philosophy: The denial that, on balance, there is anything to fear about any moral line which might be drawn, since it is strict adherence to evident personal or political interest that rewards most handsomely—the thesis that "crime pays." The position of the Jews, on the other hand, claims that moral boundaries are not only recognizable, but dangerous; that is, that the violation of such a limiting line in one's behavior is itself, on balance, sufficiently imprudent that it must be *feared*, in effect making life within the confines of moral limiting lines a matter of personal and political interest in this world—the thesis that "crime does not pay."

This remarkable claim is the subject of a parable of the rabbis to the effect that Amalek and Jethro the Midianite, Moses' father-in-law, both served as advisers to Pharaoh, each one beginning from a

position of enmity towards the Jews—"But when Jethro beheld that
God had blotted out Amalek both from this world and the next, he
felt remorse and repented."[14] The point is that various of the desert
tribes of Canaan, Midian included, live according to a paradigm
such as that of Amalek—qualifying any of them to serve as mentors
to Pharaoh, whose morally undelimited understanding of his political interest leads him to murder Jewish children at birth for concern
that the Jews have become a threat to his rule. (The midwives Shifra
and Pua, on the other hand, are distinguished from Pharaoh in their
unwillingness to participate in the slaughter, despite their obvious
interest in obeying the law, "for they feared God.")[15] What leads to
Jethro's rejection of the position of Amalek—and so to the rabbinic
suggestion that he became a proselyte to Judaism[16]—is not revelation, but prudence: So long as moral claims are aimed at convincing
him that he must sacrifice his interest in this world to secure his
position in another, he can easily deny the existence of any other
world. It is only the recognition that the paradigm of Amalek
ultimately brings destruction to its adherents in this world, as well,
which can move a pragmatist such as Jethro to think that moral
limits must be feared at all.

It is some such process of reasoning which, the rabbis suggest,
must bring a non-Jew such as Jethro to approach Moses in the
narrative in Exodus, and present him with what becomes the Jewish
alternative to government according to the Amalekite-Pharaonic
paradigm: "Take from among the entire people men of strength,
who fear God, men of truth, hating illicit gain, and place them over
them...."[17] Here, as well, the reason for the demand that the rulers
"fear God" is apparent: That they should be unwilling to abuse those
in their charge for their own self-interest.

It is important to note that the books of Moses themselves also
address the question of the superiority of the Jewish paradigm over
the Amalekite one from the perspective of secular, non-Jewish wisdom.

The position of such wisdom is represented by the conjurer Bil'am, "the man whose eyes are open,"[18] who is commissioned by an ornery Moabite king to curse the Jews. Bil'am, however, comes to examine the situation for himself and finds that, regardless of what the desert kings may wish, there is an actual truth to the matter, and it is the opposite of that which they decree. With regard to Amalek, he concludes: "The beginning of all nations is Amalek, but his end is eternal annihilation"[19]—meaning that in all the world, the powerful have always begun from Amalekite premises; but in the end these prove themselves only to be destructive. With regard to Israel he concludes: "He has beheld no iniquity in Jacob, and has seen no perversity in Israel…. How goodly are your tents, O Jacob, your dwelling places, Israel…. God brought him up from Egypt, as the horns of the wild ox is God to him, he will devour his enemies among the nations…."[20] Far from being a sacrifice of personal and political interest, Bil'am argues that the fear of God among the Jews provides them personal well-being as individuals, and translates as well into tremendous strength in the confrontation with Israel's external enemies. To "the man whose eyes are open," it is Judaism that is the path to self-interest, and Amalek the path to self-destruction.

The figure of Amalek therefore stands as the anti-Jew, caught up in the most false and destructive of idolatries: The belief that the pursuit of power is the only proper justification of human action, and that the power-idol—more correctly, the human spirit itself as idol—suffices to justify all human action in its pursuit.

Herein lies the distinction between Amalek and other idolatries to which the Jews stand in eternal opposition: Idolatry as a general case is the subjugation of moral valuation to standards dictated by partial truths deriving from a local, and therefore essentially arbitrary, perspective. As such, every idolatry is evil in principle, even if it seems perfectly benign. One can imagine a tree or a star or a man-divinity whose adherents are *not* obliged by its dictates to commit perversity and violence; perhaps they are obligated to do good. Such a theology is an evil and a snare because it denies the principle of universal and absolute moral valuations (that "God is one"), and so allows in principle for all manner of evil. But it is nevertheless possible that its disciples are, in this sense, "God-fearing"—as indeed some pagans in the books of Moses appear to be.[21] They know some version of right and wrong, and they fear to do wrong according to what they know.

In Amalek we find the reverse case. We have no idea what Amalekite idols there might be—none are named, no statues or other actual idols are mentioned. For all we know there may have been none at all. What we do know is that whatever deities may have belonged to Amalek, it was a people which did not fear any moral boundaries established by them. Unlike the most depraved of the idolaters of Canaan, they respected no limits to the desire of their own spirit to control all as it found fit.

What is frightening is to recognize how difficult this idea is to uproot—or rather, how difficult it is to implant the belief in moral limits which must be feared if man is to live. This is the reason that, while the commandment to blot out Amalek from the world is stressed again in Deuteronomy, so too is the ominous warning not to forget to do so. The irony, of course, is that God's promise to annihilate the memory of Amalek from the earth is to no small degree undermined by his promise to war against Amalek for untold generations. Like hunger and thirst, there is a sense in which Amalek, although fit to be eradicated in every generation, is nevertheless eternal. Just as man tends to turn away from what he must do to avoid hunger and thirst as soon as he is sated, so too does the willingness to set limits on his behavior erode when he feels safe and is not faced with the consequences. And we know from our own experience, too, that those who deny all limits are forever finding the beautiful words, the high phrases and the slippery and diseased thoughts needed to strengthen this beast in others, to make them appreciate and approve, and to pull them along and down, men and nations, into their abyss, these Amalekites, the anti-Jew.

Not flippantly is Haman referred to over and over as "Haman, the enemy of the Jews." For in his pursuit of power without limit, and in his willingness to destroy all the Jewish people, "the young and the elderly, children and women," in order to have his way with Mordechai, he repeats precisely the first crime of the Amalekites, who "attacked your rear and all those who were faltering behind" to have their way with the Jews. In so doing he proves himself to be a true Agagite—whose struggle to eradicate the Jews by bleeding the defenseless among them had begun in the desert wastes a thousand years before he was born.

# 9

# ANTI-SEMITISM

A CENTURY HAS PASSED since the term "anti-Semite" was invented, as though for an illness or a political party, to describe one who harbors a hatred for Jews. Today it has come into wide use, yet it conveys as little as it ever did, or less. It still takes no more effort to explain that one "hates Jews" than it does to ascribe "anti-Semitism" to him; and the Jews, of course, were never actually hated for being Semitic, that is, an eastern people. But the failure to have found a more meaningful name for the disease only reflects on how little we comprehend it. For what term can one devise to express a condition which has sought out a tiny race and hunted it out over the entire globe, generation after generation, for thousands of years, in turn seeking to abolish, expel, shame, rape, convert, torture, confine and exterminate it—and all to no apparent end other than to increase the desire to see the project through the next time around?

There have been those who claim that anti-Semitism is a byproduct of Christianity, yet it has haunted Islam from its very foundations; those who believed it was a matter of religious persecution until the Nazis made it a matter of race; those who believe it is the product of ignorance, yet it has claimed many of the most brilliant minds in history. Anti-Semitism is everywhere, and no race nor creed nor time seems impervious to it. Every people rises and falls except the Jews; and no hatred has ever been so great, so abiding, so permanent as the hatred of the Jews. What does it mean?

The Jewish people came into being with anti-Semitism. Indeed, the first time in history that we encounter the Jews as a people, it is amid the rage of an enemy, and his plot to destroy them:

> The children of Israel were fruitful and increased abundantly and multiplied and grew exceedingly mighty and the land was filled with them. Now there arose a new king over Egypt who knew not Joseph. He said to his people: "Behold, the people of Israel are more and mightier than we. Come, let us deal wisely with them lest they multiply and it come to pass that when any war should chance, they also join our enemies and fight against us and go up out of the land." Therefore they set taskmasters over them to afflict them with their burdens…. But the more they afflicted them the more they multiplied and grew, and they were mortified on account of the people of Israel…. And Pharaoh charged all his people, saying: "Every son that is born will you cast into the Nile, and every daughter will you keep alive."[1]

The account of this first decision on a final solution to the Jewish problem is startling in its prescience, its component parts all too familiar to us:

(i) The Jews succeed well beyond their numbers. Thus in a mere century or two the seventy children of Israel who came into Egypt have become tens of thousands and then hundreds of thousands.

(ii) Pharaoh assesses the Jews to be "more and mightier than we," although this is clearly an absurdity.

(iii) Pharaoh fears that the Jews will fly out of his control, rebelling, siding with his opponents, fleeing Egypt.

(iv) The continued growth of the Jews is received by the Egyptians as an emotional horror—"they were mortified."

(v) Pharaoh decides on a preliminary effort to reduce their strength by imposing special taxation of forced labor.

(vi) Finally, he determines to annihilate the Jews altogether through the slaughter of their male children and the absorption of their women into the Egyptian population.

At first glance, the entire account makes little sense. Successful as the Jews may have been, Pharaoh's assertions to the effect that the Jews had grown more powerful than all Egypt are preposterous. The Nile River basin was one of the great centers of population in the world, its people numbering in the millions. Moreover, nothing in the narrative suggests that any of the Jews had the slightest training in warfare. We are therefore left with the conclusion that Pharaoh and his entire people were drawn to slaughter the Jews among them, despite their being perfectly good slaves, for no rational cause whatever. And this despite Pharaoh's efforts to couch his argument as though it were a rational, strategic calculation.

The key word for understanding what was taking place among the Egyptians is *vayakutzu*—"and they were mortified" because of the Jews. The Hebrew word has the connotation of being stung, or stabbed by thorns—"and they were stung on account of the Jews." The response to the success of the Jews and their growth is not one of actual fear, but a burning, stinging rage which consumes the Egyptians all the more as their repeated efforts to subjugate the Jews meet with failure. It is this same hatred which we find in the book of Esther, when the vizier's sensation of perfect control is marred by his inability to control the Jew: "And all the king's servants who were in the king's gate bowed and prostrated themselves before Haman, for the king had so ordained concerning him, but Mordechai did not bow nor prostrate himself.... When Haman saw that Mordechai did not bow nor prostrate himself, Haman was filled with rage." (3:2, 5) And just as the fact of the multiplying Jewish children continues to prick at the Egyptians at every point when they consider it—the text in Exodus speaks of the growth of the Jews no fewer than nine consecutive times—so too does Haman's pain and hatred deepen upon every encounter with Mordechai:

> Haman went out that day happy and in high spirits, but when Haman saw Mordechai in the king's gate, how he neither stood nor stirred before him, Haman was filled with rage against Mordechai. Haman restrained himself and returned to his house, and he sent for his friends and for Zeresh his wife. Haman recounted to them the glory of his riches, and the great number of his sons, and everything in which the king had promoted him and elevated him above the princes and servants of the king.... "Yet all this is worthless to me, so long as I see Mordechai the Jew sitting at the king's gate." (5:9–11, 13)

It is this stinging pain of the spirit of Pharaoh and Haman, increasing unto the point of explosion, to which the rabbis alluded when they spoke of the desire to rule as a consuming crocodile which can digest anything but the Jews: "Nebuchadnezzar, king of Babylonia, had a great crocodile, which swallowed everything thrown to it. Nebuchadnezzar said to Daniel: 'So great is its might that it consumes everything that is thrown to it.' ... Daniel took straw, hid nails within it, and fed it to the crocodile, rupturing its intestines."[2] The Jews at first appear to be weak, digestible as straw. But it invariably transpires that these straws are nails: They do not melt away with digestion, instead remaining small but utterly solid, and so stinging ever more painfully the more they are pressed down upon.

Of critical importance here is the impression of relative power with which the spirit grasps the world: That which is within the bounds of control is perceived to be small and weak ("We were in our own sight as grasshoppers, and so we were in their sight"); that which is out of control is perceived to be great and powerful ("All the people that we saw in Canaan were men of great stature"). And the spirit is quiet so long as the reverse is also found to be true: That that which is small and weak is controlled in practice, obeying the dictates of the will; while only an opponent of immense and terrifying power is, for obvious and understandable reasons, in the meantime left out of control. But the spirit is most pained when that which is presumed controlled is found to be something other than expected—when one has been rejected by a loved one, when a precious possession has been discovered ruined, when one is publicly proven unequal to an activity at which one is thought to excel. The hot shame, the fear and anger of these, and their horror, are the contents of the crocodile-mind when the straws in its belly prove to be nails.

The Jew is the epitome of weakness, a slave, an exile, defeated, dispersed, despised—the first who should rightly disappear in the face of power. And this is how the ruler understands the Jews as well, for too long perceiving them, from the perspective of the materialist, or of Amalek, as being strong only in accord with the arms they can muster. Yet eventually, perhaps having been inexplicably stung by the arrogant disobedience of one such as Moses or Mordechai, he comes to look more closely and realizes that this is not the case. Instead of conforming to the will of the state, they are forever found to be clutching at some bit of their own agenda—"their laws are different from those of other peoples." And this Jewish insistence on a different authority other than the state is for the ruler a direct threat, as Resh Lakish asserted in depicting the Persian view of the Jews as forever arrogant, forever threatening: "A certain people that there is among us which, although they are the most contemptible of peoples, is nonetheless exceedingly haughty. They desire our evil and are forever cursing the king. What is the curse which they utter against us? 'The Eternal is King forever and ever, the nations are perished out of his land.' (Psalms 10:16)"[3] And it is this tiny, laughable resistance which is always there to be found, which never fails through eternity. No matter how badly he is burned and beaten, the Jew continues rasping out his foolishness, "cursing the king" and pursuing what the Czarist secret police referred to as the conspiracy of the Elders of Zion.[4]

In coming to recognize that the Jew cannot easily be brought under control, however, the ruler invariably makes the transition from considering the Jew inconsequential to vastly exaggerating his power. Since the Jew cannot be ruled, the spirit begins to sense his strength, contrary to all surface indications, to be immense, as in Pharaoh's belief that his Jewish slaves are "more and mightier than we." In Esther, this same phenomenon receives eerie expression in the soothsaying of Zeresh, Haman's wife, for whom any sign of an increase in Jewish power is, as it was for Pharaoh, a sign of imminent doom: "If he be of Jewish descent, this Mordechai, before whom you have begun to fall, you will not prevail against him, but you will surely fall before him." (6:13) Ironically, it is the very weakness of the Jews, their dispersion and lack of a government capable of defending their interests which, once the Jews are understood as a political challenge, becomes the basis for a paranoia with regard to them— that Jews are "dispersed in all the provinces of your kingdom" implies that the degree of their subversion can be virtually infinite.

Like the king's servants, the Jews are everywhere, and it is a small step from here to controlling the financial system, or the press, or hostile foreign powers, or the world. It is precisely this same sense of the mysterious power of the Jews which Haman uses to convince the king that there is no choice but to eradicate the menace: "There is a certain people scattered and dispersed among the people in all the provinces of your kingdom, and their laws are different from those of other peoples, and the king's laws they do not keep, so that it is of no benefit for the king to tolerate them. If it please the king, let it be written that they be destroyed...." (3:8–9)

It therefore transpires that there is no such thing as a *small* threat to the fantasy of perfect control. The realm of the spirit's control is either subjugated or not, and the tiniest threat, if permitted to sting long enough, is therefore total. And the Jew, in his endless consultations with old and subversive documents, his perennial reservations, his ceaseless chafing against the will of the state, his conditions, refusals and disobediences, always places the control of the ruler in doubt, necessarily offends his spirit, necessarily makes mockery of his pretensions to total power. In his tiny steadfastness, his almost pitiful solidity and indigestibility, the Jew succeeds in being the nightmare of every man of perfect rule: He is organized resistance, systematic decontrol, the smashing of the idol.

This success amid weakness of the Jew, the sting and the rage of the one who would rule, and then genocide—this is the eternal formula of anti-Semitism, the reaction of the idol whose power and whose essence the Jew denies, and which, discovering the flaws in its own power, its own falseness, must deny it at all cost; it is the lashing of the crocodile as it tries to crush the nail of which it is impotent to rid itself.

But then, this means that the hatred of the anti-Semite is not without cause. And of course this is the case. We may blame Haman for succumbing to this original sin of the political world, the temptation to let his spirit dictate to him and to the world its totalist fantasy. But once he desires such power, war against the Jew must become inevitable, as he comes to recognize in the Jew the desire and the ability to deprive him of what he believes is his right: The ability to "rule in his own house." It was this that moved Hitler to despise the Jews for constantly agitating to make Austria less the subject of the unified pan-German will, as Mordechai detracts from making Persia the subject of the will of Haman. And Stalin, too, and the endless procession of anti-Zionists in Islam—all of whom rage for the restoration of their birthright, for their rule in their house, for the unity and singleness of purpose which can belong to a nation only so long as it is not contaminated by alien elements and alien wills, constantly speaking of something else, constantly seeking a different end to a different story.

To realize this is to comprehend the incomprehensible, that the torment of the Jews in history has a cause, that no matter the time or place, the one who seeks rule will, through exposure to the Jews, relearn the anti-Semitism of Pharaoh, Amalek and Haman. And that in learning it, he will yet again set out to fight this same war, the war between the disobedient and those who can stand no disobedience; between the imposers of limits and those who can accept no limits; between the rejectors of the idols and the spirit-idol which can tolerate no rejection; between Jew and anti-Jew, as the anti-Semite is known when called by his name—a war in which every Jewish child is enlisted at birth, no matter who may wish it otherwise.

But if anti-Semitism is the inevitable false-fruit of man's spirit, the figure of the Jew always appearing to the would-be ruler in whoever threatens the heart of his power, then anti-Semitism must exist even before the existence of Pharaoh's persecution of the Jews, even before Abraham, the first Jew. And, indeed, the rabbis understood this to be the case. Thus R. Levi taught:

Cursed are the wicked, who all devise evil against Israel, each one devising according to his own idea, and then saying, "My device is better than yours."

Esau said: Cain was a fool for killing his brother in the lifetime of his father, not knowing that his father would still have children. I will not do so, "But let the days of mourning of my father be at hand, then I will slay my brother Jacob."

Pharaoh said: Esau was a fool. Did he not know that his brother would have children in the lifetime of his father? I will not make such a mistake, but I will strangle them while they are small and barely out of their mothers' wombs. And so it says: "Every son that is born you will cast into the river."

Haman said: Pharaoh was a fool for saying, "Every son that is born you will cast into the river." Did he not know that the daughters would marry and have children? I will not make such a mistake, but will decree "to annihilate, to kill and to destroy."

So Gog and Magog in the time to come will say: Our predecessors were fools for laying their plans, they and their kings together against Israel, not knowing that they have a protector in heaven. I will not do so, but I will first attack their protector and then I will attack them. And so it says: "The kings of the earth stand up and the rulers take counsel together against the Eternal, and against his anointed."[5]

Like anti-Semitism, the Jew existed before he was named, before he was born. That a man is small and weak but possessed of other higher qualities, that he believes in what is right in the face of all opposition, that he disobeys rather than succumbing to the rule of the strong, that he survives when he should have perished—this is the spectre of the Jew which is born in the breast of Cain, the first anti-Jew, the farmer who worked like an animal of burden to provide a suitable sacrifice to the Eternal. And when his brother Abel, a shepherd, labored less in the harsh sun and pondered more into the night, so that it was his sacrifice to the Eternal which was preferred, he became in Cain's eyes that spectre, that fear which had haunted his nightmares—that sting which can never be removed, and being unremovable, continues to impale the spirit, to infect it and inflame it, from Eden to eternity, a hatred so deep that for the sake of it he would murder his brother, that for the sake of it he would raze the world to its very foundations.

# ESTHER
# FOUR
[4:1 – 4:17]

When Mordechai learned of all that had been done, Mordechai rent his clothes, and dressed in sackcloth and ashes, and went out into the city, crying out a loud and bitter cry. He came as far as the king's gate, although none might enter the king's gate clothed in sackcloth. In every province, wherever the king's command and his law reached, there was great mourning among the Jews, and fasting and crying and wailing, many of them lying in sackcloth and ashes.

Esther's maids and her chamberlains came and told her, and the queen was exceedingly distressed, and she sent garments to clothe Mordechai so that he might remove his sackcloth, but he would not accept them. Esther summoned Hatach, from among the king's chamberlains, whom he had placed in her service, and charged him to go out to Mordechai to learn what this was and why it was.

Hatach went out to Mordechai, to the city square which was in front of the king's gate. Mordechai told him of all that had happened to him, and of the money that Haman had offered to pay into the royal treasuries for the Jews, to have them destroyed. And he gave him a copy of the law which had been circulated in Susa sanctioning the annihilation of the Jews, so that he might show it to Esther and speak to her, charging her to go to the king, to plead with him and to entreat him for her people. Hatach came to Esther and told her what Mordechai had said.

Esther said to Hatach, instructing him to tell Mordechai: "All the king's servants and the people of the king's provinces know that there is but one law for any man or woman who comes to the king in the inner court without having been summoned: That he be put to death, except if the king extends to him the gold scepter that he may live — and I have not been summoned to the king for thirty days now."

They told Mordechai what Esther had said. Mordechai said to reply to Esther: "Do not imagine in your heart that you, of all the Jews, will escape because you are in the king's palace. For if you insist on remaining silent at this time, relief and deliverance will come to the Jews from elsewhere, but you and your father's house will perish. And who knows whether it was not for such a time as this that you came into royalty?"

Esther said to respond to Mordechai: "Go assemble all the Jews present in Susa and fast for me. Do not eat and do not drink for three days, night and day, and I and my maids will fast as well. Then I will go in to the king, though it is against the law. And if I perish, I perish."

Mordechai took his leave and did everything which Esther had instructed him to do.

# 10

# PRESSURE

IN THE SILENT HALLS OF THE PALACE, the decree of extermination falls like the closing of the gates at sunset, and the wretched spirit of the vizier is sated. But in the streets the people are dumbfounded, Jew and gentile alike, for if Haman will now murder an entire nation on account of the refusal of one man to bow, what might he do next?

Mordechai seeks no advice and convenes no councils to discuss the decree of extermination. Upon being confronted with it, his response is immediate: He takes to the streets. Rending his clothing and smearing himself with soot, he walks through the broad places of the city screaming and wailing in grief. People rush to the windows and to the doorways. Passersby stop to take in the spectacle, to ask who is this man and what has befallen him. He makes his way through the onlookers and arrives at the palace where the guards recognize him, but prevent him from entering, for "none might enter the king's gate clothed in sackcloth." (4:2) They push him aside, threatening him, thinking he might be dangerous to the king in his anguish. Eventually, they merely push him off a distance lest any of the king's ministers catch sight of him and blame them for allowing such a breach of decorum.

Mordechai takes a number of steps back and sits down in the street. He takes up his crying again, his presence accosting all those who enter the king's gate to pursue their duties. Some who enter the palace, seeing Mordechai there, can barely hide a smile of satisfaction, for at last the insolent Jew has been put in his place. Others, with whom Mordechai has found favor in the past, whom he has advised or whom he has assisted in various ways, gather around him. Some offer him information, others advice. What kind of government is this, he interrupts them. Do you not see what has been born? Do you not see that such a one will murder any one of you who raises his head, him together with all his loved ones, even his entire people? What will become of all your interests now? And among them there are those whose hearts break to see him so, and those who understand the meaning of the thing.

Some of the rabbis stressed the religious piety of Mordechai's mourning.[1] And there is no reason to doubt the conviction of one who has been condemned to death, who may certainly come to regret his faults and fear God as he never has before. But it is not for his grief nor for his repentance that Mordechai's reaction to the decree must be considered exceptional. It is for the open, public nature of his outcry. To understand this we need only consider that other decree, of the slaughter of the Hebrew children by Pharaoh's state—which, so far as we are informed, met with no public response on the part of any Jew whatsoever: Pharaoh ordered that the Jews be reduced to slavery and hard labor, and met with no outcry worthy of having been recorded. Then he ordered that the midwives murder the male children, and still there was no reaction such as Mordechai's. Finally, when the servants of Pharaoh begin to take up the slaughter in earnest, coming into the houses of the Jews in search of the newborn infants, taking them from mothers weak from birth and hysterical from tears, carrying them past fathers with teeth and fists clenched in agony, loading them onto wagons with the howling others, howling with hunger, with dirt, with fear, and finally throwing them into the Nile to drown—when all this was actually done before the eyes of the Jews, they responded with silence.

Of course, the books of Moses recount this story in order to relate not the silence, but that resistance which did take place—how the Jewish midwives refuse to collaborate in the atrocity, lying to Pharaoh in order to avoid incurring his blame; how, once the killings have started, Jocheved and her daughter hide her baby and find him a place of refuge; and how Pharaoh's daughter protects the child against her father and the state. It is by means of the bravery of these women that a leader is born to Israel through whom the Jewish people is saved.[2] And yet these, too, are stories of silence. What resistance there is takes place behind a veil of deception, concealed from the state and its officials, as well as from the Jewish public. Moreover, the resistance of the Jewish women in Egypt is in an important sense *apolitical*—its aim being to ameliorate the effects of the decree in some limited way, while making no effort to influence Pharaoh and his advisers to alter the policy of the state itself. Of course, the reason for the lack of political resistance is clear enough: The fear of the state is so great that any such effort is thought to be useless and suicidal. But the fact remains that in the absence of any evident opposition to the decree itself, the state has no reason whatsoever to move from its course.

Resistance to Ahashverosh's decree is not in principle any more safe or certain than opposition would have been in Egypt. In fact, in making public his opposition to the decree, the only thing that

Mordechai can know with certainty is that he courts immediate punishment. Nevertheless, he chooses to take his anger and grief to the broad places of the capital, to the king's gate, perhaps even to the king himself if he had been able to do so, for a reason—for a *political* reason. And that is that a claim lodged in silence, an appeal made in silence, an interest defended in silence, is one that is not lodged, not made and not defended. The entire purpose of Ahashverosh in elevating Haman to the point where his will alone determines questions of state is to do away with politics, to silence the struggle among competing claims and truths. And if Mordechai is to prevent a repetition of the slaughter of the Jews by Pharaoh, his only hope is to find a way to break Haman's monopoly and allow another voice somehow to be heard, a voice that will speak for a different policy.

In politics, the effect of the voice which is heard by the decisionmaker is understood by means of a metaphor. It is known as pressure. When a trusted adviser threatens to resign if a policy is not changed; when a province is in rebellion over a measure promulgated by the central government; when a foreign government instructs its ambassador to threaten a boycott of the king's goods or war—these are pressure. In these cases the threat to the king is overt, the resistance not merely evident but extortionary, suggesting to the ruler what he has perhaps not wished to hear, that the course upon which he has embarked is not worth the cost. And while few are the individuals who can exert the pressure of a trusted adviser, a rebellious province, or the ambassador of a foreign power, this does not mean that others are without recourse. We know from experience that the public can succeed in exerting pressure on the state as well. This is the reason that flatterers and lobbyists come to court to press their claims with the king's advisers; that the public is urged to correspond with officials en masse; that public protest is conducted in the street, so all those who may be of influence may themselves be influenced, and at the appropriate moment take up the cause. When this chain of pressure is understood, it becomes possible to plan a political campaign, whose purpose is to muster every possible source of pressure on the ruler in favor of a change in policy, and to neutralize those forces which are propelling the state in its present direction.

Elementary though the political campaign of influence may be to politics in every society, it is astonishing that not only the skills for such work, but even the awareness of its possibility do not exist among all peoples at all times. Thus the Jews in the time of Pharaoh, even those who resisted the persecution at the risk of their lives, nevertheless could not imagine responding politically. Indeed, it is the fear of confronting the ruler, the certitude that reservations voiced will result only in punishment, which is the hallmark of the thought of a slave. The cruelties of Pharaoh's government therefore continued for upwards of eighty years before any Jew thought to approach the state with the demand that they cease: Before Moses, who had grown up amid the politics of the court—who had, as the rabbis suggested, grown up playing at removing the crown from Pharaoh's head and placing it on his own[3]—realized that even Pharaoh would change course if sufficient pressure were brought to bear. The story of the destruction of the Jews in Europe in our own time is likewise characterized by the utter lack of political pressure on the German regime and its allies to cease their atrocities. Even in the free countries the activities of the Jews to bring pressure upon their governments were minimal—while the Germans themselves were ferocious in lobbying foreign governments to the ends of the earth to destroy those Jews under their control. And when one side applies pressure to attain the execution of a policy, and this policy meets with no resistance from the other side, the results are foregone.[4]

Like Moses, Mordechai is no Hebrew slave, but a man of the court, for whom the need for the political campaign against the decree is clear and pressing. And it is this which moves him to overcome the fear and self-doubt which must grip every man rising to challenge the mighty, saying: "Who am I, that I should bring the people of Israel out of Egypt?"—to which the only answer can be that of the ministering angel, descending with a crown to place on the head of every man setting on a course of truth, and the message: "I will be with you...."⁵ And so Mordechai, too, goes down to deliver his people.

When he first goes into the public places, Mordechai has no way of knowing who will respond; or whether they will respond to the echoes of his cries in their conscience, to the memory of past favors he has done for them, or to their own interest in checking the power of the vizier. Nor can he know who among these may actually be able to exert the necessary influence to help. But he makes the case as well as it can be made, and to as many as he can reach: He dresses in mourning, that all who see him may appreciate his terror; he cries as he makes his way through the public places of the capital, that all may recognize the crisis that has come upon them, whether they have heard the decree or not; and he takes his protest to the king's gate, that every man of influence, means and resources may be directly confronted with what has been done, requiring each to make a conscious judgment that might otherwise have been avoided behind a pretense of "We didn't know"—he forces them to decide whether they are in support of the policy or against. And if they are indeed against, whether they are man enough to join in with pressure of their own.

# II

# COURT JEW

IT MAY BE THAT MORDECHAI SUCCEEDS in touching others among the courtiers in the four days he sits in sackcloth at the entrance to the palace.[1] But, as is often the case, the narrative tells us only of the one instance that in the end proves to have mattered: The queen. Upon hearing of his protest, Esther is "exceedingly distressed," (4:4) and sends Mordechai a change of clothes that he may immediately strip off the dirt in which he is attired. This he refuses to do, and only then does Esther send a trusted servant to inquire into the cause of the uproar.

The sequence of events tells us much about the mindset of the queen. Esther is "exceedingly distressed," as it turns out, not by the impending slaughter of her people, of which she is ignorant, but by the appearance of her cousin before the court carrying on so and in such attire. Knowing nothing of the background, apparently not even of the confrontation which had erupted between Mordechai and the vizier days earlier, she fears only that offense will be given against the norms of court conduct, the law and the king himself. She sees everything that Mordechai has taught her about gaining favor and influence being set to torch, and everything he has gained by years of building himself up as a loyal servant of the king about to be ruined in a single, incomprehensible act. Esther need not even know the subject in order to respond aghast, to refuse to go along, to try to make him stop.

When the chamberlain comes out to Mordechai, we find that the Jew is fully prepared to receive him. Any suspicion that Mordechai's act may have been ill-prepared and impulsive is allayed when he explains the content of the decree, relates inside information about the vizier's effort to bribe the king, and then hands him a copy of the decree itself which he has prepared. Finally, he comes forward with a demand: That Esther go in to the king and urge him to repeal the law.

Esther quickly sends the official back with a reply: She cannot do it. Of course, she is too polite to refuse outright, but refuse she does. And she explains herself: "All the king's servants and the people of the king's provinces know that there is but one law for any man or woman who comes to the king in the inner court without having been summoned: That he be put to death, except if the king extends to him the gold scepter that he may live—and I have not been summoned to the king for thirty days now." (4:11) Her reply thus consists of several responses, one tumbling over the next:

(i)   No, because it is against the law.

(ii)  No, because I will die.

(iii) No, because it will not help anyway, since I will die.

(iv)  He will not forgive me, because no one else behaves so.

(v)   He will not forgive me, because he does not care enough for me.

Here, in full view, is Esther's reaction to the threat of a confrontation over the policy of the king: She cannot imagine succeeding, she is afraid to die—and there is little else. Having learned how important it is to win favor, Esther nonetheless falters when it comes time to take the next step, using this favor to exert her own influence. In her mind, the ruler cannot be approached, his mind cannot be changed, his wrath is certain and fierce. Her self-image is nothing but the corollary: She cannot possibly challenge him, she cannot change his mind, she will be destroyed if she tries.

In this too we see the shadows of Moses' confrontation with Pharaoh. When Moses first comes to the Jews of Egypt to say he has come to liberate them, they joyously accept his leadership and his mission—for who would not agree to being quickly, easily liberated from servitude? Yet Pharaoh is not inclined to let the Jews go on Moses' first demand, nor his second, nor his third. And his displeasure is expressed not only in words: He disapproves of the resistance instigated by the new Jewish leadership and—much as does Haman at the first sign of resistance—moves with overwhelming force to crush any deviation from submission, increasing the work demanded of the Jews and threatening punishment if they do not maintain their schedule. For this bruising confrontation the Jews are completely unprepared, and rather than responding with further steps against Pharaoh, they recoil in fear over what they have done. Turning against Moses and Aaron, they say to them: "The Eternal look upon you and judge, for you have made us despised in the eyes of Pharaoh and in the eyes of his servants, putting a sword in their hands with which to slay us."[2]

The tendency to think first about the reactions of the powerful ("What will the gentiles think?") is well known in every Jewish politics. And here it is evident that this line of reasoning was already well ingrained in Egypt, at the very founding of the Jewish people itself, when two opposing and familiar political parties formed over the looming confrontation with Pharaoh: The one, led by Moses and Aaron, asserted that Pharaoh had slaughtered the Jews as children, oppressed them as adults, and now sought to break them and drive them to despair; there was nothing to be gained by appeasing him. The other, apparently comprising most of the "official" leadership of the enslaved people, argued that only greater evil would come of angering Pharaoh, and that this course would only bring senseless destruction: Better not to rock the boat. Indeed, the rabbis suggested that as Moses and Aaron walked through the street on the way to their first encounter with Pharaoh, the Jewish elders who had at first supported them stole away one by one, so that when the actual moment of confrontation came, there were none left to back them.[3] Returning to their hovels, defeated in a battle that had not even taken place, they might easily have said to one another: We were in our own sight as grasshoppers, and so we were in Pharaoh's sight as well.[4]

Invariably, the slave is afraid to fight his master. A broken spirit, even though it is broken, also seeks the sensation of stability and control—and this stability is supplied by the assurance of the solidity, the inevitability, of the ruler's will; while the ruler's anger and fear of his punishment are the greatest threats to this stability. The Jew who argues for a campaign of pressure, or any other confrontation with the power of the ruler, therefore finds that his first opponent is the leadership of the Jews themselves—those leaders who, like the elders in Moses' time, have made their careers in accommodation. In them we have the classic image of the "court Jew," whose success has always depended on the favor of the ruler, and whose life-security and self-esteem are built upon it as well. And since it is ultimately the ruler's acceptance that this leader desires above all else, the very possibility of such confrontation and the loss of such acceptance strikes him with terror.

Yet despite her condition of subservience to the king, Esther is not a slave. She is the most successful woman in the kingdom, accustomed to the dotage and service of others. Does not her constant exertion of her will in royal life set her far apart from the example of the Jewish slaves in Egypt, afraid even to lift their heads to make a request before Pharaoh, lest he destroy them?

Closer to Esther's situation is the case of Joseph. Highly talented and self-assured, Joseph at no point hesitates to defy those who stand in his way. The resentment of his brothers does not deter him from seeking to impose order on them as a boy. And as lord over Egypt, he appears to notice no man's opposition as he extorts the entire land into his command, buys the population into servitude and transfers it to the cities. Joseph is a man of immense ambition and stamina, and nothing about him suggests the character or behavior of a slave. Here, it seems at first glance, is a court Jew who is free.

But it is not as simple as it looks to become vizier to Pharaoh. As a Hebrew shepherd arriving in Egypt, Joseph is considered an "abomination"[5]—the slaughterer of the Egyptian god by trade, he is the very incarnation of the idol-smasher: Arrogant, self-absorbed, unassimilable. With remarkable skill he leaves all this behind, the narrative detailing a seemingly endless series of acquired traits and skills that render him ever more palatable to Egyptian tastes: He shaves, he interprets dreams, he adopts an Egyptian name, he wears Egyptian clothes, he adorns himself in gold and silver, he rides a chariot, he has men bow before him, he swears by Pharaoh, he marries the daughter of the Egyptian high priest, he has his father embalmed, he is himself embalmed.[6] He even names his first-born son Menashe, meaning, according to the narrative, "for God has made me forget ... all my father's house"[7]—and, indeed, he inexplicably declines to inform his grieving father that he is still alive. At virtually every turn, Joseph renders himself pleasing to his superiors so that he may find favor in their eyes, while his relationship with his people is attenuated.

But this surface conformity to Egypt calls our attention to something deeper. For Joseph is forever acting to please his lord,

zealously harnessing his will first to the interest of his father, then
that of Potiphar, then that of the keeper of Pharaoh's jails, and finally
that of Pharaoh himself. No wonder Joseph's economic proposals
"were good in the eyes of Pharaoh, and in the eyes of all his
servants"[8]—for Joseph never proposes anything which he does not
believe to be in the best interest of his master. Even in his greatest
moment of righteousness and selflessness, when he spurns the advances of Potiphar's wife, he thinks first and most naturally of the
earthly master whose interest he would be betraying, and only then
of the sin itself, saying: "Behold, my master does not inquire after
what I do in his house, and he has placed all that he has in my hand.
There is no one greater in this house than I, and he has not withheld
anything from me but you, since you are his wife. How, then, can I
do this great wrong—and sin against God?"[9]

No one considers himself a court Jew. Indeed, it is perhaps the
definitive characteristic of such a one that, in his tireless pursuit of
his master's interest, he forever believes himself to be doing what is
best for his people at the same time. Thus even as vizier in Egypt,
Joseph always speaks to his brothers of the salvation from famine
which it was his role to bring the Jews:

> I am Joseph, your brother, whom you sold into Egypt. And now,
> do not be grieved nor angry with yourselves because you sold me
> here, for God did send me here before you to preserve life. For
> these two years has the famine been on the land, and there will be
> five more years in which there will be neither plowing nor harvest.
> God did send me here before you to preserve you upon the earth,
> and to save your lives through a great deliverance. So it was not
> you who sent me here, but God.[10]

As Joseph explains it, he has spent these years accumulating power in
Egypt so that he might be able to save the lives of the Jews, and he
will now do so by taking them under his protective wing and

nourishing them through the coming years of privation:

> Come down to me, do not delay. And you will live in the land of
> Goshen, and you will be close to me, you and your children and
> your children's children, and your flocks and your herds and all
> you have. And I will nourish you there, for there are still five years
> of famine to come, lest you and your house and all that is yours fall
> into poverty.[11]

All this seems very generous at the time. Seventeen years later, however, with the great famine long past and the brothers now accustomed to life in Egypt, we see that Joseph is still repeating these claims: "You thought badly of me, but God meant it all for good, that I might this day preserve such a multitude of people alive. And now, have no fear, I will nourish you and your little ones...."[12]

There is a certain ambiguity, to say the least, in the fact that these statements are repeated again so long after the original threat has passed. Of course, as ruler of an empire which now owns the land and directly manages its entire economy, everything that Joseph has to say is true, both during the famine and long after it. With successful management he can truly pride himself on saving the lives of his people and many others year after year. The trouble with Joseph's theory is that it equates the will of God with the accumulation of economic and political power by the state. That is, so long as Joseph is operating the food production of Egypt, he is saving lives, and so long as the Jews depend on his providence, he is saving their lives as well—famine or no famine. Indeed, all this had been the official government philosophy of Egypt long before Joseph's arrival, as is evident from the records the Pharaohs left of their activities. As one of them wrote of his rule:

> I was the one who produced barley and loved the grain god. The
> Nile [the source of water] respected me at every defile. None

hungered in my years or thirsted in them. Men dwelt in peace through that which I wrought.[13]

Pharaoh's very status as god and idol was based on precisely the capacity which Joseph keeps claiming for himself: "I preserve such a multitude of people alive. I will nourish you and your little ones, as well."

Joseph's equation of the accumulation of power with the mission of the Jew in the world is problematic in other ways as well. First, since Joseph did not know that his success in the Egyptian hierarchy would result in saving the lives of the Jews until he had already been in Pharaoh's service for nine years (and in Egypt for twenty-two), there is in his statement a retroactive justification of the accumulation of all power at all times—as though it is *always* the will of God that one pursue power. By the same token, Joseph has to make sacrifices in terms of his connection to the Jewish people and faith to be able to gain this power, and this too he seems to justify as being part of God's work—since without it he would not have been able to "save your lives through a great deliverance," and could not now continue indefinitely "nourishing you and your little ones." In other words, if saving life is the highest value, and all accumulation of power is understood to be saving life, does not God then condone any and every action taken in the service of building up political and economic power—in this case the political and economic power of the Egyptian house of bondage?[14]

Now the story of Joseph is by biblical standards a massive and detailed biography, comprising almost a third of the book of Genesis. And in all this, Joseph is only once depicted as doing something that can be construed as being against the political and economic interests of his master. The event in question concerns the burial of Jacob, who calls Joseph to his deathbed after seventeen years in Egypt and makes him swear he will see to burying him in

Israel: "He called Joseph, his son, and said to him: '... Do not bury me, I pray you, in Egypt. But I will lie with my fathers, and you will carry me out of Egypt, and bury me in their burying place,' and he said: 'I will do as you say.' And he said: 'Swear to me,' and he swore to him....''[15]

Of all the biblical figures, Jacob is the one most tried in deception, and so he takes little for granted. It is clear that he suspects his son, the servant of Pharaoh, and not without reason. Pharaoh and his ministers are depicted as being enthusiastic over only two ideas during the eighty years that Joseph rules in Egypt: Joseph's proposal for meeting the emergency of the famine, and Joseph's invitation to his father and brothers to come weather the last five years of famine under his protection in Egypt. Upon hearing of it, Pharaoh reissues the invitation to the brothers, although in slightly stronger terms: "Now you are commanded: Do this...."[16] And they obey, bringing Jacob and his dependents to be resettled in Egypt. Moreover, Pharaoh orders them to leave their possessions behind, promising to replace them. His intention is to increase their dependence on the Egyptian state, but Jacob, already suspicious, ignores him and brings their possessions anyway.[17] The motive behind Pharaoh's interest in Jacob and his clan is plain: He fears that his great adviser may decide to return to his home in Canaan, and perhaps even stir up trouble on the border—and he moves to neutralize the threat by transplanting the Hebrews within easy reach. And his political calculations are apparently sufficient to justify what otherwise might have been a rather unseemly decision to import a tribe of shepherds into the land.

For twelve years after the famine abates, Pharaoh succeeds in keeping the Hebrews in Egypt. The silence of the text on this point suggests that no one dared to raise the subject, since Pharaoh was in any case not about to let anyone leave, and it would have been worse than pointless for this to be explained explicitly. The issue finally comes to a head when Jacob lies dying, the wily patriarch using his last breath to challenge the will of Pharaoh by making Joseph—the only son with the influence to press Pharaoh to do anything[18]— swear to bury him in Hebron with his fathers. For the first time in his life, Joseph finds himself bound to act against the king's interest: Jacob has demanded that the brothers all be allowed to return to Canaan, albeit only for a burial. But what if they make use of the opportunity to refuse to return? Indeed, might not Joseph himself, seeing his brothers go, succumb to the temptation and defect himself?

Trapped into a solemn commitment to his father which he cannot break, the reaction of Joseph, ruler of Egypt, is astonishing:

> When the days of mourning were past, Joseph spoke to the house of Egypt, saying: "If now I have found favor in your eyes, speak, I pray you, in the ears of Pharaoh, saying: My father made me swear, saying, Behold I die, and in my grave which you have dug for me in the land of Canaan will you bury me. Let me go up and bury my father, I pray you, and I will come back."[19]

Pharaoh does indeed consent to allow Joseph and his brothers to go up—with a military escort, while their children and herds are held hostage in Goshen.[20] But what kind of behavior is this on Joseph's part, going to Pharaoh's other servants and begging them to try to influence him, and this only if Joseph has managed to "find favor in your eyes"? The incongruity of it brought the rabbis to jest at Joseph's expense, saying: "To whom did he speak? To the queen's nurse, asking her to persuade the queen, who in turn should persuade the king."[21] And why does he blame it all on Jacob, who "made me swear," as though he, Joseph, would never have dreamed of such a thing? Is Joseph, after twenty-six years of rule over Egypt, after having saved the nation from starvation, after having concentrated all of its wealth and might in Pharaoh's hands—is he *afraid* to go in and ask the king for leave to go and bury his father?

The answer is that he is. For mighty though Joseph may be, he is not free. No longer a shepherd like his fathers, he is instead a servant to Pharaoh in the house of bondage. There is no question, of course, but that this house of bondage remains one of the great political and economic powers on earth, with the ability to give life and take it away. And there is likewise no question but that a man such as Joseph necessarily feels himself to be free, as he gives orders to others morning and night, and disposes of their lives, loved ones and property as he deems fit. But compelling as this experience may be, it is illusion. For the first among slaves may be powerful, but a slave he remains, subject to annihilation by his master at a moment's notice, in Pharaoh's house no less than in that of Potiphar. And when, once, Joseph realizes that he must act contrary to the will of Pharaoh, when once he is faced with a possible *loss* of favor, and the wrath that comes to Pharaoh when he senses betrayal, Joseph is struck with the self-same terror of the Hebrew slaves facing that other Pharaoh generations later. Before this terror Joseph gives in, dooming his people to slavery and atrocity at the hands of a Pharaoh that he—unlike his father Jacob—could not bring himself to challenge. For this reason, the rabbis observed that "as soon as Jacob our father died, the enslavement of Egypt began for Israel."[22]

In the end, it seems that Joseph, too, knew that he had been defeated, for as he lay near death, looking back at the results of his life's efforts, he felt compelled to say to his brothers: "I am dying, but God will surely remember you and bring you up out of this land … and you will carry my bones out from here."[23] Joseph had succeeded in fulfilling his dreams, but he had ultimately delivered no one, not even himself. The work of redeeming his people he left to someone else, to someone who would succeed where he had failed, to Moses.

The sense of loss which permeates this ending to the story of Joseph, the most gifted leader the Jews had ever had, is captured in a parable of R. Levi:

It can be compared to a man who brought his wine into the cellar, and thieves came and took away the barrels and drank their contents. When the owner of the wine found those who had stolen the barrels of wine, he said to them: "You have drunk the wine. At least return the casks to their place."[24]

And what of Esther? Was she not also as wine, stolen unfinished in youth, to be drunk by strangers? And might her end not be such as this, as well—her gifts and her beauty spent in futility, drained to the dregs in the service of one not her maker?

Rarely is any man privileged to grasp the iron relationship between his decision of the instant and the greater effects which the decision stands to bring upon the rest of his life. And Esther too, in the rush of the moment, at first fails to see and falters, thinking of the favor of her ruler, fearing its loss: "All the king's servants and the people of the king's provinces know that there is but one law for any man or woman who comes to the king in the inner court without having been summoned: That he be put to death...." (4:11) Yet her character is, in the final analysis, of a different sort than Joseph's, and Mordechai has been able to offer her lessons in politics that Jacob, separated from his son too early, was never able to provide.

# 12

# THE DECISION

THE PERSIAN POLITICAL BOOKS of the Bible were written in the wake of the destruction of Jerusalem, for a Jewish people once again confronted with the terrifying dilemmas of Joseph in Egypt: Whether to attempt to use the worldly power of the state-idols for the sake of Jewish survival—despite the fact that it is precisely such supposedly "productive" use of idolatry which the Jews had set out to abolish. And while all of them, Daniel, Nehemia and Esther, accepted Joseph's premise that if the Jews were to make it through the exile, they would have to collaborate with the state in order to gain power for Jewish ends, they rejected the ending to the Joseph story as the only possible outcome. Surely, they argued, one should have been able to achieve favor and wield power in Egypt—and yet have been strong enough, when the moment of terror came, to defy the idol and deliver one's people.

In the book of Daniel, in fact, facing up to Joseph's dilemma is made to look easy. The leaders of the Jewish exile in Babylon, Hanania, Mishael and Azaria, are brought before Nebuchadnezzar, the emperor who had destroyed the Jewish kingdom, and ordered to bow before the golden idol that he has erected. The law decrees that they should obey or die. In the critical moment of decision, they muster a defiant and disobedient response almost without concern or hesitation, so powerful is their faith that God will assist them if they do the right thing: "O Nebuchadnezzar, we have no need to answer you in this matter. For our God whom we serve is able to deliver us…. But even if he does not, let it be understood, O king, that we will not serve your gods, nor worship the golden image which you have erected."[1] When the Persians seize the city, Darius becomes emperor and promotes Daniel to high office. But eventually, he too finds himself being ordered under law to desist from saying prayers to God and to pray only to Darius. Learning of this law, he also refuses obedience, although he knows that he will be thrown to the lions.[2] In both cases, the Jewish response to the demands of the idolaters is obvious, and a miracle takes place so that all ends well.

In Nehemia, on the other hand, there are no miracles to be had, and the question of whether to risk the ruler's wrath for what is right appears difficult and frightening. Nehemia is serving as cupbearer to the Persian king Artahshasta,[3] a sensitive position requiring a substantial measure of confidence on the part of the king, since it entails ensuring that his cup has not been poisoned. But as in Esther, Nehemia's special relationship with the king turns into a crisis of conscience when his brother comes to Susa, bringing him news of the misery of the Jewish remnant in Jerusalem: "The survivors who were not taken into captivity are suffering terrible hardship and degradation, and Jerusalem's walls are broken and its gates burned with fire."[4]

Jerusalem had been destroyed for being rebellious, and the narrative makes it abundantly clear that the effort to rebuild the ruined city—which would in practice amount to the resurrection of Jewish military power—could easily be construed as a threat to the empire and rebellion against the king.[5] Indeed, numerous diplomatic efforts had been made by the enemies of the Jews to persuade the Persian kings that it was a security risk to allow such work to proceed.[6] Nehemia, whom the subsequent account reveals to be a gifted statesman, is thus rightfully terrified to make an approach to the king on Jerusalem's behalf, realizing that he could easily be taken for a traitor and lose everything. Yet if he, whom the king trusts with his life, will not go in to intercede for Jerusalem, then who will?

Upon hearing his brother out, Nehemia decides to try to use his influence, although it may mean forfeiting his position or his life: "It came to pass, when I heard these words, that I sat down and wept, and I mourned for days, and I fasted and prayed before God in heaven: … Prosper your servant this day, and grant him mercy before this man. For I was the king's cupbearer."[7] Only after these trials does he go in to the king and make precisely that request which Joseph was never able to utter in all his years in Egypt: That the king permit him to leave his service and go up to the land of Israel to be governor there for the sake of his people. The king responds by asking Nehemia how long he will be gone.[8]

In Esther's case, the stakes are even higher. She faces a king who has already made a decision, a vizier who has staked his career on ensuring that the plan is executed, and a prescribed penalty of death for herself if she makes the wrong move. For her, the decision to approach the king will open a political war within the palace, something with which she has no experience, and upon which depend the very lives of the Jews of the empire. We know that the decision to take the gamble is particularly painful for Esther on another level as well, for like Joseph, she is a personality that thrives on attracting the favor and affections of powerful people.

Nevertheless, Esther's story is ultimately a rejection of Joseph's course as well, not only because of his failure of nerve in not confronting Pharaoh, but because of the problematic philosophy which seems to render his failure inevitable: Joseph is unable to act where his deeds are likely to displease his master, because of his tacit assumption that the good of the Jews (and of the world) depends on the preservation of his power. That is, since, as he repeatedly claims, it is God's will that the Jews be saved through him, it is always his duty to do whatever it is that will preserve his power in tact.[9] Ironically, it is just this faith in his own divine mission which paralyzes Joseph, preventing him from using his power lest he lose it—and as becomes evident, power that one is afraid to use is not power at all.

It is this theory, of the divine will singling out a single person as the sole possible savior, that Mordechai categorically rejects—in a passage dramatically emphasized by virtue of its being the only place where he is quoted verbatim in the entire narrative. In contrast to Joseph's self-assurance that the divine plan is manifest and that he is it ("God did send me here before you to save your lives through a great deliverance"), Mordechai argues that while one may have a critical role to play in some divine plan, this cannot be known for certain ("Who knows whether it was not for such a time as this that you came into royalty?"); and that if one proves unwilling or unable to fulfill such a role, it will be played by someone else ("For if you insist on remaining silent at this time, relief and deliverance will come to the Jews from elsewhere." (4:14))

Had Mordechai sought to advise Esther on the basis of Joseph's understanding, he would have argued as follows: Since, as queen of Persia, Esther is in a unique position to assist the Jews and others, there is virtually nothing so important as the maintenance and advancement of her position. Any action that could jeopardize her favor with the king would be nothing more than a reckless dissipation of the only hope of the Jews' being saved. Esther should therefore refrain from challenging the king, and await an opportunity when her influence might be of use.

But the consequences of such a position are far-reaching. If the influential Jew, considering himself to be indispensable, begins weighing his every action exclusively on the basis of how it affects his own power and the favor of those on whom his power depends, the result will be the helplessness amid the illusion of freedom that is the bottom line in Joseph. It is simply absurd to imagine that the needs of the Jews as a people will at every crucial moment coincide with the interests and inclinations of Pharaoh, of Ahashverosh, or of any other foreign ruler or state upon which the Jews depend. A Jew whose only understanding of his service to his people is to build ever greater monuments of favor and authority within the power structure of a foreign state must inevitably find himself facing situations in which the vital needs of the Jews are ignored, while he himself remains silent for fear of offending those who could deprive him of his position.

In disavowing this theory, Mordechai's first line of attack is a counterintuitive one. He seeks to deflate the importance that the individual in a position of power naturally tends to assign himself. By emphasizing the Jewish belief that the Jewish people is in any case eternal,[10] and the survival of the Jews therefore foregone with or without Esther's help, he ironically renders her free to act. Only if it is clear to her that the Jewish people does not need her to retain her position at all cost, is it possible for her to take risks which might very well end in the weakening or even elimination of that influence.

But the belief in the eternity of Israel has its problematic aspect as well. For if the relief and deliverance will surely come from elsewhere, then what possible reason can there be for Esther to act at all? It is from just such fatalism that religious quietism arises: The belief that God will take care of everything, that man is in any case too small to alter the course of events, that God's will is done with or without one's involvement. Here, too, the tendency is towards paralysis. It seems that boldness is so difficult that in any case a reason will be found to avoid it.

As against this tendency, Mordechai makes a second argument in the same passage. His entire speech is rendered as follows:

> Do not imagine in your heart that you, of all the Jews, will escape because you are in the king's palace. For if you insist on remaining silent at this time, relief and deliverance will come to the Jews from elsewhere, but you and your father's house will perish. And who knows whether it was not for such a time as this that you came into royalty?" (4:13–14)

The argument he makes with regard to Esther's destiny as the savior of the Jews, then, is twofold:

(i) *Perhaps* it is in order to save the Jews that you have risen to power, but—

(ii) if you are silent, you and yours will *certainly* be lost.

At first glance, Mordechai's insistence that inaction will lead to Esther's destruction seems contrived. Of all the Jews in the empire, Esther stands the best chance of being spared. The king adores her and is unlikely to let a second wife go the way of the first.[11] Moreover, no one in the court is aware that she is a Jew. If anything, Esther's position seems itself to be the best guarantee of the persistence of the Jewish line. In asserting, again against all intuition, that while others may be saved, it will be Esther whose doom will be sealed by her inaction, is he merely trying to scare her into motion?

But Mordechai is not just trying to scare her. He is in deadly earnest. For although the fate of the Jewish people as a whole cannot and should not be understood to be in Esther's hands alone, there is nevertheless a portion whose fate may very well depend on her. After all, had not Joseph's silence permitted Pharaoh to massacre the Jews in their thousands—despite the fact that relief and deliverance did eventually come from elsewhere, from Moses? That the Jews as a people will in some way be saved in no way assures that Esther and her father's house—and even six million of her father's house—will not be lost through the inaction of those who could have acted but did not. No one can know what will come of his efforts, and yet with hindsight, Esther may find that her deeds saved, not the Jewish people, but her "father's house" in a large sense, that portion of the Jews that she loves and knows, and that constitutes her people in her time and place. When one recognizes that such power nevertheless does reside in the individual, one has no choice but to consider and reconsider: "Who knows whether it was not for such a time as this that I have been placed here?"

It is precisely the retention of one's shepherd freedom, the ability to act *against* the interest of worldly power in the service of something higher, which is the source of man's greatness. It is not Joseph's building of Egypt which is unique in history; for there is virtually no man who does not work to build up the place in which he lives. What is unique is Moses' rejection of Pharaoh's court, with all the power that it offered him, in order to protect a slave who was being treated unjustly, and in order to lead his people into the wastes of Sinai. Without Moses, Joseph's empire-building would not even have made a scratch on the collective memory of mankind.

But there is more to it than this. For Mordechai's words are carefully chosen: If Esther is silent at such a time, then, who knows, perhaps she will have missed the opportunity to save thousands. But one thing is certain—that she herself will be "lost," and with her, the house of her father Avihail in the literal sense, of which she is the only surviving member. How does Mordechai know this?

Mordechai's certainty comes from an understanding that the battle of the court Jew is ultimately the struggle to save, not the Jewish people, but himself. Exposing himself to the relentless encroachment of foreign values, allowing himself to become preoccupied with the pursuit of favor, in effect transforming himself into the tool of an alien master rather than of his own conscience, he balances himself on a precipice in the hope that there he will be able to do good. Perhaps, as Joseph claims, he will sometimes be able to achieve that good in the course of executing his assigned duties. But the proof that he lives as a Jew comes not when he executes his assigned tasks on the path to worldly power. It comes when he *cannot* pursue these tasks as expected—when the demands of power, expedience and the interest of the state are opposed to what is Jewish and what is right, when he stands to lose everything as Abraham lost everything in rejecting Mesopotamia. Only then does it become clear whether he is yet fighting the battle of the Jew, or whether this cause has been sacrificed to the enslaving idol. In the rejection of the idol, *only* in the rejection of the idol, does the Jewish soul persist.

This is why, while Esther may or may not succeed in saving numbers of Jews by interceding with the king, the only one who will be lost for certain through her silence is herself. Remaining unmoved when tens of thousands of innocent people, her own people, stand to die, she will have finally and completely returned to that condition of powerless, spiritless bondage, which as a Jew she should have left behind in Egypt. Remaining unmoved before the cries of the persecuted, her heart like a stone, her face like a carving of wood, she will serve a lie which, by her own subservience, she makes as a god. And this is the meaning of the biblical teaching with regard to idols: "Mouths have they but they cannot speak; eyes have they but they cannot see; ears have they but they cannot hear.... Like them will be those who make them...."[12]

It is when she understands that such is the choice before her that the greatness of the queen is revealed. Esther, who has ever sought the favor of others, who always did as she was told, who would never ask anything for herself, faces the moment of truth. She must choose between building up the horror which has reared itself up before her, the fear of it, the numbing paralysis and amnesia of it; and picking up a stick to swing with all her might, with anything and everything she has ever had in her, to smash it. Recognizing what she must do, she breaks with her past, and for the first time in her life issues the order which Mordechai immediately obeys: "Go assemble all the Jews present in Susa and fast for me. Do not eat and do not drink for three days, night and day, and I and my maids will fast as well. Then I will go in to the king, though it is against the law. And if I perish, I perish." (4:16–17)

# ESTHER
# FIVE
[5:1 – 5:14]

It came to pass on the third day, that Esther dressed in royalty and stood in the inner court of the king's house, facing the throne room, while the king was sitting on his royal seat in the throne room, facing the entrance to the chamber. And it came to pass that when the king saw Esther the queen standing in the court, she won favor in his eyes, and the king extended to Esther the gold scepter in his hand, and Esther approached and touched the tip of the scepter.

The king said to her: "What is your concern, Queen Esther, and what is your request? Even if it be half the kingdom, it will be given you."

Esther said: "If it please the king, let the king and Haman come today to the banquet that I have prepared for him."

The king said: "Hasten Haman to do as Esther has said." And the king and Haman came to the banquet that Esther had prepared.

*The king said to Esther during the banquet of wine: "Whatever your wish, it will be given you. Whatever your request, up to half the kingdom, it will be done."*

*Esther responded and said: "My wish and my request —. If I have won favor in the king's eyes, and if it pleases the king to grant my wish and to fulfill my request — then let the king and Haman come to the banquet that I will prepare for them, and tomorrow I will do as the king has said."*

*Haman went out that day happy and in high spirits, but when Haman saw Mordechai in the king's gate, how he neither stood nor stirred before him, Haman was filled with rage against Mordechai.*

*Haman restrained himself and returned to his house, and he sent for his friends and for Zeresh his wife. Haman recounted to them the glory of his riches, and the great number of his sons, and everything in which the king had promoted him and elevated him above the princes and servants of the king. Haman said: "Even Esther the queen brought no one with the king to the banquet she had prepared other than myself, and tomorrow, too, I am invited*

to her, along with the king. Yet all this is worthless
to me, so long as I see Mordechai the Jew sitting at
the king's gate."

Then Zeresh his wife and all his friends said to
him: "Let a tall gallows be made, fifty cubits high,
and in the morning tell the king to have Mordechai
hanged on it. Then go with the king to the banquet
in good spirits."

The idea seemed good to Haman, and he had
the gallows erected.

# 13

# THE PLAN

THERE THEN FOLLOW TWO TERRIBLE DAYS in which Esther prepares herself to go in to the king. We know that Esther was fasting, and we may surmise that she prayed a good deal as well.[1] But the most important part of her seclusion is the long hours she invests in poring over what she knows of the king, searching for a way to counterbalance the interest he believes he has in harming the Jews. From the information she has, it is apparent that the scheme is the vizier's, and that Ahashverosh's acquiescence comes of his desire to promote Haman and permit him to consolidate his control over the empire. And if the king considers it crucial at this stage to rely on Haman's judgment, then there will be no point in arguing with him about a policy whose actual content probably matters little to him. What is needed is to damage Haman's favor with the king, so that

Ahashverosh feels he has something to lose in so quickly accepting Haman's goals as his own. Only then will it be possible for another voice to be heard.

It is from this trail of reasoning, followed doggedly through the mists of fear and exhaustion, that Esther's plan begins to emerge.

When the queen enters the inner court of the palace less than three days after the promulgation of the decree, there is little to be seen of the beauty for which she is known throughout the empire. Pale, haggard, weak, she has been without food or water for days.

The king gazes in her direction and points to her with his scepter, lifting the decree of death. He loves her "more than all the other women" in the kingdom (2:17), and having already suffered from the loss of his first wife because of an impulsive application of law, he is in no rush to go through this again. Moreover, as when Nehemia comes before Artahshasta,[2] Esther has made sure that her appearance is irregular and pitiable, so that the king can clearly see something is wrong. The king, who delights at nothing so much as a display of magnanimity where he has nothing to lose, makes a show of welcoming her into his presence, and Esther "won favor in his eyes." (5:2) Now the drama truly begins.

The king understands that Esther would not risk her life without having some terribly important matter to take up with him, and so he asks her: "What is your request," and then adds his standard, hyperbolic form of pretended largesse: "Even if it be half the kingdom, it will be given you."

The queen responds according to plan: "If it please the king, let the king and Haman come today to the banquet that I have prepared for him."

The king is pleased to comply, ordering that Haman be "hastened" to appear. But it is obvious that not for such a gathering did Esther transgress the king's law. Or did she? Ahashverosh is ready to get to the bottom of the matter, and upon taking part in the banquet of wine hours later, he repeats his question, again asking Esther what her request might be.

Esther reaches for the next line in her script, but instead comes forth with only a terrible stammer, rifling through a series of meaningless hesitations before coming to an answer, evidently not the one which she had prepared:

> "My wish and my request—.
> If I have won favor in the king's eyes,
> And if it pleases the king to grant my wish
> And to fulfill my request—
> Then let the king and Haman come to the banquet that I
>   will prepare for them,
> And tomorrow I will do as the king has said."

At the end of all this, she arrives at the same point where she had been in the throne room that morning: "Let the king and Haman come to the banquet that I will prepare for them." Lest the king think that she is playing with him, she adds: "And tomorrow I will do as the king has said"—that is, reveal the concealed request which is behind her initiative. (5:3–8)

Why does Esther invite the king to come to a pair of wine-sodden dinners with her, in the company of his vizier, instead of coming out and demanding that the decree be repealed and the Jews saved?

The reason is that she does not believe he will grant the request. While Esther is well liked by the king, and he may be willing to hear her out, a direct assault against the decree means pitting her own untried credibility on matters of policy against the settled opinion of the vizier—whom the king has appointed, after all, to conduct policy. Moreover, such an attack would force Ahashverosh to choose between

Haman's policy and a different one proposed by Esther—precisely the kind of politics he has sought to avoid. Having staked his kingdom on the belief that Haman's advice is preferable to hearing out competing claims, the chances are excellent that the criticism of a young queen whom he calls to visit him only sporadically will only anger the king and result in her own discreditation.

What is needed is to drive a wedge between the king and the vizier, something that will give Esther the leverage she needs to pry Ahashverosh away from him. To do this, she must avoid the trap of arguing policy directly, and find a way of challenging Haman's trusted status on personal grounds, causing the vizier to appear flawed in judgment or even suspect in the eyes of the king. It is to achieve this that Esther proposes that Ahashverosh come to her dinner, telling the king that she wishes to invite "the king and Haman to the banquet that I have prepared for him."

Behind a superficial innocence, Esther's intention is to make a highly unusual, even disturbing request: For why should the queen, who has not had the benefit of seeing her husband for a month, wish to organize a cozy, romantic dinner for three? Moreover, she invites "the king and Haman to the banquet she has prepared for him." Which of her guests is the "him"? Him *whom*?

The trouble is that the invitation and its acceptance occur too quickly, and within hours the three of them are together, the king again inquiring as to Esther's request. Has Ahashverosh understood any of the implications of what the queen has said to him, of the event taking place before his eyes? She cannot tell, and she has no reason to think so. He shows no signs of having understood any-thing. He just sits there drinking, laughing, opining, as though all is well. When the moment comes, and the fate of her strategem and her people hangs in the balance, Esther balks. The vizier's favor with the king is still as it was, far too great for her to move against him, and she determines to try again. Another banquet, the same message, this time with one measure less subtlety: "Let the king and Haman come to the banquet that I will prepare for them."

If he does not understand this time, she will no longer be able to wait. By the next afternoon, she will already be running the danger of the king feeling toyed with.

For them, for *them*.

This bizarre locution of the queen's is not lost on Haman, who immediately feels the power of the wine, the power of the queen's words. Drunk on what she has said, he immediately runs to his friends and preens: "Even Esther the queen brought no one with the king to the banquet she had prepared other than myself, and tomorrow, too, I am invited to her, along with the king." (5:12) But will the king be quick enough to perceive the threat?

Esther has made her move, the die is cast. Either the night will do its work, or she will have to confront Haman as he is—standing against her with the full backing of the king and all the might of the empire still tightly in his hands.

# 14

# THE REACTION

THE VIZIER NOW HAS AN ENEMY, whose moves he can only follow in part. To use the contemporary phraseology, Mordechai is engaged in creating public pressure against him, while Esther works to undermine his position through quiet diplomacy. And although Haman misses the connection between the queen's flattery and the Jews' war, he understands something else: That the complete failure of the decree to stem Mordechai's public campaign—to induce him to come before the vizier begging for mercy, to cause him to disappear in degradation, or even to alter his posture of public contempt—is a sure sign of deeper trouble brewing, unseen and yet *felt* beneath the surface. The decree is scheduled to be implemented only in eleven months' time, and in politics eleven months is an eternity, during which a concerted resistance can generate sympathizers at all levels. It is this feeling, the intensifying sensation of uncontrol before a menace not understood, which appears in Haman's soul as the thrashing of his crocodile spirit, a nail stuck in its innards, unable to reassert rule despite the application of the most venomous pressure.

Distressed, Haman summons his friends and advisers to hear what should be done. He recounts to them his recent successes in consolidating ultimate power in the empire, but concludes with a fit of inspired hatred: "Yet all this is worthless to me, so long as I see Mordechai the Jew sitting at the king's gate." (5:13)

Recognizing the threat to the vizier's position, Haman's advisers propose a surgical strike to neutralize Mordechai's opposition: "Let a tall gallows be made, fifty cubits high, and in the morning tell the king to have Mordechai hanged on it." (5:14) Their intention is twofold. First, the threat from Mordechai must be eliminated as rapidly as possible. So long as the Jew continues to be a player at the court, he will work to discredit Haman and incite dissension; even courtiers unfriendly towards the Jews will be encouraged by the vizier's failure to impose his order, and will begin generating their own excuses for weakening his rule and bringing him down. Unless Mordechai is eliminated, there is no way of assuring that the decree, and even Haman's position itself, will be safe. Second, the height of the gallows, which will tower over most of the buildings of the city, is intended to produce public pressure as against that which Mordechai has been broadcasting. Where Mordechai's campaign has been aimed to show that there can be resistance, Haman's gallows is aimed to demonstrate that such resistance is chimerical, standing out as a warning: Disobedience no sooner stirs than it is doomed.

The move proposed by Haman's advisers is not, however, without risk. The vizier, although in full favor with the king, must also make sure that his requests are couched in terms of the king's interest and not his own. While Ahashverosh is determined to secure for Haman absolute authority over others, he is himself hardly in awe of Haman, whom he is careful to abuse in little ways—having him "hastened" here and there by the chamberlains, for example—in order to remind him whence his authority derives. (5:5, 6:14) In hoping to have Mordechai eliminated, Haman is, ironically, in a position similar to that of Joseph requesting to go up to Canaan to bury his father: The request is obviously not a demand for national strength but a confession of personal need and insecurity—and this had been the very reason that "it was disdainful in his eyes to lay hands on Mordechai alone" to begin with (3:6); whereas the Jews as a people can be supposed a security threat to the entire empire, the vizier's desire to rid himself of an opponent who, after all, is known to object principally to Haman himself, is difficult to interpret as anything other than the political assassination of a rival member of the court.

That Ahashverosh, who generally concerns himself with appearing magnanimous and disbursing gifts, may not appreciate this particular policy is an open possibility. But against the need to eliminate the leader of his opposition before he can rally allies and pose a genuine threat, this concern pales and is passed over. The meeting of the vizier's camp ends with a resolution of consensus: against the opposition, a swift, brutal reaction, from which the Jews will be unable to recover. In the morning, Haman will go in to request Mordechai's execution.

# ESTHER
# SIX
## [6:1 – 8:2]

That night, the king could not sleep, so he ordered that the book of records, the chronicles, be brought out and read before the king. There it was found how Mordechai had denounced Bigtana and Teresh, two of the king's chamberlains of the guardians of the threshold, who had plotted to lay their hands on the king Ahashverosh.

The king said: "What honor or promotion has been conferred upon Mordechai for this?"

And the king's youths, who attended him, replied: "Not a thing has been done for him."

The king said: "Who is in the court?" And Haman had come into the outer court of the king's house to ask the king to hang Mordechai on the gallows he had prepared for him.

The king's youths said to him: "It is Haman standing in the court."

And the king said: "Let him in."

Haman came in and the king said to him: "What should be done for the man whom the king desires to honor?"

And Haman said in his heart: Whom should the king desire to honor more than me?

Haman said to the king: "The man whom the king desires to honor —. Let a royal robe be brought which the king has worn, and a horse upon which the king has ridden, and with the royal headpiece on its head. And let the robe and the horse be entrusted to one from among the king's most noble princes, and let him attire the man whom the king desires to honor, and lead him on the horse around the city square, proclaiming before him: Thus will be done for the man whom the king desires to honor."

The king said to Haman: "Hurry, take the robe and the horse as you have said, and do so for Mordechai the Jew, who sits in the king's gate. Omit nothing from all you have said."

Haman took the robe and the horse and attired Mordechai, and led him around the city square, proclaiming before him: "Thus will be done for the man whom the king desires to honor."

Mordechai returned to the king's gate, and Haman returned to his house, aggrieved and with his head covered. Haman told Zeresh his wife and all his friends everything that had happened to him, and his advisers and Zeresh his wife said to him: "If he be of Jewish descent, this Mordechai, before whom you have begun to fall, you will not prevail against him, but you will surely fall before him."

While they were yet talking with him, the king's chamberlains arrived, hurrying to bring Haman to the banquet which Esther had prepared.

The king and Haman came to drink with Esther the queen.

The king again said to Esther, on the second day of the banquet of wine: "Whatever your wish, Queen Esther, it will be given you. Whatever your request, up to half the kingdom, it will be done."

Esther the queen replied and said: "If I have found favor in your eyes, my king, and if it please the king, let my life be given to me as my wish, and my people as my request. For we have been sold, I and my people, to be annihilated, to be killed and to be destroyed. Had we been sold as slaves and serving women, I would have remained silent, for this suffering would not have been worth the injury to the king."

The king Ahashverosh spoke, saying to Esther the queen: "Who is it, and which is he, who has inclined his heart to do so?"

Esther said: "A tormentor and an enemy — this evil Haman." And Haman was struck with fear before the king and the queen.

The king rose in his rage from the banquet of wine and went out into the palace garden, while Haman stayed to plead for his life with Esther the queen, for he saw that the king had determined ill against him.

The king returned from the palace garden to the pavilion of the banquet of wine, and found Haman fallen upon the divan on which Esther lay. And the king said: "And would he even conquer the queen with me in the house?"

The words left the king's mouth, and Haman's face fell.

Said Harvona, one of the chamberlains before the king: "And there stands the gallows which Haman made for Mordechai, who spoke well for the king — in Haman's house, fifty cubits high."

And the king said: "Hang him on it."

They hanged Haman on the gallows he had prepared for Mordechai, and the rage of the king subsided.

On that day, the king Ahashverosh gave the house of Haman, the persecutor of the Jews, to Esther the queen.

And Mordechai came before the king, for Esther had told what he was to her. The king slipped off his ring, which he had retrieved from Haman, and gave it to Mordechai. And Esther placed Mordechai over Haman's house.

# 15

# POWER SHIFT

WITH THE CLOSE OF THE MEETING of Haman's faction, the struggle over the future of the decree and the future of the Jews has reached its height. On the morrow, both parties plan to launch their decisive moves: Haman will go to the king in the morning to demand the immediate execution of the leader of the opposition; in the afternoon Esther plans to attempt to dislodge the king from his unconditional support of the vizier and his decree. It is the disposition of the king that will be decisive, and in the effort to sway this, it is the Jews who have managed to land their blow first.

"That night the king could not sleep…" (6:1)—for as he lies in bed turning over the day's events, the provocation of the queen finally finds its mark. What was the purpose of the banquet? Why had she so desired the presence of the vizier? Had she indeed said, as he remembered, that the banquet was intended to honor both of them? If she were indeed so desirous to see the vizier, perhaps she had an interest in him—or he in her.[1] And if this were indeed the case, perhaps here was another conspiracy on his life?[2] Could this be the purpose of the banquet? But Haman would never dream of taking the place of his king, who had raised him to such prominence. Or would he? As the hours wear on, the king is tossed and torn between the two great fears that have haunted his reign: The loss of his queen and the loss of his life, both threatened once again at the hands of those closest to him. And had he not taken Haman, the wretch, to protect him from precisely these terrors, to make his world stable for him? To whom could he possibly turn?

With this, the king for the first time comes to understand the weakness of the political position in which he has cornered himself. For it is in his authority to decide among the competing views presented by his advisers that the king maintains his power: Each adviser depends on the king to secure his view against those of the others. Once the king has granted one of his men the right to eliminate all opposition, he has granted him complete freedom of action—freedom which, sooner or later, becomes the power to do without the king. Panic-stricken over this revelation, the king comes clean awake and calls for his youths. Would it not be better to have another minister who might keep an eye on the vizier?

He orders that his servants bring the chronicles to be read, in the hope of finding some hint of Haman's treachery against him, some hint of someone who can protect him. They begin to read, and in this way he returns to the attempt on his life which had triggered Haman's installation: "There it was found how Mordechai had denounced Bigtana and Teresh, two of the king's chamberlains of the guardians of the threshold, who had plotted to lay their hands on the king Ahashverosh. The king said: 'What honor or promotion has been conferred upon Mordechai for this?' And the king's youths, who attended him, replied: 'Not a thing has been done for him.'" (6:2–3)

In reviewing the events leading to Haman's rise, the king begins
to piece together the case against the vizier. Was it not Haman who
had informed him that it was "of no benefit for the king to keep the
Jews," when here the Jew had in fact been responsible for saving the
king's life? Perhaps Haman had even been involved in the plot which
the Jews had succeeded in foiling? And then there is Haman's
suspicious mania for control, which had led the king to elevate him
in the first place—but which has now succeeded in laying a hand on
his signet, and on his banquets with his wife, and on who knows
what else.

Moreover, in mulling over the attempt on his life, the king finds
evidence of something else: the presence of others in the court who
are willing to side with him in adversity, others who are perhaps
more loyal than the vizier. Troubled and frightened, Ahashverosh
weighs advancing them, taking them in.

It is in this moment of doubt, as Ahashverosh struggles to grasp
his world by adjudging competing theories and claims, that the
politics of the empire begins to return. In the answer of the king's
youths, that "Not a thing has been done for him," is the first voice of
any adviser reported in the narrative since Haman's elevation. Face-
less, nameless, they are at least opinions other than that of the
vizier—opinions which intrude on the king's apolitical honeymoon,
as Rava suggests, not out of any especial sympathy for Mordechai,
but because they detest the monopoly of power which has been
granted Haman.[3] With this intrusion, the king begins the laborious
effort of listening to others again.

By the time Haman arrives with the dawn to make his move
and try to recoup control, the king has already shifted into a
contrary state of mind. Haman seeks to elevate himself yet further,
but the king is weighing whether the vizier would not benefit from
being taken down a notch or two. Perhaps by being forced to make
room for another, Haman will understand who rules and who is

the servant. The vizier enters to speak to Ahashverosh, but the king's agenda is not Haman's. The exchange that follows is a verbal elaboration of the shift in political favor which has taken place during the night.

"What should be done for the man whom the king desires to honor?" the king asks, as if to seek advice, when in fact his eye is already set on a humiliation. The sport is in learning what kind of humiliation it will be, turning Haman's own desire to rule against him, letting it devour itself.

Haman's conception of the ordering of the Persian state allows for only one interpretation of the king's question: Truly an idolater to the core, he continues to identify the good of the realm with his own perfect control. For him there is in fact only one appropriate address for all honor. To honor someone else is to create rivalry and danger, allowing another to vie for the favor of the king, to him an impossibility. Thus "Haman said in his heart: Whom should the king desire to honor more than me?" (6:6)—and he responds with that infamous fantasy of self-indulgence and usurpation: "The man whom the king desires to honor—. Let a royal robe be brought which the king has worn, and a horse upon which the king has ridden, and with the royal headpiece on its head. And let the robe and the horse be entrusted to one from among the king's most noble princes, and let him attire the man whom the king desires to honor, and lead him on the horse around the city square, proclaiming before him: Thus will be done for the man whom the king desires to honor." (6:7–9)

With each word, the king, now looking upon Haman for the first time as a possible rival, becomes more convinced that his suspicions are well-placed. It is with evident satisfaction that he carefully pronounces the doom that demotes Haman once more to the position of a courtier among others, one voice among the many interests of Persia: "Hurry, take the robe and the horse as you have said, and do so for Mordechai the Jew, who sits in the king's gate. Omit nothing from all you have said." (6:10)

And so it is done. The vizier, the paradigm of total power, seeks out the dissident Jew and publicly carries out the doom of submission to him—just as the other men of power in the court had humbled themselves before Haman in the preceding weeks.

But there is more here as well. For Haman's humiliation is also a confession, before a city that had gaped at the height of his gallows only that morning, that all for which Haman had hoped is in fact vanity. The Jew cannot be defeated because in the end his word does stand. No man may claim for himself the authority to dictate truth, to elevate his perspective into the absolute. The parade through the streets in which the idolater concedes the potency of the truth beyond himself, outside himself, is none other than the retelling of the dream of the Jewish faith: That the idol be brought down to its proper size, that the figurine of gold be recognized as a lump of metal in the hand of man; that each idol, as the rabbis had it, should bow down in recognition of the truth, in so doing bringing upon itself oblivion.[4]

It is Haman's advisers, in their anti-Semitism, who understand the meaning of the vizier's humiliation better than anyone. For as soon as the Jewish message of limiting his power is accepted in principle, Haman's dream is finished. His effort to kill off the Jew and achieve perfect rule has come too late, and now he can only fall: "If he be of Jewish descent, this Mordechai, before whom you have begun to fall, you will not prevail against him, but you will surely fall before him." (6:13)

The configuration of power in the state has now shifted, with another faction moving ahead of the vizier's, pressing its advantage. Events are no longer in Haman's control.

# 16

# DOWNFALL

NOT ONLY AMONG HAMAN'S ADVISERS but in the Jewish camp as well, the humbling of Haman is understood to signal a shift in power and the moment to act—before Haman should have the chance to revive, defend himself and recover his losses.

Haman is brought to the queen's banquet, and there the king repeats his query for the third time: "Whatever your wish, Queen Esther, it will be given you. Whatever your request, up to half the kingdom, it will be done." (7:2)

This time, the narrative records no hesitation in the queen's voice. The king will give her a fair hearing now or he never will. She makes her appeal in words she has rehearsed a hundred times: "If I have found favor in your eyes, my king, and if it please the king, let my life be given to me as my wish, and my people as my request. For we have been sold, I and my people, to be annihilated, to be killed and to be destroyed. Had we been sold as slaves and serving women, I would have remained silent, for this suffering would not have been worth the injury to the king."

A terrific silence reigns as the king struggles to ingest what she has asked of him. Could someone wish to murder the queen? Should he be forced to go through such torment again? He asks so that he should be able to understand:

"Who is it, and which is he, who has inclined his heart to do so?"

"A tormentor and an enemy—this evil Haman." (7:3–6)

Ahashverosh seethes, the temperature rises. Livid, shaking with rage, he storms out into the garden. The vizier is struck with terror— the very same terror of standing alone before the wrath of the king with which Esther has lived every day, every hour since learning of the decree.

But why does the king leave the room? What does such behavior really mean? Storming out if insulted or embarrassed, slamming a door behind, or similarly, not speaking with someone for years, abandoning a flagging marriage without a word, resigning from high office, and in the extreme, suicide—all these are familiar, and they are the same. Hardly ever does it make sense to act this way, strictly calculating benefits against costs, but these are not actions of reason and interest. They are actions of the spirit which, finding no possible recourse for the reestablishment of control, establishes mastery, at the *expense* of self-interest, through the demolition of the situation itself. In departure, that which cannot be controlled is nonetheless brought to bow to one's will. Even in suicide, the action of the spirit is the same, its need to control winning over the needs of the body, control being firmly and finally regained in the purposive destruction of all that has heretofore resisted control. Such an action is therefore not only one of self-destruction, but also of powerlessness—since it proves that control cannot have been imposed in any other way.

Ahashverosh leaves because he has lost all control. His wife, it transpires, is a Jewess. And Haman—did he know this?—has tried to murder her. All his efforts to gain security have come to nothing, and he is once again alone. But how can he rule now? Whom is he to rely on? Surely the vizier is dangerous, is insane. In his lust to rule he would murder the queen.

The king, obsessed from the outset with the need to "rule in his own house," lest he find that he rules nowhere—and to have control of his own wife, as the foundation on which the stability of his world is based—finds that he has lost control of her yet again, this time to the vizier.[1] Esther's stratagem, her arousal of the king's jealousy and suspicions, has therefore brought appearances into line with the truth: Haman has in fact sought to take the queen with the king in the palace—not sexually, but, similarly enough, because of his inability to tell that which is his to lay his hands on from that which is not.[2]

And now the king understands this as well: "The king returned from the palace garden ... and found Haman fallen upon the divan on which Esther lay. And the king said: 'And would he even conquer the queen with me in the house?'" (7:8)

# 17

# ALLIES

AT NO POINT IN THE BOOK OF ESTHER is Ahashverosh depicted as making a decision for himself, and the crisis that brings about Haman's ruin is pointedly no exception. Even at the height of his wrath, when the king determines that the vizier has arrogated to himself the authority to murder the queen and ruin his life, Ahashverosh still does not determine policy. Instead, it is one of his chamberlains, Harvona, who suddenly materializes from nowhere in order to determine the course of events: "Said Harvona, one of the chamberlains before the king: 'And there stands the gallows which Haman made for Mordechai, who spoke well for the king—in Haman's house, fifty cubits high.' And the king said: 'Hang him on it.'" (7:9)

Who is this Harvona and what does he want? He is mentioned once before as one of the king's inner circle of attendants and advisers, (1:10) but he, like all the king's other loyal servants, disappears from the tale with Haman's elevation. Like the others who have been pushed aside by Haman, Harvona keeps close track of what takes place in the politics of the court. Here we see that, like Mordechai, he knows the finest details of what has been taking place, including that which should not have been public knowledge: What Mordechai did for the king, the grudge which Haman held against the Jew, and even the precise height of the gallows which looms over the city. Yet his name does not appear because he remains silent throughout the development of the conflict. When Haman is appointed, he acquiesces in the new reality, paying whatever shameful homage is required, swallowing the insult and nursing his resentment out of sight. When Mordechai resists, he does not join him, and when the Jew appeals for help against the liquidation that Haman has ordered, Harvona refuses to deploy himself in the Jews' camp. In every instance, in fact, Harvona is of abject uselessness, except that when the king's wrath is kindled against the vizier, and the question which hangs in the balance is how this anger will expend itself, Harvona directs it and transforms it into a decision, a policy, playing a part similar to that of Memuchan in the Vashti affair. It is Harvona, in fact, who hands Haman the final blow which ensures that he is executed, where he might otherwise have somehow escaped with his life.

The reason for Harvona's actions is not hard to identify. Regardless of where his personal sympathies lie, Harvona understands himself to have no interest in risking his own position in the struggle against Haman while the opposition to him is weak. Certainly, the vizier's authoritarianism means a deterioration in his own personal station, and as such is unlikely to have made Harvona much disposed to sympathize with him. But as the public displays of obeisance to Haman are meant to indicate, it is in Haman's hands that power lies, and those who would seek favor in the court would do well to seek it with him. So long as the vizier has sole access to the ear of the king, Harvona sees little choice but to ingratiate himself with him to whatever degree possible and certainly to avoid any friction.

Harvona's move to come to the assistance of the Jews—both emphasizing the good that Mordechai has done for the king, and serving the death-blow to their mortal enemy—is therefore a defection from the camp of Haman's supporters to that of the Jews. He recognizes the shift in power that has taken place, and determines to place his bet on the ascendant party, the party he believes will soon enough be in control: Esther and Mordechai.

A similar approach is taken by Pharaoh's cupbearer in the Joseph narrative. Joseph, having been unjustly condemned to the dungeon for his purported misdeeds in Potiphar's house, makes every effort to be of service to the king's adviser when the chief steward likewise provokes the anger of his master and is incarcerated. Having done the king's cupbearer a good turn in relieving him of the fear that had resulted from his uninterpreted dream, Joseph tries to turn this favor into support for his own efforts to win release from prison:

> But remember me when it is well with you, and show me kindness, I pray you, and mention me to Pharaoh, and bring me out of this house. For I was stolen out of the land of the Hebrews, and here too have I done nothing that I should be cast in the dungeon.[1]

Yet the cupbearer turns a deaf ear to Joseph's pleas for assistance. Neither the favor Joseph has done him, nor his appeal to "kindness," nor his appeal to justice succeeds in moving the king's adviser, who sees fit to forget the Hebrew and his troubles for two full years while Joseph continues to languish. In this case, too, it is the strict political interest of the chief steward that determines the degree of his allegiance to Joseph. Having narrowly avoided death for incurring the disfavor of the king, he is hardly interested in exposing himself to intercede on behalf of others. He feels his position and his life still to be in the balance—although this may not be any more true of him than it is of the king's other servants—and his every effort is in the direction of pleasing Pharaoh, not in making demands of him. It is only after the king has reached a peak of frustration over his uninterpretable dreams, having failed to obtain a useful interpretation from his advisers, that the steward decides he has something to gain, and probably nothing to lose, by returning the favor that Joseph did for him: If the king is pleased with Joseph, it will only increase his estimation of the steward, whereas if he is not, it was only out of desperation that the steward suggested "the young man, the Hebrew slave."[2]

The critical moves, both in bringing about Haman's downfall and in Joseph's rise to power, are therefore supplied by interested parties whose concern for the well-being of the Jews is questionable or nonexistent, and whose assistance is provided out of strict concern for what will be of benefit to them. That politics makes for strange bedfellows is well known, but the more important implication of this maxim that is emphasized in the biblical texts is this: In order to secure the success of any political campaign or effort, regardless of the loftiness of the goal, one must cultivate and make use of such allies—the great majority of men who will side with power, and who will never lift a finger to help the Jews, or anyone else, unless it is made evident that such support is in their own interest. This is the case so universally that it amounts to a natural law of politics: That strength attracts strength, and power attracts power. And this is a law to which we will have reason to return.

Harvona's intervention on the side of the Jews allows for an outcome that Esther would not likely have suggested herself. The king immediately orders that Haman be taken out and hanged. But

Esther, having scored a decisive gain with the king, does take advantage of his confusion to push through a second, fateful decision without which the story might still have ended in tragedy: The elevation of Mordechai to the position of vizier. "On that day, the king Ahashverosh gave the house of Haman, the persecutor of the Jews, to Esther the queen. And Mordechai came before the king, for Esther had told what he was to her. The king slipped off his ring, which he had retrieved from Haman, and gave it to Mordechai. And Esther placed Mordechai over Haman's house." (8:1–2)

It suits the king well to place Esther and Mordechai over all that had been Haman's at this moment, making use of the Jews, the vizier's enemies, to degrade his memory. Ahashverosh thus gives Haman's position and his property, even the signet ring that should rightly have gone back to the king's hand, to those the vizier despised to emphasize how completely his will has been erased. Yet all this is to a large degree show, containing far more hatred of Haman than respect for the Jews. Ahashverosh has no intention of granting Mordechai the extraordinary position of authority he had intended for Haman—there are no proclamations that place the Jew "above all the princes" or require "all the king's servants who were in the king's gate to bow and prostrate themselves." (3:1–2) Instead, Mordechai's promotion to a more conventional position signals the rebirth of history, the restoration of the politics of the empire to where it had been before Haman's elevation. Mordechai had saved the life of the king from those who were disloyal to him, and now, belatedly, he is rewarded with a position of trust and responsibility, as one important voice among many.

With Haman out of the way, the queen having demonstrated her influence, Mordechai positioned in the highest political post in the kingdom, and Harvona and others close to the king turning to side with the Jews, there can be no question but that the constellation of power has improved decisively. Haman's rule has not lasted even a month—his ruin the product of his own idolatrous aspirations. And yet the machinery of extermination which he has set in motion has not yet been turned aside, as his many, many allies and sympathizers remain to do the work he has begun.

# ESTHER
# SEVEN
[8:3 – 8:17]

Yet again did Esther speak before the king, and she
fell at his feet, and cried, and pleaded with him, to
avert the evil of Haman the Agagite, and the scheme
which he had devised against the Jews. The king extended to Esther the gold scepter, and Esther rose and
stood before the king.

She said: "If it please the king, and if I have found
favor before him, and if the thing seems right to the
king, and if I am worthy in his eyes, let it be written
to revoke the letters devised by Haman, son of
Hamedata the Agagite, which he wrote to destroy the
Jews who are in all the king's provinces. For how can
I bear to see the evil which will befall my people?
And how can I bear to witness the destruction of my
kindred?"

The king Ahashverosh said to Esther the queen
and Mordechai the Jew: "Behold, I have given

*Haman's house to Esther, and he himself has been*
*hanged on the gallows because he would lift a hand*
*against the Jews. And you, write concerning the Jews*
*as seems good in your eyes, in the king's name, and*
*seal it with the king's ring. But an edict written in the*
*king's name and sealed with the king's ring cannot be*
*revoked."*

*The king's scribes were summoned there and then,*
*on the 23rd day of the 3rd month, the month of Sivan,*
*and it was written exactly as Mordechai instructed,*
*to the Jews and to the satraps, and to the governors*
*and the princes of the provinces from India to Ethio-*
*pia, 127 provinces, to each province in its own script*
*and to each people in its own tongue, and to the Jews*
*in their own script and their own tongue. He wrote in*
*the name of the king Ahashverosh and sealed it with*
*the king's ring, sending letters by couriers on horse-*
*back, riding the swift thoroughbred steeds of the king's*
*service: That the king had permitted the Jews in every*
*city to organize and to defend themselves — to anni-*
*hilate, to kill and to destroy the forces of every people*
*and province that threatened them, children and*

women, and to take their property for plunder — in a single day in all the provinces of the king Ahashverosh, on the 13th day of the 12th month, that is the month of Adar. The contents of the letter were to be circulated as law in every province, and were to be published among all peoples, that the Jews should be ready on that day to avenge themselves upon their enemies. The couriers, riders of the swift steeds of the king's service, went out with great haste by order of the king, and the law was distributed in Susa the capital.

Mordechai went out from before the king dressed in royal garments of blue and white, with a great crown of gold, and a robe of fine linen and purple, and the town of Susa rejoiced and was glad. The Jews had light and gladness, and joy and honor. And in every province, and in every city, wherever the king's command and his law reached, the Jews had gladness and joy, a feast and a holiday, and many from among the people of the land became Jews, for fear of the Jews had fallen upon them.

# 18

# THE LAST APPEAL

ESTHER'S COUP SUCCEEDS in deposing the vizier and placing her cousin at the top of the Persian government. But it does not save the Jews. Indeed, in her principal mission—convincing the king to allow the Jews to escape his decree with their lives, she has failed completely.

It is true that Esther does approach Ahashverosh at her second banquet with the demand that she and her people be saved from Haman. But the king's reaction has nothing whatsoever to do with the Jews—for whom, if one were to judge by his original complicity in having them all murdered, he would appear to care very little. When he responds to Esther's plea by asking "Who would presume to do so?" he is referring not to the annihilation of the Jews but to the threat to the queen. It is the protection of the queen which is, after all, an issue of immediate, burning interest to Ahashverosh. The rest

of the Jews, and even the fact of Esther's being a Jewess, appear
hardly to scrape his consciousness.

And so it seems for quite a while. After Haman is hanged and his
duties as vizier are transferred to Mordechai, the king returns to
ignoring the issue of the impending destruction of the Jews, just as
though Esther had never broached the issue. His anger over the
threat to him and his household has been appeased by Haman's
death, and with this, the case is closed. It is not even clear that he
heard the second part of Esther's plea: That her people be delivered.

A month goes by, and then a second. Yet the decree of destruction against the Jews remains in force, unchanged. The king is
immersed in the business of making order in a politics which has
been convulsed by two swift changes in government, and Mordechai
finds himself with the pressing and ponderous concern of making a
responsible impression in his new post. The narrative stresses that
Ahashverosh is generally far more concerned with his honor than
with the status of the royal treasuries—giving out "royal wine
aplenty, from the hand of the king" for half a year, (1:7) granting a
remission in taxes and giving out gifts "from the king's hand" in
honor of his wedding, (2:18) waiving away Haman's offer of a vast
contribution to the state budget as though it were nothing, (3:11)
and preferring to respond to petitions with offers of "even if it be
half the kingdom, it will be given you." (5:3) Indeed, the only time
Persia is portrayed as securing sources of financing for all the king's
gestures is under Mordechai's tenure as vizier when, like Joseph, he
raises taxes and sets the state on the path to solvency and power:
"The king Ahashverosh levied taxes on the land, and on the islands
of the sea." (10:1) But this new policy may not have been an easy
sell with the king and the court, and Mordechai must not have
dared raise subjects other than those needed to obtain the
contradictory aims of pleasing the king and responsibly operating
the state.

Only after two months of frustration and worry over the fate of the decree does it become apparent to Mordechai and Esther that there is to be no response. Ahashverosh is simply not concerned to alter this policy. Having returned with his tail between his legs from his experiment in totalitarianism, Ahashverosh clings like a child to the old rule of the laws, under which even the king does not alter a law once it has been decreed. Moreover, he has little interest in humiliating himself by rescinding the edict even if a way out can be found—an act which would amount to a public admission of his own confusion and weakness. What is more, he may not have been convinced that Haman was all wrong about the Jews, who after all have proven to be a deadly opponent. Perhaps it is still "of no benefit for the king to tolerate them"? (3:8)

Whatever the explanation, it becomes clear that without a further effort from Esther and Mordechai, the decree will remain in force and the enemies of the Jews will have their way in spite of everything. It is difficult to imagine a more miserable realization. For all that Esther had done, her people were not to be saved. For all her belief that time was of the essence, that she should immediately risk her life rather than let a day go by with the terrible decree in place, here the time was dragging on, the awful date approaching, and nothing was being done.

While Mordechai has used the intervening time to do everything in his power to gain the confidence of the king, it is nevertheless obvious to him that if another appeal is to be made on behalf of the Jews, it is Esther who stands the better chance of influencing Ahashverosh. Yet even this may not have been so clear. If Esther had been able to approach the king without once more entering the throne room unsummoned, she certainly would have, which suggests that the king may have been avoiding her for some time—perhaps even since Haman's downfall. We can only guess whether this was from embarrassment, or from a desire to restore his illusion of control over events, or because he was still nursing a grudge over what had happened, or because he did not wish to discuss the fate of the Jews with his politically partisan wife. Or for all of these reasons. And if, when she first approached the king, it had seemed highly likely that he would not want to do away with her, the brooding silence now put everything in question.

Spring has given way to the deep Persian summer, and sixty-six precious days have gone by before Esther and Mordechai finally reach the conclusion that there is no choice but for Esther once more to gamble with her life.[1] Realizing that this is the last chance for her and her people, Esther again decides to act. She enters the throne room and collapses in tears at the king's feet, pleading the cause of the Jews in public for the first time, even before the king is able to react to her presence.

This time, there is no feint on Esther's part. She leaves no doubt in the king's mind as to what she wants: He can choose to spare her life and confront her face to face on the issue of her people—or he can avoid the subject for good at the cost of having her executed.

Although Ahashverosh still has no interest in discussing the Jews, his hand is forced. The humiliation of losing his queen would be too great, and he extends the scepter to her a second time. But this time he says nothing, grudgingly refusing to ask her what her request is, according to the accepted formula. Passive, morose, he just lets her talk.

Esther's second appearance in the throne room barely resembles the first. Gone are her hesitation and stammering, her lack of confidence in herself; gone are Ahashverosh's pompous displays of his power to grant her things. They both now recognize the power that she herself has in the court. Politely, but forcefully, she presents a demand which she believes he has to accept: "If it please the king, and if I have found favor before him, and if the thing seems right to the king, and if I am worthy in his eyes, let it be written to revoke the

letters devised by Haman, son of Hamedata the Agagite, which he
wrote to destroy the Jews who are in all the king's provinces. For how
can I bear to see the evil which will befall my people? And how can I
bear to witness the destruction of my kindred?" (8:6–7)

Esther's carefully rehearsed address has three parts, each corresponding to a different instrument of political pressure to which the
queen appeals: The king's interest in those things which he desires;
his presumed interest in the cause of justice; and his fear of losing her:

*Interest:*

(i) If it please the king;

(ii) If I have found favor with the king;

*Justice:*

(iii) If it seems right;

(iv) If I am worthy;

*Fear of Esther herself:*

(v) I cannot bear to see this evil;

(vi) I cannot bear to witness this destruction.

It is obvious that some of these expressions have appeared in Esther's
earlier approaches to make requests of the king—the invitation to
her first banquet, (5:4) the invitation to her second banquet, (5:8) and
her first plea for the deliverance of her people (7:3)—but there is also
much here that she has never been willing to say to Ahashverosh
before.

The first part, appealing to the king's interest, consists of standard formulations for making a request from a king, which Esther
has always used before in her dealings with Ahashverosh. (i) "If it
please the king" constitutes an appeal to whatever the king likes and
considers to be desirable for him, and serves to dress up her opinion
that the proposed course should be pleasing to him because it is in his
interest. Esther herself has used this formulation each time she has

made a request of the king, beginning with her first approach to invite him to her banquet. It is also used in every other political appeal in the narrative, whether by Memuchan, Haman, Esther or the king's youths.[2]

The second appeal to interest, (ii) "if I have found favor with the king," is more personal and less direct, drawing the king's attention to the fact that it is in his interest to act for the sake of someone whom he desires to please, even if the requested action is in itself of no interest to him. This is the kind of vicarious interest of which "boss" politics is made, with favors constantly being disbursed to keep various clients and vassals in line. Even this mild effort indirectly to focus on someone other than the king seems to have been a bit presumptuous, however, since no one dares make use of it other than the queen, and she herself musters the courage to do so only upon making her second and third requests of the king.

The other components of Esther's speech are unique to her history, as well as being unique in the entire tale, demonstrating how far she has come both in her political wisdom and in her willingness to confront the king. Esther makes two appeals to justice, which mimic the pattern of her appeals to interest: (iii) "if it seems right" and (iv) "if I am worthy"—turning first to the objective question of the justice of sparing the Jews (even if the king has no political interest in doing so), and then to the question of whether she herself is deserving of having this done for her (even the king has no interest in granting her such a favor).

Issues of justice are a critical factor in political pressure, because they appeal to emotions which are capable of inducing the listener to rise above the constraints of his own petty self-interest, and not few are the men who can be induced to take at least some action on these grounds. Yet appeals to justice are also important in the case of a rascal such as Ahashverosh, although his actual concern for justice is demonstrably trivial, because they play to the interest of every ruler in *appearing* just to maintain the respect of his subjects.[3] Ahashverosh in particular is known for his cultivation of the appearance of justice, consulting with the learned, at least whenever such are present, "for such was the king's habit before all who knew law and judgment." (1:13)

But there is more to this part of the confrontation than an effort to embarrass the king into doing the right thing.

In both of these cases, Esther refers to the moral judgment of the king ("if it seems right to the king," "if I am worthy in his eyes"), but this formal consideration for the honor of the king affords him little cover. Questions of justice deal not with personal perceptions, but with objective issues of what is right and wrong, good and evil in the world. No matter how politely the point may be phrased, Esther is steering the king's attention to things that exist outside of his infantile desires: If saving the Jews is right, then any other determination on the part of the king is wrong. If Esther, after years of devoted service, including saving the life of the king, is not to be considered worthy of having her request granted, then Ahashverosh is obtuse in his ability to judge those around him. And it is important that he sense that such are her opinions.

To broach questions of objective truth before the king is in itself a challenge to the feeling of omnipotence with which Ahashverosh likes to pamper himself—as it had been a challenge to Haman before him. But it also reflects an accurate reading of the strength of the man. Ahashverosh, for all his rages, is afraid to make decisions, afraid of exposing himself, afraid of embarrassing himself, and afraid of losing control. Esther correctly guesses that the more strongly he is aware of the steadfastness of her position, the more likely he is to take it as a given and respond favorably. That is, she must appeal to justice in order to make it clear to Ahashverosh that a decision based solely on what he believes to be in his own personal interest is unacceptable. The policy of the state must square with reality—*her* reality.

Among other things, Ahashverosh's personal weakness suggests a fear of rejection as well, and it is to this fear that Esther appeals in the third, climactic part of her speech, when she asks: (v) "How can I bear to see the evil which will befall my people? How can I bear to witness the destruction of my kindred?"

By this point, all pretense of the king's interest is incredibly dropped, and Esther, perhaps alone among the petitioners whom Ahashverosh can remember, steps forward as an independent player with an independent interest to which she demands that he attend: The queen wants the Jews saved because she herself cannot stand having it otherwise. Ahashverosh can save the Jews because it suits him, or he can save them because it is right. But if he does not, the queen will not be able to "bear" it—whatever this may mean—and it is he who will have to cope with the consequences.

The full force of the queen's threat cannot be appraised without remembering Vashti, who would not show off her beauty before the drunken crowd at the king's summons. She, too, had publicly pitted her independent interest against his command. The throng, the advice, the drink, the humiliation, all had braced him to fight, to eliminate her independent will and restore his own rule. But in securing victory for his spirit Ahashverosh had lost, paying for his refusal to accommodate her for years. This time, there is no throng, no advice, no drink: Only the humiliation of backing down and rescinding his foolish law, standing as against the power of the queen—understated, hidden, mysterious, but there to be felt—the eternal, imponderable power of the weak over the mighty.

Ahashverosh has only two choices as he sits before the watching eyes of the courtiers: He may try to discredit Esther and distance himself from her position, as he did with Vashti. Or he can seek conciliation with Esther and the Jews, by distancing himself from Haman's law.

As he looks down from his throne at Mordechai and the others, he recognizes that there is no way of avoiding the issue. Refusing to respond to Esther is a negative response, and he is not strong enough to open up such a fight. His hand forced, the king fumbles for a defense that will allow him to accept the queen's position while minimizing the damage done by an about-face. He professes to have done everything within his power to protect the Jews: "I have given Haman's house to Esther," he announces to the court, "and he himself has been hanged on the gallows because he would lift a hand against the Jews." (8:7)

Upon hearing these words, anyone present in the court would have instantly recognized the victory Esther had won. For two months, the empire had dealt with Haman's death as one brought about by his treachery against the royal family. The well-known rivalry between the deceased vizier and the Jews had been considered irrelevant to the story of his downfall, since the king's own intention to exterminate the Jews had been well known.

Yet to hear the king now, he never was the scourge of the Jews, having actually championed their cause, bringing Haman down "because he would lift a hand against the Jews." In so saying, Ahashverosh officially accepts the premise that the persecution of the Jews is unjust and undesirable. The extermination order itself is still on the books, he implies, not through any fault of his own, but only because "an edict written in the king's name and sealed with the king's ring cannot be revoked." Had it been up to Ahashverosh, the kingdom is now to believe, it would all have been different. Indeed, as far as the king is concerned, Mordechai, the new vizier, can "write concerning the Jews as seems good in your eyes, in the king's name...." (8:8) It is not he, but the law of the land which stands in the way of saving the Jews.

This is political legerdemain at its finest, but there is no one in the court who has the will and the authority to challenge the revolution which has just occurred in imperial policy. Like Harvona, the king himself has now recognized which way the winds are blowing, and switched sides—marking the actual political watershed from which point a favorable conclusion of the story becomes a real possibility, the odds actually shifting in favor of the camp of the Jews for the first time.

# 19

# POLITICAL POWER

BY THE TIME OF THE KING'S "CONVERSION" to the cause of the Jews, barely eight months remain before the day Haman had promised his followers would see their final triumph over this people.[1] With the king's nominal support of the Jewish cause, it now becomes possible for Mordechai to work openly to undermine the forces which, even without the assistance of Haman, continue organizing in preparation for the massacre.

Although as vizier Mordechai has at his disposal the influence of the central government of the empire, it is easy to underestimate the enormity of the task that lies before him. For while the belief that Ahashverosh wants all the Jews murdered has been abroad for only about ten weeks at this point, it is nevertheless clear that the machine that has been set in motion has been much longer in the making. It is evident from the narrative that fear of the Jews and hostility towards them were not something new to Haman's followers, or to others in the kingdom.[2] The king's decree was therefore not an instruction to do something to which none might otherwise have been inclined; in the manner of state-sponsored pogroms elsewhere, it was rather an official assurance that the state would stand aside if individuals and local governments did as they had otherwise wished to do for years. With an imperial decree in force to the effect that the Jews were to be massacred, there had been no shortage of enthusiasts from one end of the earth to the other who had set to work preparing for the great day; nor had they had any difficulty in persuading the fence-sitters to join in. The fact was that the machine Haman had set in motion would not be so easy to turn aside under any circumstance.

Moreover, Mordechai's political aims at this point are not so simple as might be supposed at first glance. While a military triumph for the Jews might seem a fine thing in comparison to the scorched-earth defeat that had been promised, Mordechai cannot satisfy himself with this. It is not enough that he achieve military superiority, win the critical battles and prevent the threatened holocaust. He must somehow secure the life of every individual Jew, wherever in the empire he might be. It is clear that any scenario in which an overwhelming victory for the Jews and their allies is not a foregone conclusion will end in disaster. The date designated by Haman will trigger warfare against the Jews throughout the empire, in which the casualties on both sides will be massive, and the weaker among the Jewish communities will have been destroyed before the fighting has ended.

Without the ability to alter Haman's decree, Mordechai has before him only one way to prevent such a catastrophe. There can be no hope of preventing massacres without bringing the might of the empire to bear against the anti-Semites—as would have been the case if they had tried to organize the murder of innocents without the encouragement of an official decree. He has to build an alliance of pro-Jewish forces so vast that the anti-Semites will find themselves abandoned by their following, and without the capacity to mount a serious assault in any province. But how can this be done?

Herein lies the fundamental question which is the subject of politics: How can the individual, weak as he is, move the group of the many to act in accordance with his will?

In politics, weakness does not attract the interest of strength, does not bring strength around to its cause, does not move strength to action. But strength attracts strength, and power attracts power. The strong have every reason to be attracted to those they believe to be strong, to help them: (i) That they may win favor with them and later receive assistance from them in return; (ii) that they may avoid arousing the ire and ill will of the strong; (iii) that they may be perceived as being influential with the strong, and thus powerful themselves; and (iv) that they take part in winning combinations in which they may claim a share of the spoils. None of this can be said to apply to the weak. They can rarely return favors of value; they can rarely do damage worthy of fearing; there is little value in being perceived as having influence with them; and there are no spoils to be gained in joining in their moves, since it is ever apparent that they will lose.

And thus to the fundamental question of all politics, there is only one possible answer: The weak, to the degree they can make themselves seem strong, can attract the support of the strong, thereby becoming strong in reality; and to the degree that they fail in this, they can expect no help from men.

It is in a sense to the credit of contemporary readers that this most basic political truth often strikes them as being so alien, that it at first appears unintelligible. For those unschooled in politics, it is ingrained that precisely the opposite should be the case: That it is weakness that should attract strength—that one should strive to defend the weak and assist the poor. But such moral principles are necessary precisely because they remedy nature as we find it, the natural law coming as it does to repair that which we find intolerable in the way the world works—and in the ways of politics especially.[3]

Of course, there are always exceptions to any law presuming to predict man's behavior, and the Bible in particular emphasizes the righteous few, Jews and non-Jews, who have always made it their business to use their strength to protect the weak. But as is clear from the biblical narrative, these powerful are the exceptions. The reality is as Machiavelli became notorious for insisting: The world does not much run according to these precedents.[4] The book of Esther sticks close to the gritty functioning of the common political world—one in which no one stood to defend Vashti when the king was poised to destroy her, in which no one stood to defend Esther or the other women when they were to be raped by the king, in which no one joined Mordechai in refusing to bow to Haman, in which no man stood with Mordechai to openly oppose the extermination of the Jews at the word of the king. Indeed, not one among the mighty and the many of the empire dares to stand up against Haman in anything so long as he is strong, and Harvona, the first to break ranks and openly turn against him, does so only after "the king had determined ill against him" (7:7)—not until *after* it is clear that Haman is already doomed.

It is from the grim consistency with which considerations of political interest prevail over every other motive—even more than from the absence of explicit mentions of God—that the narrative of Esther draws its eerie feeling of the abyss. It is in such a world that man lives unless he makes it otherwise, and it is according to its rules that Mordechai must play to win.

The narrative describes six ways in which Mordechai acts to fight and win the political war, rallying the strength of the empire to his side and causing the anti-Semites to despair and give up on implementing their scheme. The first three acts of Mordechai are described in the account that follows Esther's second appeal for the lives of the Jews: (i) Mordechai's decree (8:9–14), (ii) Mordechai's public appearances in Susa (8:15–16), and (iii) the public celebrations among the Jews (8:17).

In the next chapter, which treats the course of the war itself, an additional passage makes it clear that these are only the first successes of a concerted political campaign which Mordechai wages over the subsequent months in order to make the military victory possible: "The Jews organized themselves in their cities in all the provinces of the king Ahashverosh, to lay their hands on those who sought to harm them, and no man could stand before them, for fear of them had fallen on all the peoples. And all the princes of the provinces, and the satraps, and the governors and those that conduct the king's affairs supported the Jews, because the fear of Mordechai had fallen upon them. For great was Mordechai in the king's house, and his reputation had gone out to all the provinces, for the man Mordechai grew greater and greater." (9:2–4)

Thus to add to the events immediately surrounding the decree, Mordechai also engages in three other aspects of a political offensive to save the Jews: (iv) Military organization (9:2), (v) rallying the support of provincial and local governments (9:3), and (vi) building up his own reputation (9:4).

It is worth looking at the way these elements are assembled to form a comprehensive political campaign. The first efforts of any political offensive must be aimed at the morale of the faithful—for unless the Jews are psychologically prepared for the coming fight, there is no chance of projecting whatever strength they may have in potential. That is, to have a real chance of coming out of this ordeal victorious, the Jews must first believe that they can win; and only if they believe that they can win can they impress upon their enemies that they may lose.

No one understands this as well as Haman, whose original decree was crafted to fight just this psychological war—robbing the Jews of their self-confidence by demonstrating that their independence and power amounts to a nullity, instructing: "To annihilate, to kill and to destroy all the Jews, the young and the elderly, children and women, in one day—on the 13th day of the 12th month, the month of Adar—and to take their property for plunder." (3:13)

This first decree had consisted of three parts, each forged in the image of the obsessed anti-Semite's lust for the complete degradation and disempowering of his opponents: (i) To annihilate, to kill and to destroy the Jews, (ii) to kill their children and women, and (iii) to take their property for plunder.

Thus the almost comical emphasis on (i) how the Jews, every one, were not only to be "annihilated," but also "killed" and "destroyed," was intended by Haman to connote perfect rule, without exception, without hope of escape. The emphasis on (ii) "children and women" was a further step in the terror, demonstrating that nothing would be left of anything which the annihilated Jews had valued and hoped for during their lives. And the almost anticlimactic insistence on (iii) taking "their property for plunder"—which one might have thought to be an issue of little interest to people who were being informed of their own deaths and those of all their loved ones—was intended to deepen their anguish. Rather than ordering that the properties be handed over to the king's treasuries, Haman chose to leave the possessions of the Jews in the hands of those who had murdered them. The Jews were to understand that not only were they to be murdered, but that others, their murderers, would reap the benefits of all they had hoped for and labored towards in their lives.

The contempt for issues of property comes from a perspective in which things are measured in terms of their supposed objective worth: How can one compare property ("things") to the value of the life of a man? But the narratives of the Bible are more sensitive than we tend to be to the *subjective* value of things to the individual. People spend their entire lives building up a home or a business, using materials they have inherited or chosen to buy at their own expense, in order to create things which are the fruit of their lives, and which they will bequeath to those people most precious to them. For the individual, the property in question is not a material object at all, just as the children in question are not merely individual lives. The property, like the children, is an achievement of his spirit. It has come to be what it is through his own rule—not merely his labor, but his labor as the process through which his control and rule, his decisions and creativity, his power, are exerted on the world. Because both the children and the property continue after his death, they are the ways in which every man may evade the mortality which hangs over all men: If the objective mortality of man confirms his power-lessness, his subjective ability to create that which will endure, even that which stands as a contribution to the eternal, robs death of its absolute power; it relieves man of his absolute powerlessness before the eternal, restoring his spirit, which would otherwise drown in a perpetual hopelessness.

While an "objective" estimation should place murder as the greatest of crimes, the biblical narrative is therefore often aware that from the point of view of the murdered, whose life was in any case to end some day, there may be other crimes which are more terrible. Thus the book of Kings relates the story of Navot the Jezreelite, whose vineyard Ahav, king of Israel, determined to have for a vegetable garden because it was near his house. Ahav offered to give Navot money, or else a "better vineyard than this one," in exchange. But the fact that Ahav was offering an objectively good deal in the form of a "better" vineyard was of no interest to Navot, for whom such a trade was reprehensible. He had spent his life from childhood building up a vineyard, as good a one as he could make, so that it could be passed on. Should he now agree to have his life's work destroyed so that the king could have vegetables nearby? He responds: "The Eternal curse me if I should give you the inheritance of my fathers."

Like Ahashverosh, Ahav finds not having his way unbearable, and like Ahashverosh, he has advisers prepared to goad him to perfidy over such opposition to his authority. Jezebel the queen sends out letters in Ahav's name, sealed with his signet, ordering that Navot be killed, and then triumphally announces that he may now go down and begin uprooting the vines. When the prophet Elijah finds the king in the vineyard, he is enraged: "So says the Eternal: Have you murdered, and then taken possession as well?"[5]

Here, too, it is possible to ask how a property issue can be on the prophet's mind when a man has been murdered. And the answer is that Elijah understands the evil king's deed from the perspective of the slain man, for whom the greatest pain would not have been the ending of his life, but the erasure of all that he had achieved in it, as though he had never been—so that another with no sympathy or appreciation for what he had built could plant his own shoots and grow in his stead. Elijah understands what has happened here to be not only a crime of the body, but a crime of the spirit as well. And such is also the judgment of other biblical thinkers when they consider the meaning of property to men: Kohelet, for example, considers the fact that the product of one's labors will be inherited after death, and then mistreated by men who are likely to be fools, to be one of life's great evils;[6] and Jeremiah, in seeking to impress upon Jerusalem the terror that is to come, depicts God as saying: "Therefore I will give their wives to others, and their fields to those who will take them...."[7] Enjoyment of one's life's work by his conquerors can be seen as the most potent expression of ruin and defeat—and, in fact, it is to precisely this sense of ultimate ruin that Ahashverosh wishes to appeal when, at his own initiative, he hands Haman's estate over to Esther.

Recognizing this, we can now understand the purpose and effect of Haman's decree. For ten furious weeks after its promulgation, the streets of every city in the empire reverberated with scenes in which the anti-Jews worked the brutal psychology of the king's edict for all it was worth. The enemies of the Jews—not only the enemies of the Jewish people, but the enemies of every particular, individual Jew as well—swaggered about the public places, trumpeting their intentions in the face of every Jew who had ever insulted them, or edged them out for a public post, or charged them a price they believed to be too high, in accordance with the three parts of the decree: "I will have your house when you are gone, Jew," "I will have your daughter before she dies, Jew," "I will dance on your grave, Jew." And worse. And with the taunting began the acts of vandalism, of theft, of desecration, testing the Jews, humiliating them, preparing them.

The effect of this campaign was first on the anti-Semites themselves, as it had been in Pharaoh's Egypt, as it was in the Germany of the brownshirts. It gave the anti-Jews what they wanted more than anything else: The drunken, boundless sense of vengeful rule which is the motive heart of all great evil. It provided them with the sense of empowerment, of license, of freedom without which they never would have dared to speak as they did, and without which they could never have done as they planned to do. For many are the dark thoughts which men nurse in silence; but to act when the bitter day came required not only organization, but psychological preparation. Every day in the streets, they prepared themselves to accept, to anticipate, to desire, to *believe* in what was coming.

But perhaps the greater effect was on the Jews themselves. The natural reaction of a man under attack is to become angered, to rise up in power, to fight; these are the reactions of any animal which can still hope to have power over others, at least to have power over itself. But beyond anger lies despair, the emotion which accompanies the belief in the hopelessness of one's cause, and the powerlessness of one's self. And as the campaign of humiliation gained strength and popularity in the streets, so too did the Jews feel more isolated every day. As friends began to distance themselves, as those who had feared them began to laugh, as those who owed them debts of gratitude turned their backs, they began to feel the despair in the air, the hopelessness and the death. The Jews turned in on themselves, grew numb, grew powerless, grew tired of life, became objects, became dead. For many of them in those terrible weeks, their annihilation gradually became a fact, and they began to say to themselves: Tomorrow we die.

When Esther finally succeeds in extracting a grudging statement in support of the Jews from the king, Mordechai recognizes that much will have to be done to transform this shift in the palace into a different reality in the provinces. Without a dramatic act to break the momentum of events, the deterioration in the condition of the Jews and the rapidly growing power of their enemies will continue, and massacres of the Jews will take place in various parts of the empire despite everything that has happened in Susa.

Unable to revoke the king's first decree, Mordechai chooses to give force to the king's new policy by giving anti-Semites a dose of their own methods. He constructs a decree of his own, informing the empire that the king will allow the Jews "to annihilate, to kill and to destroy the forces of every people and province that threatened them, children and women, and to take their property for plunder—in a single day in all the provinces of the king Ahashverosh, on the 13th day of the 12th month, that is the month of Adar." (8:11–12)

While seeking to stress the fact that the Jews are being given permission "to organize and to defend themselves," (8:11) the wording of the missive which Mordechai dispatches is hardly defensive. Being copied straight out of the first letter composed by Haman, it grants the Jews permission (i) "to annihilate, to kill and to destroy" their enemies, (ii) to slaughter their children and women, and (iii) to seize their property. Neither the assault on the families of would-be assailants nor the clause concerning property has anything to do with defense in any obvious sense, nor does the brutal hyperbole of

annihilation, killing and destroying immediately seem to have much
in common with this purpose. Indeed, Mordechai's letter reeks of
Haman's style and substance, and its language is the language of
terror. When first these formulations were sent out, their purpose
was clearly to inspire fear and despair. In this second instance, this is
no less the case: Mordechai reasons that the Jews need a shot of
confidence, and that the anti-Semites need a slap in the face to
deprive them of their certainty of victory. And if the Jews must stay
up nights wondering whether their children will be alive a year from
now, whether someone else will be living in their home a year from
now, the anti-Semites can afford to lose some sleep as well.

In achieving this, Mordechai's decree is extraordinarily successful. There immediately follows a giddy, surreal account of Mordechai's
stepping into the streets of the Jewish quarter after the promulgation
of the decree, virtually radiating with a majestic power which revives
the languishing Jews of the capital: "Mordechai went out from
before the king dressed in royal garments of blue and white, with a
great crown of gold, and a robe of fine linen and purple, and the
town of Susa rejoiced and was glad. The Jews had light and gladness,
and joy and honor." (8:15–16)

Mordechai had certainly been functioning as vizier before this
point, and there is no reason to think that his personal appearance
had actually changed much after his letter had been issued. But the
narrative refers to the subjective understanding of the Jews, for whom
even Haman's death could have been scant comfort. So long as the
king was determined to go through with the promised outrages, the
appearance on the street of a court Jew such as Mordechai—having
once been paraded through the streets on the king's horse, now
dressed in the king's finery, in fact nothing better than an accomplice—
was certainly the subject of ambivalence, and probably even scorn
Mordechai himself must have seemed to many in those weeks a rath
pathetic and grasshopperish figure, a subservient court Jew if not a

traitor. It is only with the appearance of the decree, and the shift in the policy of the king towards the Jews, that Mordechai in fact begins to gain the stature that until then had only been formally his. Most of the Jews, living outside the city walls, have seen the meaning of imperial power up close only once in their lives—when Ahashverosh invited them to immerse themselves in his wealth and majesty in the palace, amid "hangings of white, of fine cotton, and blue, suspended with cords of fine linen and purple from silver rods and marble columns, divans of gold and silver...." (1:6) But now they have the chance to see this strength being wielded on their behalf by one of their own. No coincidence then, that they now perceive Mordechai "in royal garments of blue and white, with a great crown of gold, and a robe of fine linen and purple," and that as a result, "the Jews had light and gladness, and joy and honor"—not merely happiness, but honor, the sense of pleasure which results from a renewed belief that they have control over their lives. And while they do not take the same pleasure in it, it is likely that the anti-Semites, too, catch the electric scent of the supernatural in this reversal of fortune.

Mordechai's brutal decree is the first step in establishing him as the leader who would destroy the enemies of the Jews, his march through Susa the second. By nightfall, celebrations had been organized which were then repeated throughout the empire as word of Mordechai's decree reached the other provinces. And everywhere that the celebrations reached, the Jews began to feel themselves reviving. At Mordechai's behest, "The Jews organized themselves in their cities in all the provinces of the king Ahashverosh, to lay their hands on those who sought to harm them," and the first vestiges of genuine strength began to be felt.

This did not, of course, mean that the anti-Semites gave up on their plans. Some of them only grew in their determination to have their way with the Jews, and the harassment of the Jewish communities of the empire did not immediately come to an end. But what had until now been a simple edict of annihilation became a test of strengths, with that of the Jews on the ascendant, and wherever the anti-Semites sought to humiliate the Jews and test their mettle, they now collided with a tide of increasing confidence—the taunts were thrown back in their faces, and some of the more hot-tempered Jews responded to the hatred of the anti-Semites with blows. And with every bruising confrontation, the reputation of the Jews and their leader increased, and confidence in the inevitable fact of their destruction and its desirability withered. And as this process took place, one and all could glimpse the uncanny, almost physical growth in the appearance of Mordechai, as "the man Mordechai grew greater and greater"—and this slowly began to be true of the Jew in the street of every city of the empire as well. Where only weeks before, both the Jews and much of Persia would have laughed to know that the rabbis of later times referred to Mordechai the Jew as a dragon,[8] now the distinct contours of the dragon's armor, its talons, its mass, its breath and its guile all began to emerge.

With this change in public image, Mordechai had the strands of power he needed to barter for greater political assets, taking his political campaign to "the princes of the provinces, and the satraps, and the governors and those that conduct the king's affairs," whose support in each province would mean the difference between life and destruction. In some cases, he immediately found himself speaking with those who were sympathetic, or who could at least read the writing on the wall. Consolidating this support and encouraging it to go public, Mordechai turned to the harder cases, seeking harsher methods of persuasion, pointing to the military preparations under way, to the support for their cause which was now the policy of the king, to the foolhardiness of the anti-Semites' plans—pushing every official who could have a hand in the business to believe that anti-Semites could not win, that those who aided them would only suf in the end.

And one by one, they came to believe, for "his reputation had gone out to all the provinces, because the fear of Mordechai had fallen upon them." And one by one, those who had sympathized with the Jews began to do so openly; those who had been uncertain began to sympathize; those who had been derisive and had calculated the benefits of the coming catastrophe grew silent; and those who had preached against the Jews grew afraid. And the sense grew in Persia that the Jews were going to win.

In the end, the image of Mordechai did reach the proportions which had characterized Haman during the reign of his terror, when none of the king's servants could resist prostrating himself. The empire believed in the power of Mordechai, and so they believed in the power of the Jews, and "no man could stand before them, for fear of them had fallen on all the peoples"—"and all supported the Jews."

And the Jews saw this additional, remarkable effect of the law that in politics, strength attracts strength, and power attracts power: "And many from among the people of the land became Jews, for fear of the Jews had fallen upon them." (8:17)

# ESTHER
# EIGHT
[9:1 – 9:16]

On the 13th day of the 12th month, the month of
Adar, when the king's command and his law were to
be enforced, on the day that the enemies of the Jews
had expected to rule over them, the situation was reversed, and it was the Jews themselves who ruled over
those who hated them.

The Jews organized themselves in their cities in
all the provinces of the king Ahashverosh, to lay their
hands on those who sought to harm them, and no
man could stand before them, for fear of them had
fallen on all the peoples. And all the princes of the
provinces, and the satraps, and the governors and
those that conduct the king's affairs supported the Jews,
because the fear of Mordechai had fallen upon them
For great was Mordechai in the king's house, and h
reputation had gone out to all the provinces, for
man Mordechai grew greater and greater.

*The Jews struck at all their enemies with the sword, killing and destroying, and they did as they pleased to those who hated them. And in Susa the capital the Jews killed and destroyed five hundred men — along with Parshandata, Dalphon, Asphata, Porata, Adalia, Aridata, Parimashta, Arisai, Aridai and Vaizata, the ten sons of Haman, son of Hamedata, the persecutor of the Jews, but the spoils they did not touch.*

*That day the number of those killed in Susa the capital was reported to the king.*

*The king said to Esther the queen: "In Susa the capital the Jews have killed and destroyed five hundred men, and the ten sons of Haman. What have they done in the rest of the king's provinces? — and whatever your wish, it will be given you, and whatever more you may request, it will be done."*

*Esther said: "If it please the king, let the Jews in Susa do tomorrow according to the law for today, and let Haman's ten sons be hanged on the gallows."*

*The king said to do so, and the law was given in Susa, and Haman's ten sons were hanged. The Jews* in Susa assembled on the 14th day of the month of Adar as well, and they killed in Susa three hundred men, but the spoils they did not touch.

The rest of the Jews in the king's provinces organized and defended themselves, gaining respite from their enemies, and killing seventy-five thousand of those who hated them, but the spoils they did not touch.

# 20

# THE JEWS' WAR

BY THE THIRTEENTH DAY OF ADAR, the Jews have turned political defeat into political triumph, and the power to emerge from battle victorious is theirs. When the day comes, they use this strength to deal a death-blow to anti-Semitic power in the empire, killing seventy-six thousand men, laying waste to its leadership and establishing a deterrent against future threats to the Jewish communities of Persia. Perhaps most significant, the crushing of the anti-Semitic nemesis establishes the position of the new Jewish vizier with the king, ensuring that Ahashverosh's authority will be wielded for the good of the Jewish interest for years to come.

The narrative touches on only the most essential aspects of these final stages of Mordechai and Esther's coup, but these are enough to understand what happened. After months of feverish diplomatic work, Mordechai had succeeded in parlaying the fact of the new decree's existence and the feeble mumblings of Ahashverosh into a widespread belief that he in fact had the influence, authority and power to make good on it: "The man Mordechai grew greater and greater," "his reputation had gone out to all the provinces," and with that "the fear of Mordechai had fallen upon them." By the opening of the actual war, it was clear to all that the influence of the Jews in the empire had become overwhelming. The hard core of anti-Semitic power had been isolated, as "all the princes of the provinces, and the satraps, and the governors and those that conduct the king's affairs supported the Jews." Those that had been willing to support the anti-Semites had switched sides or disappeared into the woodwork, and it had become obvious that in the case of an actual physical contest, the Jews and their allies would score a terrifying victory. Thus the "fear of them had fallen on all the peoples," and "no man could stand before them." (9:2–4)[1]

Presumably, Mordechai now had the option of restraining the fury of the promised Jewish onslaught. There was no longer much question of a real anti-Semitic assault, and if he feared an anti-Semitic resurgence at the first sign of his weakness, he could have opted to arrest or execute a few hundred gang-leaders across the empire. Would this not have sufficed?

In this, Mordechai's decisions are straight out of Machiavelli's textbook of power politics:

> For it must be noted, that men must either be caressed or annihilated; they will revenge themselves for small injuries, but cannot do so for great ones; the injury therefore that we do to a man must be such that we need not fear his vengeance.[2]

Moreover, a ruler or a prince

> must not mind incurring the charge of cruelty for the purpose of keeping his subjects united and faithful; for, with a very few

examples, he will be more merciful than those who, from excess of
tenderness, allow disorders to arise, from whence spring bloodshed
and rapine.... And of all princes, it is impossible for a new prince
to escape the reputation of cruelty....[3]

In politics, a minimalistic response to a real threat all but ensures two
undesired consequences, both of them deadly: (i) the defeated enemy
nurtures the hope of revenge, and continues to be an active threat as
he seeks an opportunity to reassert his challenge; and (ii) the mildness of the response encourages others to take advantage of what can
be perceived to be hesitancy or weakness on the part of the ruler. The
only hope to avoid future outrages is thus the assertion of overwhelming power in the first instance.

And this is what Mordechai chooses to do: "The Jews struck at
all their enemies with the sword, killing and destroying, and they did
as they pleased to those who hated them. And in Susa the capital the
Jews killed and destroyed five hundred men—along with Parshandata,
Dalphon, Asphata, Porata, Adalia, Aridata, Parimashta, Arisai, Aridai
and Vaizata, the ten sons of Haman.... The rest of the Jews in the
king's provinces organized and defended themselves, gaining respite
from their enemies, and killing seventy-five thousand of those who
hated them." (9:5–10, 16)

Throughout the empire, the Jews enter into battle with the anti-
Semitic forces, in most cases with the active assistance of the allies
who have rallied to support Mordechai's position. Abandoned by
most of their former supporters in the populace and in the government, the anti-Semitic inciters and those who had actively advanced
their cause are brought low in province after province. The carnage is
so great that (i) the anti-Semitic basilisk is in fact beheaded, its life
and leadership burned out of the body politic, and (ii) the lesson is
learned by all future challengers to the safety of the Jews and the
power of Mordechai in the king's court. Nowhere in all the vast

reaches of the Persian empire does there any longer exist a leader capable of inspiring the peoples to rise and harm the Jewish communities, nor can anyone imagine becoming such a one while Mordechai's influence persists.

But there is a third reason for the decision to go to war which perhaps even surpasses the others in importance: (iii) The position of the king himself towards the Jews and towards Mordechai as their leader.

When last Ahashverosh had expressed an opinion on the subject of saving the lives of the Jews of Persia, he had managed to leave no question as to how little the subject concerned him. Pushed by the queen, the best he had been able to do was to reply that he had already done something good for the Jews once ("Behold, I have given Haman's house to Esther, and he himself has been hanged on the gallows"), and that although there was nothing else to be done ("an edict written in the king's name and sealed with the king's ring cannot be revoked"), Mordechai and Esther were free to try if they so chose ("And you, write concerning the Jews as seems good in your eyes"). (8:7–8) If this answer does not in itself suffice to transmit a message of disdain and disregard, one need only compare it to the account of Darius' response when confronted with similar circumstances in the book of Daniel. Upon learning that he has issued an irreversible royal edict which will result in the death of his Jewish vizier in the lion's pit that night, Darius is "much distressed," labors futilely until sunset to rescue him, spends the sleepless night in fasting, rises at dawn "in anguish" to see what has become of his servant, and in the end orders that the advisers who pushed him to issue the murderous decree be tossed to the lions themselves.[4]

Ahashverosh is indeed a scoundrel, even for a Persian king. Not only is there no reason to believe in his present sympathy for the cause of the Jews, but his original complicity in their destruction, especially when combined with his subsequent statements on the

subject, suggests that there is every reason to fear for the future: Who
is to say that some turn of events will not bring the Jews out of favor,
and return Ahashverosh to the original course he and Haman had
set? With these facts constantly before him, Mordechai has another,
critical reason to bring the war against the enemies of the Jews to its
spectacular conclusion: *Strength attracts strength, and power attracts
power; thus the weak, to the degree they can make themselves seem strong,
can attract the support of the strong, thereby becoming strong in reality.*

Ahashverosh has made it clear that he is not the slightest bit
inclined to become the protector of the Jews, so long as they are a
diffuse and contrary minority, and therefore, "it is of no benefit for
the king to tolerate them." (3:8) If Mordechai is to make the reversal
of the Jews' fortune complete—and if he is to lend this reversal a
measure of stability and permanence—he has no choice but to make
it perfectly obvious to Ahashverosh that the Jews are strong, and that
it *is* of very real benefit to him to tolerate them, to ally himself with
them, and to protect them against future threats that may arise.

This, the final transformation in the king's relationship with the
Jews, is depicted in the narrative in an exchange between Ahashverosh
and his Jewish queen at the height of the tension on the day of the
war. Reports from the provinces have not yet begun to arrive, but the
dimensions of the catastrophe that has befallen the anti-Semites in
Susa have already become known. Ahashverosh seeks out Esther to
report to her: "In Susa the capital the Jews have killed and destroyed
five hundred men, and the ten sons of Haman. What have they done
in the rest of the king's provinces?"

Immediately thereafter, there tumbles from the king's lips a
statement which one is tempted to mistake for a non sequitur. He
says to Esther: "—and whatever your wish, it will be given you, and
whatever more you may request, it will be done." (9:12)

The change in the man is obvious when one considers what he
has said on the three previous occasions on which he has used this

expression in speaking to Esther in the past: Upon her first forbidden approach to him in the throne room, and at the two banquets of wine which she had prepared for him. On all three previous occasions, the king had responded to the queen's approach with a variation of the formula: "Whatever your wish, it will be given you. Whatever your request, up to half the kingdom, it will be done." (5:3, 5:6, 7:2)

Ahashverosh's largesse on this occasion differs from his previous gestures: The king seeks out Esther's behest in the absence of any initiative on her part. Indeed, his words in the Hebrew text are packed into the same verse as Ahashverosh's previous thought—about the numbers of anti-Semites who must have died throughout the empire in the Jews' war—and the association between the two is unmistakable. With visions of blood dancing before his eyes, and afraid as to what may happen next, Ahashverosh's relationship with his Jewish queen undergoes a final, traumatic revision: It is Esther who now embodies power in the king's eyes, and it is he who offers his favors—his *service*—in an effort to gain favor with her. Their relationship is finally and perfectly reversed: Esther, who had come into Ahashverosh's bedchamber five years earlier in search of a way of winning him over so as to avoid a life as a discarded harem girl, now finds the king anxiously seeking to win *her* pleasure.

In this context, it is obvious that Ahashverosh demonstratively (or perhaps unconsciously) drops the hedge, setting an upper bound on her request of "only" half the kingdom; the implication is that she might now ask for the entire kingdom. In practice, once it is he who is seeking out her favor, he does not even need to offer all this: It has already been granted. In fact, Esther asks for much less. "If it please the king, let the Jews in Susa do tomorrow according to the law for today, and let Haman's ten sons be hanged on the gallows." (9:13)

Both parts of Esther's answer are straightforward. Like the king, she has no way of knowing what has happened in the rest of the

empire. In the best case, the war in the provinces will have come to
an end that night with the anti-Semitic menace eradicated; in the
worst, the war will have to be extended by a decree from the palace.
Her request is that the Jewish reign of arms in Susa be allowed to
continue until there is news of what has happened in the rest of the
empire. The point is that in the capital, at least, the initiative should
remain in Mordechai's hands until he is able to determine what
should happen next. The Jews are therefore permitted to continue
holding the streets of Susa at swordpoint for another twenty-four
hours, flushing out of hiding another three hundred of their enemies. Moreover, the bodies of Haman's sons, in life the very symbol
of the remainder of anti-Semitic power, are transformed into a
symbol of Jewish effectiveness when these grisly relics are put on
display for potential opponents to consider.

By the time the streets of Susa have grown quiet after the second
day's battle, reports have begun to arrive from the other corners of
the kingdom. Everywhere, the victory of the Jews has become a
rout. Men have been hounded out and struck down, the spectre of
the massacre of which Haman had dreamed is dead, the decree
which has hung over the heads of the Jews for so long has been
lifted. And the day on which the enemies of the Jews had hoped to
rule over them has been transformed, miraculously, into a day of
honor and glory, with the Jews themselves achieving rule over those
who hated them.

# 21

# THE MORALITY
# OF THE WAR

ALL THIS IS CONSIDERED A TRIUMPH by the narrative itself and by later Jewish tradition. Yet there can be no mistaking the discomfort with which the account of the war is approached by contemporary readers, who tend to lose interest in the story with the death of Haman—this despite the fact that Haman is hanged well before the political turning point in Mordechai and Esther's struggle to save the Jews, and long before the actual war itself, which is the event that in fact brings the Jews redemption.

There is good reason why the account of the Jews' bloody, one-sided, and overwhelming victory—which in other societies would be remembered and savored with pleasure—tends to be underemphasized, passed over in discussion, or even, in some cases, avoided as if it were an object of shame. Jews today, as well as others who come to read Esther, are often men who conceive of themselves as being at peace. The vast democratic societies of our time are societies founded on the principle of non-violent resolution of disputes, political and otherwise. The doctrines of the social compact, of the rule of law, of the voluntary division of labor and the mutual benefits of contractual exchange—all these are the basis of what has already become a prevailing consciousness, growing stronger as one approaches the more educated strata. The young who grow in the core of this rising international culture have no life experiences which suggest to them first-hand a need for force, violence and war, and their education, generally at the hands of society's most genial men, stresses and strains to inculcate the virtues of "outgrowing" force. The self-awareness of such men identifies the appetites and reason as familiar and desirable springs for action, and in the experience of industrialized and libertine societies, all the aims of these impulses—food, possessions, sex and knowledge—can be obtained in quantities by most members of society without recourse to force, or even, it is thought, without the subjugation of any individual by any other.

For these, the functioning of the spirit, which for lack of under-standing they invariably refer to with pejoratives such as "the lust for power," is a mystery. They tend to deny the existence of a real need for power and control within themselves, and they sincerely profess incomprehension when such needs manifest themselves in others. Thus a great many men at peace, recognizing no need for power, force and war in themselves, come to consider these things to be, as they say, objectively undesirable. Then evil, to the extent that it continues to exist as a concept at all, comes to be associated with power, force and war, and with those who have recourse to them.

Among Jews the accession of the international-democratic con-sciousness has been accelerated far beyond that in any other culture. The Jewish classics first introduced the ideal of non-violence into the world, with Isaiah calling for swords and spears to be beaten into agricultural implements, and Jeremiah going so far as to call for a "new covenant" to be instilled in every breast at birth, that man should no longer desire iniquity.[1] Jews have always been exposed to these ideas, and the long history of the last centuries, in which they were completely cut off from the experience of armed conflict and high politics—and driven into the ever-deeper familiarity with the realm of ideas—did much to refashion the Jews as a caste of dream-thinkers and idealists within Western civilization, for whom every step towards the establishment of international-democratic society has served to reconfirm the unnecessity of power and violence in the world.

For such readers, the story of Esther up until Haman's demise is supposed quaint and harmless. Not being able to understand the terrifying contest of spirit and rule which leads to Haman's execution, they find in it only a dead coincidence: The king's wife turns out to be a Jew and so Haman's plot is foiled. The fact that Mordechai and Esther then go on to orchestrate a rampage which soaks the empire to its farthest reaches in blood is for them an embarrassment and a mystery. What need was there for this? What rejoicing and holiday could there be in this? What moral teaching could there be in this?

Yet the narrative itself is unambiguous in making the power and control which the Jews consolidated in the bloodletting a cause for celebration—and one of the book's central *moral* themes. The summary which immediately precedes the account of the war therefore touts the fact that "on the day that the enemies of the Jews had expected to rule over them, the situation was reversed, and it was the Jews themselves who ruled over those who hated them." (9:1) The passage which caps the war footage speaks of the relief gained in "killing seventy-five thousand of those who hated them," making the morrow "a day of feasting and gladness." (9:16–17) And the summary which accompanies Mordechai's official interpretation of the events underscores the fact that Haman's "evil plan, which he had intended against the Jews, should be turned on its head, and they hanged him and his sons on the gallows" (9:25)—where "turning the evil plan on its head" means the liquidation of all those who planned to perpetrate the massacre against the Jews. Moreover, it is impossible to miss the effort of the narrative to associate the war with Saul's campaign against Amalek, in which it was considered a moral imperative to kill every member of the tribe. This in itself invokes even harsher images from the earlier periods of the Bible, in which it could be considered a command from God to destroy an entire people, or even, as in the case of Joshua, to drive out all the peoples of an entire land.

The difficulty in reconciling the overt militarism of Esther and the other war accounts with a defensible morality is not, however, a modern invention. At least as early as the time of the rabbis, these difficulties were raised. R. Mani, for example, suggests that moral qualms may have played a part in Saul's failure to carry out the war against the Amalekites as prescribed, the Jewish king asking himself prior to the battle: "If the people have sinned, what have the cattle done? And if the adults have sinned, what have the children done?" But in this telling, at least, the grim decision to carry out the war is sealed when a voice from heaven—the traditional arbiter of absolute truth in such discussions—comes forth and tells him: "Be not overly righteous."[2] In contrast, R. Mani refers to a later incident in which Saul's men lay waste to the priestly town of Nov, which the king believes to be guilty of treason, killing women, children and livestock. Here, too, the voice from heaven intervenes, this time to cry out: "Be not overly wicked."[3] In this view, the biblical narrative cannot condone warfare against innocents, and doubts in this regard are well in order—but then, there are also apparently cases in which these doubts must be set aside.

The trouble with all such speculation is that one simply cannot be a good person or a good Jew in our own age—or in the period of the rabbis, either, for that matter—and "understand" genocide. Being good is today very closely allied with the revulsion we have learned towards the killing of children, the aged, and other non-combatants in war, and it is very clear that our own moral sensibilities are in this sense "higher" than those which drove the wars of liquidation in Joshua and Samuel, and even the Jews' war in Esther. On the other hand, one only need recall the foolishness of certain pacifists, ecologians, vegetarians and abstentionist sectarians who insist that the use of force, the expansion of industry, the killing of animals or sexual intimacy is inherently immoral, in order to recognize the possibility of wandering lost in endless, false and dangerous "higher" moralities whose pursuit bears no fruit other than destruction. As the saying of Kohelet has it: "Be not overly righteous, and strive not to be too clever, for why should you destroy yourself?"[4]

Is there not some terrific hypocrisy in this, that we take such pride in the moral heights we believe ourselves to have climbed with respect to others; yet we find ourselves appalled and annoyed at the demands of so many of those who, in their sanctimoniousness, their naïveté, their utter *irrelevance* to the world and its doings, hawk their ever-more-suffocating formulas, providing, where good and truth should have been, only strangulation?

Whenever we recognize in ourselves this aversion to the grisly warrior moralizer, this shuddering at the ghostliness of the priests, our moral vertigo, which prevents us from "understanding" much more than a certain adjustment in our own behavior in either direction—whenever we see this, it begins to appear as though the accepted belief in the linearity of this scale—from the so-called higher moralities down to the lower, non-moralities of the lower worlds—is ill thought out, and even greatly mistaken. Indeed, the fact that either pole repels suggests that there is not one ideal of morality, but two, with our truth lying in the balance. And upon examination, such proves to be the case: That behaviors derive their

normative qualities—their "should," their "ought," their divine command—from two separate directions or ideals, each vying with the
other and against it, and which must be kept distinct in order for
religion and ethics to be able to speak coherently: The ideal of
*morality* and that of *purity*. Let us consider what these are and how
they affect our question.

Man's subjective consciousness is challenged by objective conditions which prevent him from living in an inertial introspection,
conditions which continually pull him, often against his will, towards action in the world. These conditions are essentially two: (i)
The needs and urges of his body, and (ii) the needs of others, of his
family, his people, and his world. It takes little experience to discover
that these two influences of the world are fundamentally and irrecon-
cilably contradictory, producing antithetical impulses within philosophy and religion—the one being held as a virtue to the degree
that it is minimized, the other being held a virtue to the degree that it
is maximized:

(i) The needs and urges of one's body and spirit have always been
seen as demanding that man pull away from ideas and truths to
occupy himself with eating, digestion and excretion, infatuations
and sex, clothing and shelter, natural and chemical intoxications,
sleep, discomfort and illness of the various kinds, honor and anger,
phobias, depressions and other impairments of the spirit, and death.
They are a bottomless pit, into which all life's energies and abilities
easily disappear without a trace. After a lifetime preoccupied with the
pursuit of them, man finds that he has nothing to show for his efforts
other than having worn out a body which had started its career fresh.
It has therefore been considered a virtue to minimize one's concern
for the needs and urges of the body and of the spirit to whatever
degree possible in order to free the mind for its confrontation with
higher things. This virtue, when found in men, has been called *purity*
or *holiness*—the Hebrew word for holiness being *kedusha*, meaning

"separation," from the body, from the concerns of men and from the world. And its most basic ethical form is the command of the books of Moses: "Holy shall you be."[5]

(ii) The needs of the world, on the other hand—the protection of innocent life, the dissemination of truth and the establishment of justice, the alleviation of suffering, the development of productive talents and capacities, the facilitation of happiness and the attainment of peace—all these have been held to be the noblest of efforts, and the pursuit of them has been held to be a virtue. Yet if they are to be pursued to any worthy effect, they demand the greatest possible concentration of the individual's worldly resources, the maximal use of his body and his spirit to attain high levels of experience and skill, reputation, respect and wealth, allies and power, in order to have a hope of achieving that perfection of the world which can possibly be achieved. And this virtue has been called *morality* or *justice*—the Hebrew word for justice being *tzedek*, meaning "that which is right," its purport being one of involvement with the concerns of men, and of the world. And here, too, the books of Moses speak in the language of a command: "Justice, justice, shall you pursue."[6]

The crux of the contradiction between the two ideals is man's relationship to power. Purity requires that man renounce power; but morality requires that man have power in order to pursue right. This is true on the individual level, in which one can only give to others if one has what to give. But it is even more true when one considers moralities of scale, which require vast amounts of political power, economic power, military power. Without power, there is no police force capable of defending the innocent, no court capable of doing justice, no army capable of wresting peace from the aggressor, no surplus capable of feeding and clothing the poor, nor of paying to teach truth to the young. Morality requires power, and morality on a vast scale requires power on a vast scale.

For the saint, the man of perfect study and prayer, power is essentially exorcised as a motive, and so the entire world of spiritual blemishes—the obsession with honor and wealth, tantrums and rages, depressions, competitiveness, cruelty—all these are not found in him. But power is lost to him as a tool: He may give charity from what he has, but the good he can do is of necessity circumscribed; he may wish to do right in the world, but he has few resources and does not really know how. For the hero, the man of great deeds, the endless game of accumulating power and the preoccupation with wielding it, of learning the rules and building alliances, of consolidating the wins and recovering from the losses, of gradually growing to the point where one is in fact able to move an immovable world, all this leaves him relatively little time for contemplation, for study and thought, for prayer. He may include such activities in his daily routine, but he finds it difficult to concentrate as the world presses in on him, demanding that he return to it. The saint and the hero may be religious men both. Yet the saint makes a token effort towards power and leaves the rest to God, while the hero leaves nothing to God until he himself reaches exhaustion.

Purity and morality are untranslatable ideals, a vertical axis against which man measures how inwardly removed he is from the world, and a horizontal one measuring the degree to which he outwardly affects it—so that it is forever difficult to advance in one direction without doing damage in the other, a dilemma which appears in Jewish tradition again and again. Thus David, Israel's greatest king, was responsible for the moral achievement of uniting the fragmented Jewish tribes and leading them to victory against the enemies that had caused them such suffering; yet the Bible held that these very acts disqualified him from building the Temple in Jerusalem because he had "shed much blood upon the earth"[7]—so that the construction of the sanctuary was left to his son Solomon.

Even grimmer is the rabbinic story told of the arrest of R. Eleazar ben Parata and R. Hanina ben Teradion, who are to be brought to trial for their activities by the Roman authorities. R. Hanina was a well-known representation of saintliness, of whom it is said that his only sin was that he once allocated Purim alms as though they were regular charity, and then replaced the alms with his own money.[8] Yet according to the tale, he tells his cell-mate: "Happy are you who have been arrested on five charges but will be delivered. Woe is unto me, who have been arrested on one charge but will be condemned. For you have occupied yourself with study of Tora as well as deeds of kindness, whereas I have occupied myself with Tora alone." When R. Eleazar is brought before the tribunal and accused, this more worldly rabbi refuses to give a straight answer, dodging and maneuvering until he succeeds in confounding the court, eventually winning his release. But when R. Hanina is asked by the court why he occupies himself with Tora though it is against the law, he replies with words of purity: "Because I was commanded to do so by the Eternal, my God." Having confessed his guilt, he and his wife are put to death, and his daughter is consigned to a brothel.

Lest the point somehow be missed, the Talmudic account refers in this context to the opinion of R. Huna: "He who only occupies himself with the study of Tora is as if he had no God":[9] That is, even divine assistance depends on making sacrifices in purity in order to gather ability in the ways of tribunals, dissemblances and occupying armies. And if there were ever an exemplar of one who benefits from such assistance, it is Joseph, who spends his life immersed in and becoming expert in the politics and impurity of Pharaoh's court. As the oft-repeated dictum of R. Jose ben Hanina has it: "As the waters cover the fish in the sea, so that the evil eye has no effect on them, so too does the evil eye have no effect on the descendants of Joseph."[10]

From the earliest times, the response of the Jews to the inherent conflict between the demands of purity and the moral need to achieve power in the world was for each individual to strive for a balance between them: Seeking power in the world for six days in the week and seeking purity by withdrawing in the seventh; seeking worldly power through sexual relations and raising up heirs, yet maintaining purity through the institution of marriage and periods of monthly abstinence; seeking power through the consumption of meat, yet striving for purity in the choice of the livestock and the manner of the slaughter, as well as periodic fasts. But if men were to succeed in this effort to find and maintain course on the middle path, it was also clear they would have to rely on the instruction and leadership of those whose life's efforts consisted of attempting to embody the one ideal or the other, the possibility of embodying both simultaneously apparently being intolerably remote. Thus from the time of Moses, the Jews instituted what amounted to a division of labor between the guardians of each ideal, distinguishing between the judge and the priest, between the man of morality and the man of purity—and even between Judah and Joseph, the tribes responsible for the pursuit of justice and national well-being, and Levi, the tribe of purity. And when the Jews finally entered the land and became a nation, the rabbinic tradition has it that there were three strategic necessities which became incumbent upon them as a collective: That they appoint a king, build the Temple, and destroy Amalek—these representing, respectively, the establishment of justice in the land, the establishment of purity among the people, and the securing of limits on these—and therefore a balance between them—through the establishment of the fear of God.[11]

Needless to say, the recognition of the dire need for men of power and rule is not easy for a people which sees itself as "a kingdom of priests and a holy people."[12] But much as the Jews wished to be ruled by none but God, the unmistakable message of the centuries when the Jews first entered the land—without a king and with their resources diffused among the tribes—was that precious little of the dream of a nation of priests can be achieved without wielding immense worldly power: Neither the construction of the Temple in Jerusalem nor the concerted effort against Amalek becomes possible until the Jews unite their resources by placing them in the hands of a singularly unpriestly moral figure, the king.

The idea that the political and military leader is essential to morality and religion—that he is, for better and worse, an important moral and religious figure in his own right—sits uneasily with our tendency to believe that politics is "immoral" or amoral, an opinion that is itself at least thousands of years old.[13] The last centuries have seen endless confusion on this score, as moral thought, which in the time of the prophets and the philosophers had been inseparable from political thought, has become the preserve of priests and professors—men who have intentionally removed themselves from the affairs of the world, the better to pursue "pure reason" and such things. Contrary to their own protestations, it has by now been amply demonstrated that neither of these make for usable moral thought, precisely because they have so little experience with what is required to achieve anything in practice. Kant in particular insisted on the equation of morality with the eradication of self-interest—that is, with purity—and thus was forced by his own reasoning to conclude that worldly actions are perhaps never actually moral.[14] But this has not prevented generations of his disciples from applying this pseudo-tautology to every action ever undertaken by a government or a politician—every one of which is "self-interested" in the sense that it is taken in order to enhance one's own power and advance one's own cause—and determining them all to be "immoral."

Lending plausibility to an argument which would otherwise have little to recommend it is this: Politics is "dirty." That is, people who are not known to lie, cheat, defraud, deceive, break agreements, blackmail, blacklist, to engage in dual loyalties and false loyalties, in campaigns of espionage and character assassination, in bribery and peddling influence, even to incite to violence, suddenly find themselves doing so and more when political power is at stake. There is an objective sense in which what is accepted and even necessary in the political arena is neither necessary nor acceptable among family or friends, nor even among rival businesses. Politics is dirty because it is in fact impure, relative to the world of family, school or business in which a person normally lives.

But this does not make it immoral. There are many activities which are impure in this sense: The modes of behavior accepted in the bedroom, the gravesite, the operating room, the slaughterhouse, the lavatory and the battlefield are none of them activities suited to relations of family, school or business. And not because any of them are inherently immoral, but because they are impure. They are activities which focus attention on the body, its various organs, their functioning and malfunctioning, their decay and mortality—whereas family, school and business are relatively pure, allowing us to focus on the minds of those who are with us, their hopes, insights and personalities, and the unique human relations in which we are engaged with them.

The ability to distinguish the purity of one environment from that of another is the fundamental concept which allows man to step into civilization, leaving behind the physical organs and secretions, the corpse and death itself, in order to enter a "safe space," a bubble "separated" from the world in which it is possible to concentrate on things that are more essential, more personal and more eternal. In the Jewish tradition, it is considered to be that distinction which allows man to emulate the divine in his own life, as he sets aside certain times and places for behavior which is purer and in this sense higher. At such times and in such places, the appearance of things associated with impurity breaks the spell of the higher being which man is trying to be, and so such intrusions are also frequently held to be immoral.

The same must be said for the accepted behaviors of politics. There, too, many of the activities are brutal, and in fact they have often been referred to as "naked power," verbal actions whose meaning is pure force, acts of the spirit which are in their essence violence, whether accompanied by physical blows or not. Yet in order to achieve power in order to do good, one must be experienced, talented and expert in the ways in which power is in fact allocated and applied. One must know war as it is waged by others, and be able to wage such wars more effectively than they. One must know finance as it is waged by others, and be able to build an economy more effectively than they. One must be able to gain influence and wield it as it is wielded by others, but be able to use this influence more effectively than they. Power is a matter of beating "them" at their own game, and using the results for good. Participating in the ways of the political world as one finds it is not inherently immoral, any more than the activities of the lavatory are immoral. In neither case does a habitually pious person desire to behave in such ways; he does it neither for pleasure nor for some kind of personal gain, but because there is presumably no choice. And it would be absurd if each time an individual took it upon himself to achieve right and justice, even at the expense of his own personal purity, he would also have to be castigated for being immoral besides.

Indeed, the biblical narrative and subsequent rabbinic tradition reserved the appellation of *tzadik*, meaning "the righteous," for precisely those figures whose lives are spent in outward political and moral action, immersed in power and evil, but who nonetheless manage to maintain a level of *relative* purity in this state. This is the meaning of the oft-repeated Talmudic appellation, "Joseph the righteous":[15] Not, as is often supposed, that Joseph surpasses others among the Jews in the purity of his life; rather, the significance of his great act of self-discipline—the refusal of the Egyptian temptress—is in that he is able to maintain any standard of purity at all in the polluted realm in which he flourishes, and despite the ways in which he must accommodate this realm to attain success. Others referred to as "righteous" are of this sort as well: Noah, who saves mankind from the flood, is referred to as righteous in the books of Moses despite the fact that in his time "the wickedness of man on earth was great, and all the inclinations of his heart were only to perpetual evil";[16] Lot, who risks his life and that of his family to save perfect strangers from the mob, is referred to as righteous in the books of Moses despite living amid the depravity of Sodom;[17] Jacob, who wrests control of his father's inheritance from his powerful brother and makes a fortune at the hands of the Mesopotamian idolaters, is called righteous by the rabbis despite spending the best years of his life serving his father-in-law surrounded by immorality and idolatry;[18] and Mordechai, who saves the Jews of Persia, is called righteous by the rabbis despite likewise living every day with the perniciousness of the Persian court.[19]

Of course, the existence of the political world as a sphere of lesser purity does not legitimize every means to any political end. One cannot make such deep sacrifices in one's purity and humanity for trivial moral goals; the political struggles of municipal zoning boards or the notorious politics internal to academia cannot justify relinquishing civilized behavior. In high politics, on the other hand, it is, as Joseph says, "the preservation of the multitude of men alive"[20] that is in fact at stake, so that it can always be reasonably argued that willful departures from our accustomed standards of purity are justifiable, and even obligatory. Left to the hands of others who would use the power of the state for their own gain, the law would serve the few, the country would engage in oppression and unjust wars, and thousands would die for naught. Indeed, it is the political

world, with all its impurity, which makes it possible for the normative civil world to exist as it does. It is politics which musters the ugly
power necessary for higher society to live oblivious, just as the body
marshals the resources needed for the mind to work, much of the
time without caring for its body's functions. If the political world
should one day fail in its impure task when faced by dark challenges
from outside society or within, the bubble of civilization in which we
spend most of our adult hours would come crashing down into the
lava of impurity below.

There is no point in attempting to count the strata of impurity
upon which our world floats, and upon which it depends for its
existence. But it bears emphasizing that the impure sphere of politics
floats atop other, impurer worlds upon which it, too, floats like a
bubble: The realm of wars, both foreign and domestic, is one such,
in which even today nations use the most gruesome means in order
to survive—means that would be unthinkable even in a dirty arena
such as that of domestic politics. And beneath this lies another, even
fouler world, which exists now only in the farthest reaches: That of
the idolaters, in which murderous violence was a norm even within
the family, and in which no safety truly existed anywhere. It was this
realm in which the genocides of antiquity took place: In which Rome
murdered every citizen of Carthage and sowed the soil of its lands
with salt so that no human being should ever be able to persist there
again. And it was in this world, according to the hideous exigencies
of its politics, that Joshua entered the land with an imperative to
secure a stable Jewish nation and faith.

The biblical narrative is sufficiently aware of the severity of this
moral teaching to depart from the usual method of the books of
Moses and explain the precise intention behind this imperative:

> You shall beat them and you shall utterly destroy them, you shall
> sign no treaties with them, nor shall you show them any mercy.

> And you shall not make marriages with them: You shall not give
> your daughter to his son, nor shall you take his daughter for your
> son. For they will turn your son away from following me, that they
> may serve other gods.... You shall destroy their altars, and break
> down their images, and cut down their asherim, and burn their
> idols with fire.... The idols of their gods shall you burn with fire,
> do not desire the silver and gold that is on them nor take it for
> yourself, lest you become ensnared by it, for it is a horror to the
> Eternal your God. You shall not bring a horror into your house,
> lest you become accursed as it is, but you shall loathe it and abhor
> it, for it is an accursed thing.[21]

The point is all too clear: "They will turn your son away," "lest you
become ensnared," "lest you become accursed as it is." Without the
annihilation of the murderous Canaanite presence in the land, the
"higher" morality of the Jews cannot come into existence—for the
Jews themselves would rapidly become Canaanites themselves: Perverse, murderous, idolatrous. Indeed, the subsequent narrative tells
precisely this story: How the Jews, having failed to live up to the
imperative of driving the Canaanites from the land, sank into a
thousand years of assimilation to the ways of the idolaters.

The modern world is quick to decry the war against the
Canaanites. But contemporary warfare has resorted to the categorical
destruction of innocents for less. The "countervalue" warfare against
Hiroshima and Dresden was not aimed at saving Western civilization or even the United States. The war had long since turned in
favor of the Allies. Yet these enormities were deemed necessary to
bring the war to a speedier conclusion. German children were
considered worthy of destruction in order to save the lives of Ameri-
can servicemen. The premise of the war against the Canaanites is far
less cynical, since it presumes what was clearly not the case when the
decision was taken to drop the bomb: That the possibility of Jewish

civilization—indeed, of moral civilization itself—could not persist without the eradication of the worst level of impurity on the land.

That there may be a place in moral argumentation for such acts is not easily assimilated. Within the confines of our own world the rules are different: One may not murder an innocent person to save one's own life under any circumstance. To challenge this in the case of the individual is rightly understood as the greatest of crimes. Yet most of us can glimpse our own descent into the realm where our own norms dissolve in scenarios in which the contemporary West is faced with annihilation, or in which the State of Israel is to lose against the Arabs. Would we refuse to order a nuclear strike in such a case? The harsh truth is that the immorality of such a strike, killing millions of innocents to save a civilization, cannot be deduced from the immorality of murdering an innocent individual to save another.

From this it is evident that the political arena is not merely "dirty." In certain cases it leads us rapidly into a pollution in which man is transformed into a beast of the lowest grade: not merely killing individuals for his own survival, but annihilating cities, nations. It is the curse of politics that in certain cases precisely such monstrous acts of impurity may be the acts most *moral* given the paucity of alternatives. But it is always possible instead to preserve one's own purity and allow the world to fall into ruin.

Mordechai's war is a war of morality, a war fought in the world and by its rules—because any other choice in his time and place would have been folly. Thus if one were to ask why so many men had to die on the day of the fighting, if the results were by then practically assured, the answer is that this is the way of politics. Without decisive action against his enemy, Mordechai would have guaranteed himself a reputation of hesitancy and mildness—a reputation which would have breathed new life into the anti-Semitism of the empire and left the king doubting the Jewish vizier's abilities. And if one were to ask why Haman's ten sons had to die, it is wishful thinking to argue that every one of them was active as a leader in the camp of the anti-Semites. Rather, their deaths are sought, as was accepted in the course of warfare and politics in antiquity, to prevent Haman's enmity from leaving heirs, as well as to degrade his memory and emphasize the enormity of his defeat. The book of Daniel tells of Darius issuing a parallel order for the destruction of those who persecuted Daniel, along with their families: "And the king commanded, and they brought those men who had accused Daniel, and they cast them into the lion's den; they, their children and their wives."[22] In Herodotus, Artabanus, uncle to Xerxes, similarly offers to wager his life and those of his children on the outcome of a war he opposes: "If things go well for the king, as you say they will, let me and my children be put to death; but if they fall out as I prophesy, let your children suffer, and you too, if you come back alive."[23] And if one insists that Mordechai should have conducted the war without resorting to the impure methods of Persian politics, even though such a nod to purity might have jeopardized the endeavor, the first answer must be that of Kohelet: "There are righteous men who perish through their righteousness, and there are the wicked who flourish by their wickedness. Be not overly righteous...."[24]

Yet harsh as is Mordechai's onslaught, he nevertheless does demand that the Jews carry on their war on a purer level than that which they expected to have waged against them. Thus Mordechai's decree, copied more or less verbatim from Haman's, speaks of the death of children and women, as well as the appropriation of all the property of their enemies, all with the intention of inspiring counter-terror in the enemy camp. When the day comes, however, the text pointedly avoids mention of casualties among the dependents, which were apparently minimal, repeatedly emphasizing that the Jews did not even touch their property.[25]

The issue of respecting the property rights of one's enemies and their families is one which has its roots in the earlier stages of the plot, when Haman first approaches Ahashverosh with the hope of convincing him to destroy the Jews. In making his case, he relies on every interest of the king's to which he can appeal, concluding with a possible financial interest: "If it please the king, let it be written that they be destroyed, and I will weigh out ten thousand talents of silver into the hands of those who have charge of the business, to bring it into the king's treasuries." (3:9) This is an outrageously large sum, in the range of what Herodotus reports to have been the income of the entire Persian empire for a year,[26] and the only imaginable source for such a fortune would have been the plunder of the Jews' property. Yet Ahashverosh, ever eager to demonstrate his power by wasting state moneys, assures Haman that: "The silver is given to you, and the people, to do with them as you see fit," (3:11)[27] thus clearing the way for the vizier to offer the Jews' property as an incentive to the murderers. In so doing, he greatly expands the circle of those who will potentially be willing to do the work of annihilation, including not only those who hate Jews, but those who like property.

All of this is in contrast to the wars against the Canaanites and Amalek, in which plundering was proscribed. In the case of the Canaanites, the fear was principally that in claiming property of the idolaters, the Jews would end up with idols in their homes and be drawn to them. But in the case of Saul's effort to destroy Amalek, there is no mention of idols, and the issue, once the plundering takes place, seems to be completely different: "But Saul and the people took pity on Agag, and on the best of the sheep, and the oxen, and the fatlings, and the lambs, and all that was good, and did not destroy them, but everything that was of little value and poor, they destroyed." When confronted by the prophet Samuel, Saul explains: "I have transgressed the instruction of the Eternal and your words, for I feared the people and listened to their words."[28] For this crime, of giving in before the desire of the people for plunder, Saul is stripped of his kingdom.

At stake in the argument over the right to plunder is the *motive* which moves the Jews to liquidate an entire people. According to Samuel, Amalek's history of unlimited terror, its being a nation of evil-doers, and its record of state murder justify what is otherwise a horrendous act.[29] But if the Jews begin claiming Amalekite cattle for themselves, the war is in fact fought for another reason altogether. Far from engaging in an act of morality which aims to make the world safe for a life of purity, they are in that case engaging in acts of murder for the sake of stealing—itself understood to be a great evil.[30] Samuel instructs Saul to kill for the sake of his truth and his people, and his fighters tell him to kill instead for plunder; his choice is between right and evil, and he chooses the latter.

The fine distinction between just war and murder is today referred to as the "purity of arms," and this is what is at issue, too, in Esther, where Mordechai's war against the Persian anti-Semites is told as a replay of the Amalekite war in Samuel. Here, the emphasis on not touching the property of the anti-Semites is intended to indicate the purity of the cause. Men are killed because they had been planning to murder the Jews, and as a preemption against future threats. The fact that this is understood by the Jews to be the sole motive raises their warfare to a level of purity far higher than that of Haman, and higher too than that which had been practiced by their ancestors. It is for this reason that the tradition refers to Mordechai as "the righteous": Because in raising the Jews to impressive purity amid the fearsome acts of politics and war required in his place and time, he provided precisely the kind of political leadership for which the Jews should hope in every generation.

# ESTHER
# NINE
[9:17 – 10:3]

This was on the 13th day of the month of Adar, and they gained respite on the 14th day, making it a day of feasting and gladness. And the Jews in Susa assembled on the 13th and 14th, and they gained respite on the 15th, making it a day of feasting and gladness. That is why Jewish villagers who lived in unwalled towns celebrate the 14th day of the month of Adar as one of gladness and feasting, a holiday and one for sending foods to one another.

Mordechai recorded these events and sent letters to all the Jews in all the provinces of the king Ahashverosh, near and far — charging them that they should keep the 14th and 15th days of Adar every year: As days on which the Jews gained respite from their enemies, and as a month which was transformed for them from sorrow to gladness, and from

mourning to holiday, and to make them days of feasting and gladness, and for sending foods to one another, and for giving gifts to the poor.

The Jews undertook to do as they had begun, and
as Mordechai had written to them.

For Haman, the son of Hamedata the Agagite,
persecutor of all the Jews, had planned to destroy the
Jews, and had cast a pur, that is a lot, to terrify and
destroy them. But when she came before the king, he
did decree in his letters that his evil plan, which he
had intended against the Jews, should be turned on
its head, and they hanged him and his sons on the
gallows.

Thus they called these days Purim, after the pur,
and thus, because of all the events in this letter and
what had happened to them: The Jews enacted and
undertook, upon themselves and upon their descendants, and upon all those who might join them, that
they should not fail to keep these two days, according
to their writings and according to their season, each
and every year. And these days are remembered and

*performed in each and every generation, in every fam-*
*ily, in every province, in every city, and these days of*
*Purim will not fail from among the Jews, nor will*
*their memory perish from among their descendants.*

Esther the queen, the daughter of Avihail, and
Mordechai the Jew, wrote with all due emphasis to
enact this second letter of Purim: Letters were sent
to all the Jews, to the 127 provinces of the kingdom
of Ahashverosh, with words of peace and truth.
Enacting these days of Purim in their season, as
Mordechai the Jew and Esther the queen had
enjoined them, and as they had undertaken, for
themselves and for their descendants, with regard
to the fasts and their lamentations. And Esther's
decree enacted these matters of Purim and it was
written in the book.

The king Ahashverosh levied taxes on the land,
and on the islands of the sea. And all his acts of might
and power, and the account of the greatness of
Mordechai, whom the king had promoted, are recorded
in the book of chronicles of the kings of Media and

Persia. For Mordechai the Jew was second to the king
Ahashverosh, and great among the Jews, and popular
with the multitude of his brethren, seeking the good of
his people and speaking peace to all his descendants.

# 22

# THE FESTIVAL

AS THE BATTLE DREW TO A CLOSE, it became clear throughout the empire that the Jews had achieved a frightful victory. In every
land, the forces that had sought to eradicate the Jewish presence were
uprooted. The Jews, who had at the outset appeared beyond help
and hope, had over the course of less than a year mustered the
political and military strength to defeat some of the greatest men in
the empire. By the end, the plan for their annihilation had been
"turned on its head," and "Mordechai the Jew was second to the
king, seeking the good of his people...." (9:25, 10:3) The Jews had
positioned themselves to secure their own safety and to dominate the
politics of Persia for years to come.

The narrative records the reaction of the Jews to the end of the
nightmare, as well. Feelings of relief and gladness contributed to the
eruption of celebrations and feasts in every province where Jews had

been delivered from their enemies. Many Jews apparently expressed their joy even on that first occasion by sending gifts to one another, as a spontaneous response to the new gift of life which they had all been given.

But it rapidly became evident that the events had a more profound significance than the immediate deliverance itself, and Mordechai and Esther moved to instate the victory as days of holiday in the annual cycle of Jewish festivals—to be "remembered and performed in each and every generation, in every family, in every province, in every city," so that the days marking the ultimate effects of Haman's purim "will not fail from among the Jews, nor will their memory perish from among their descendants." (9:28) According to the narrative, Mordechai and Esther each send out a letter in the years subsequent to the events themselves, asking that the Jews observe the days on which the original celebrations had taken place as a festival, and giving legal significance to practices which had been spontaneous among those delivered from death on the first Purim.

All of this is a rather unusual twist for a biblical text. All of the other Jewish holidays which merit explicit imperatives in the Bible are already commanded in the books of Moses, a thousand years before the events described in Esther took place. While the subsequent accounts of Jewish history are filled with victories and deliverances of various kinds, none of the heroes of these other stories ever tries to create a holiday which "will not fail from among the Jews." Mordechai appears to have been the first Jewish leader since Moses to establish such a festival.[1]

In addition to the question of why Mordechai and Esther should have insisted on so unusual a move as the establishment of a religious festival, the text itself focuses on a rather peculiar aspect of how this new holiday was legislated into Jewish tradition. It is clear that Mordechai and Esther favored its establishment, and that as the leaders of the Persian Jewish community they used all their influence to make sure that the holiday was observed throughout the empire, with Mordechai "charging them that they should keep the 14th and 15th days of Adar every year," (9:21–22) and Esther later writing "with all due emphasis to enact ... these days of Purim in their season." (9:29–31) Yet the narrative insists on mentioning, no fewer than three times, that the establishment of the festival was actually in the form of an "undertaking" (9:23, 27, 31)—that is, that despite Mordechai and Esther's lobbying, the acceptance of this commitment among the Jews was voluntary.

Both the motive for the establishment of Purim and the importance of its voluntary acceptance can be understood best against the political context in which Mordechai and Esther found themselves responsible for the well-being of the Jewish people. The long exile into the Babylonian empire (and its Persian successor) was not the first massive deportation of Jews from the land of Israel, but the second: A century and a half before Mordechai's family had been exiled by the Babylonians, the northern kingdom of Israel had been forcibly removed from its land by the Assyrians.[2] The result of the Assyrian exile had been the rapid obliteration of much of the northern ten tribes, which, when dispersed throughout the east, had succumbed to the peoples around them and disappeared. By the time of Mordechai and Esther, the magnitude of the catastrophe which had befallen the Jews of the northern kingdom had become clear, and the burning question was how to prevent the new exile— constituting the majority of the Jews remaining in the world—from disappearing into Persia as well.

We know that the pressures and temptations of a cosmopolitan society such as Persia were immense. Like Daniel and Nehemia, Mordechai found himself deeply involved in the mainstream of Persian political life. Like Daniel, Esther bowed to Persian culture by adopting a gentile name. The hatreds of the society caused Esther to hide her Jewishness, as Mordechai, to judge from the fact that he later "reveals" his Jewishness to the courtiers, seems to have done as well. True, the Jews of the Babylonian exile were far stronger in their knowledge and observance of Judaism than had been their brothers in the northern kingdom, and they had among them far greater intellectual and spiritual leaders. And yet the issue was alive and well: In the face of anti-Semitism, and the difficulties of observing Judaism in an empire which occasionally persecuted its practitioners, and with every door open if one's Judaism were hidden away or renounced altogether, would not the Jews of Persia eventually disappear as well?

The fact is that in Persia, being a Jew became—for the first time in history—a matter of choice, and a choice that had to be faced by every individual. In Egypt, the Jews had been a slave caste living in segregated Jewish ghettos. In Canaan, the Jews had always lived as tribes surrounded by alien cultures with which they were constantly at war. And once the Jews had established themselves as a kingdom, every individual's identity as a Jew became even more secure. In the thousand years since Sinai, the Jews had strayed from observance of the law of Moses time and time again, but their *identity* as Jews had never been subject to their own volition. It was only after the dispersal throughout Babylonia and Persia that a child born as a Jew found himself in immediate, constant and personal contact with other possible identities—and had to choose for himself whether his Jewishness would be something he would maintain, or something he would hide.

This explains why the great talmudist Rava argued that the Jews had accepted the law of Moses twice: Under duress at Sinai, and voluntarily "in the days of Ahashverosh."[3] Sinai was the founding of a Jewish people whose members have no real alternative but to be Jews, and to take part in the unique history of their people. The Persian empire represented the re-founding of the Jewish people on an entirely different basis: Since each Jew was from birth exposed to other options, his entry into the history of his people would perforce be voluntary.[4]

On the surface of it, the narrative in Esther repeatedly refers to the voluntary undertaking of the Jews with regard to the festival of Purim, and not to the entire law of Moses as Rava suggests. But such a simple reading leaves dangling the question of why Mordechai and Esther should have been so concerned to establish a new festival, and why they should have placed such emphasis on pursuing its observance that it should be virtually the only act in their subsequent careers worthy of mentioning in the closing passages of the narrative. On such a narrow understanding of what is taking place, self-glorification is the only motive which readily suggests itself.

The answer seems to be that Mordechai did indeed consider his campaign to secure widespread voluntary observance of Purim to be tantamount to a quest for renewed acceptance of the covenant of Moses. Until the Babylonian exile, the dispersion of the Jews in foreign diasporas had ended only in two ways: Enslavement and persecution in Egypt, and absorption and dissolution in Assyria. In either case, the clear meaning of the diaspora for the Jewish people was death. In Mordechai's time the greatest challenge for the Jewish leadership was to create the conditions under which the unwanted dispersion might mean something else.

Mordechai understood that under conditions in which an individual Jew has every incentive and every means of hiding his relationship with his people, the old themes are not necessarily sufficient to inspire continued allegiance. Purim added a cosmopolitan message for Jews far from their homeland and their God: If the Jew will stand up for himself and fight for his faith, the diaspora can allow power and life—not only for individual Jews, but for the Jewish people as a whole.

Purim was the story of the Jewish people's success in Persia. Just as it had brought "many from among the people of the land to become Jews" when first it took place—out of respect, fear and enthusiasm for this success—Mordechai understood that in its retelling it would deepen this sense of pride and purpose, among the Jews of the dispersion in future generations; that the ambitious and strong would remain Jews only if being a Jew were a badge of strength, for power attracts power, and strength attracts strength. More than any other festival, Purim would express to the Jews that it was worth fighting to be a Jew, because even in exile, the fight against Israel's enemies was one that could be won. As the rabbis preached in the centuries that followed:

> 'And it will be to the Eternal for a memorial' (Isaiah 55:13). This refers to the miracle which the Holy One, may he be blessed, performed on this occasion [Purim], the like of which there had never been before. For was there ever in history such a miracle, that Israel should wreak vengeance on the other nations and do with their enemies as they pleased?[5]

For any Jew in the exile who could hear this message, Judaism would not only be something that had to be hidden away in fear. Even in the exile, a Jew could make use of the tools of politics and power to become "second to the king, ... seeking the good of his people."

The successful establishment of Purim therefore suggests a second great deliverance infrequently mentioned in connection with the political achievements of Mordechai and Esther, yet which ranks with the more visible triumph over the enemy, Haman the Agagite. In establishing a celebration of Jewish victory and power in the annual calendar of the Jews of the dispersion, Mordechai and Esther opened the way to an exile which, though bitter, might ultimately offer triumph and life to the Jewish people.

It is thus no coincidence that Mordechai required the Jews to make the days of Purim "days of feasting and gladness, and for sending foods to one another, and for giving gifts to the poor," all these legal provisions of the holiday being ones which inspire a sense of well-being, control and power. In the narrative, all three laws of the holiday—feasting, the granting of gifts and the giving of charity to the poor—appear as expressions of royalty and rule on the only occasions when Ahashverosh feels himself to be fully in control of his personal life and his realm: The 180-day feast and the wedding feast. (1:3–5, 2:13) Indeed, even the grotesque activities associated with the festival in later times—drunkenness, comedy cabarets and masquerades of various kinds—are every one of them designed to allow cruder individuals to share in the sense of power which Purim originally sought to instill in the Jews of the Persian diaspora.

# 23

# POLITICS AND FAITH

OVER A THOUSAND YEARS and a thousand pages, the Hebrew Bible relates the history of God as he appeared to the Jews and among them: As creator and mentor, as redeemer, warrior and fortress of refuge. Only in Esther does the trail grow faint, the pen weary, the sense of things irrevocably blurred. History continues, but the Bible ends. It is the Jews who are sent into exile from their land, but it is God for whom there no longer seems to be any place. What does Esther have to teach us that we do not already know—of the emptiness and grief of the old tale as it drags on, with man now the only actor, with the enemy now facing us across the stage, squinting with pleasure to have found us so alone?

What can be the meaning of a book of the Bible in which there is no mention of God, however so incidental, if not to inform us, two thousand years before Nietzsche, that the evidence of God's actions in the world has ceased—that the earth has been unchained from its sun, that it has grown darker, colder?[1] For this much, one has no need for Esther, which, coming as it does a century after the reduction of Jerusalem, can seem hardly more than a bitter redundancy. Had not Jeremiah, speaking of the end of the eternal city, already written that all that had been achieved in creation had now been ruined? "I saw the earth, and behold it was void and unformed, and the heavens with no lights in them…. I saw, and behold there was no man, and all the fowl of the skies wandered away. I saw, and behold, the fruitful field was the desert, and all its cities vanquished…."[2] Had not even the books of Moses foretold this same end, of the departure of God from among men? "My anger will burn against them in that day, and I will abandon them and hide my face from them, and they will be devoured and many evils and torments will befall them, so that they will say on that day: Are not these evils come upon us because our God is not among us?"[3] What more is there to add to the horror of God's absence after these?

The truth is that in the great Hebrew tale of the formation of the world and its abandonment, as it seems, by its maker, Esther ranks barely as a postscript. It is no part of this story; if anything, it contradicts it and drains it of meaning. For what is left of Jeremiah's pathos once one has feasted and drunk with Mordechai and Esther—in celebration of the possibility of Jewish rulership and power *without* Jerusalem? In celebration of the possibility of Jewish victory *without* God? If taken seriously, the events in Esther serve as a denial of all that the earlier writings had come to teach.

Yet for all this—indeed, because of all this—Esther is the classic text of Jewish continuity: It speaks of a different place and a new time, of Jews with no land and no revelations from on high, and yet the story line is eerily familiar: Amalek, the arch-idolater and anti-Jew, returns to seek dominion, the Jew stands to resist evil against all odds, the people return from their daydreams and wanderings to unite behind their truth, and for all his worldly might the enemy is brought low, leaving the Jews free to rule themselves under new conditions that permit them what they desire most, "words of peace and truth." (9:30) Esther is a world removed from the story told in the rest of the Bible, but it is not a different story. It is the same story, that of Moses, that of Saul, told again in a different bible, of which Esther is not the last book, but the first.

To understand this, we must return to the dictum of Rava, that the Jews accepted the Tora twice, once at Sinai when there was no choice other than to accept it, and again "in the days of Ahashverosh" when they accepted it voluntarily.[4] For the first thousand years of Jewish faith, the insular nature of the community of Jews meant that the word of God could hardly be escaped. A man could observe the law or fail to do so, but he lived in a culture which was bombarded by the thought of the priests and the prophets, and so always had to reconcile his behavior with the knowledge that somewhere, somehow, someone was judging him according to the covenant. Thus Jeremiah could testify to the people on the eve of the destruction of Jerusalem that they had heard God speaking to them night and day since their fathers had left Egypt eight hundred years earlier: "On the day that I brought them out of the land of Egypt.... This thing I commanded them, saying: Obey my voice ... and walk in all the ways I have commanded you, that it may be well with you.... From the day that your fathers came out of the land of Egypt, unto this day, I have sent to you all my servants the prophets, sending them to you from morning until night. But they did not listen...."[5]

What changed in Persia was not only that prophets ceased to frequent the marketplaces of the east, but that the majority of the Jewish people was for the first time well beyond earshot. Even had prophecy survived the catastrophe of the exile, the mere fact of being dispersed to the ends of the six-score Persian provinces would have meant that most Jews would never have an opportunity to hear a prophet in their lives. When added to the constant pressure of foreign concerns and ideas which was the daily grist of exile, the heightened sense of God's speaking—commanding, berating, imploring—dissolved and was gone, so that the rabbis concluded that "whoever lives outside the land of Israel can be considered as though he has no God."[6] With dispersion, God's voice quite literally ceased to be audible to most Jews. And if they truly wished to keep listening, the responsibility would of necessity be theirs to find a way to hear it.

While the collapse of Jerusalem had been political in nature, its fundamental meaning was therefore theological. Up until the exile, the Jews had been *pursued* by their God. It was he who prescribed to them the moral law, and they who passively received it; it was he who called the spiritual leadership, and even the political leadership, and they who responded to this call; it was he who saved them "with an outstretched arm,"[7] and they who struggled to keep up with history. Certainly, there had been among the Jews men of spectacular personal initiative, and the ideal of a Jew had always been that of a man who has "contended with God and with man, and prevailed."[8] But the essential tenor of the Bible is one in which God approaches man in order to elicit spectacular responses, and the text faithfully reflects this relationship as it seemed to the Jews living in that time and that place: God approached, and the individual could choose between duty and, as in Jonah's case, flight.

In Persia in the days of Ahashverosh, God had "hidden his face" from man, had ceased to appear at all. But this did not mean that the world somehow ceased to need instruction or direction; God's withdrawal from man was met with no commensurate extinguishing of the voice of evil. If anything, the opposite could be said: Not since Pharaoh had Israel been so helpless before a nemesis so monstrous as Haman. In the aftermath of the destruction and the exile, the world continued as before, revolving around its flaw, and the same eternal task remained to be done. But now there was only one force that could bear the responsibility for doing it—man himself.

Many are those who have tried to read the book of Esther as though nothing had changed from the preceding age, as though God's absence were merely a literary device in a story otherwise laced with divine intervention: The enemy is set to destroy the Jews, but by means of a series of inexplicable coincidences—the king happens to be married to a Jewess, for example—his efforts are brought to naught and he perishes himself. Every coincidence is thus understood to be a minor miracle, and the overall effect is not much removed from the deliverance from Egypt: The Jews would have perished had it not been for the active intervention of God.

Yet this reading obscures more than it explains. For the truly great events in the book of Esther are not those instances where the clever convergences of the plot can be interpreted as hidden divine activism. Rather, they are found in the initiatives of Mordechai and Esther, who repeatedly *choose* to risk everything for the sake of right and truth: Mordechai's decision to stand against Haman's elevation; his willingness to violate the king's law to draw public attention to the Jews' anguish after the decree has been issued; Esther's decision to go in to the king twice, both times knowing that she may die before even having explained her cause; and her final, face-to-face confrontation with her enemy. It is these actions which ultimately bring about the fall of Haman and the lifting of the decree—and it is glaringly clear that all of these are, according to the narrative, the political initiatives of men, and no one else.

A number of events suggest that Mordechai and Esther understood this shift in responsibility from God to man, and were willing to shoulder it in full—taking initiative not only in political actions, but also in making critical philosophical and religious determinations in order to give moral force to these actions. Thus it is Mordechai, and no earlier Jewish source or authority, who determines that prostrating himself before Haman is an evil so great that it is worth risking his life and his people over; Esther willingly maintains the king's favor despite the Jewish prohibition violated by such liaisons; and Esther also declares a three-day fast which means the obliteration of the festival of Passover that year.[9] Moreover, Mordechai and Esther's crusade to institute a new Jewish festival flies in the face of an explicit injunction in the books of Moses forbidding any effort to "add to the law."[10] The rabbis said of this unprecedented human incursion into the legislation of divine law: "Forty-eight prophets and seven prophetesses prophesied to Israel, and they neither took away from nor added anything to what is written in the Tora—except for the reading of Esther."[11] There can be no question that in all of these initiatives, ultimate values were at stake—idolatry and tyranny, life and death, the survival of Judaism and of their people—and that without the religious and moral responsibility Mordechai and Esther were willing to accept in the crisis, all would have been lost.

And herein lies the key to Esther. The most remarkable aspect of the book is not God's absence itself, but the fact that this absence does not induce defeat and despair. Quite the contrary, in fact: Mordechai and Esther prove that even in the grim new universe of the dispersion, the most fearsome evils may yet be challenged and beaten—so long as man himself is willing to take the initiative to beat them. Thus while Esther adheres faithfully to the message of earlier Jewish teachings in terms of the outcome of the story, it heralds a dramatic shift in the burden of responsibility for this outcome. Man may still find out what God wishes of him, but he will not be given the answers; he will have to seek them. Man may still participate in the actions of God in history, but he will not be called to them; he will have to initiate them. And man may still see God's justice and peace brought into being in the world, but it will not be handed to him; he will have to build it. Thus R. Assi taught: "Why was Esther compared to the dawn? To tell you that just as the dawn is the end of the whole night, so is the story of Esther the end of all miracles."[12] Where before, the story of man had been conducted in darkness, with an occasional sign from heaven illuminating the night, now these signs have gone. There is yet to be light in the world, but this light must be brought as it was brought to the Jews of Persia—by Esther. As the rabbinic tradition told it:

> At night, despite the fact that it is night, there is light from the moon and the stars and the constellations. When is it truly dark? At the dawn. The moon disappears and the stars disappear and the constellations go, as well. There can be no darker hour than this one. Then it is that the Holy One, may he be blessed, answers the world and its inhabitants, bringing forth the dawn from the darkness, and illuminating the world. And why, then, is Esther compared to the dawn? Like the dawn whose light is about to break forth, at first it comes little by little, and then it bursts forward and arrives, and then it intensifies and grows great, and then it is excellent and ever stronger. So too was the deliverance of Israel by Esther....[13]

Esther is the dawn because that light which comes to the Jews comes from her, of her own creation and her own power. Neither the seething firmament of the old Jewish night, nor the astrological fatalism of idolaters such as Haman casting their lots, will now be the final arbiter of events; for Esther is herself a star, if only she wills it, a sun in her own right.[14]

In the Jewish tradition, the ideal of man acting as God acts is summarized in the exhortation to "walk in all his ways," which is found in the books of Moses, and which the rabbis understood to mean "to behave in the same ways in which he directs his world—and these are righteousness and justice."[15] If the Jews succeed in this, the result is promised to be power and success in this world: "You will inherit nations greater and mightier than yourselves.... No man will be able to stand before you, for the fear of you and the dread of you will the Eternal your God cause to fall on all the land...."[16] And it is possibly the most cutting expression of what the book of Esther seeks to instill in the Jewish people that the words of this promise are the same ones used to describe the victory of Mordechai's forces over the anti-Semites: "No man could stand before them, for fear of them had fallen on all the peoples." (9:2) The implication is that Mordechai and Esther had indeed succeeded in walking in all God's ways.

Yet one cannot help noticing that there is something frightening in this message. In accepting it, does not man seek to usurp the place of God, deciding on right and wrong for himself, and seeking to chart the course of history? And does not man thereby reconcile himself with a Godless world, with atheism?

It seems that even in Mordechai's time, the Jews were not all that comfortable with the activist line he advocated in thought and deed. It is rather glaring, for instance, that in Mordechai's decision not to prostrate himself before Haman, he acts by himself: No other Jews joined him in refusing to pay obeisance to the vizier. Indeed, the Jewish community as a whole remains silent up until the day of the actual decree ordering their extermination—at which time the mourning and fasting finally begin. (4:3) Even after this, no Jews seem to join Mordechai in his protest at the palace gate. Other than the fasting, there is no discernible Jewish activity whatsoever until two months later, when the decree allowing the Jews to defend themselves is issued and Mordechai sets to work organizing them into a fighting force. On the religious front, too, the issuance of the second letter of Purim "with all due emphasis" (9:29) strongly suggests a protracted struggle within the Jewish community over the acceptance of the new holiday. No wonder, then, that the rabbinic tradition interpreted the book's closing comment concerning Mordechai's being "popular with the multitude of his brethren" to mean that he was accepted only by the *majority* of his brethren—and opposed by many others.[17]

In this argument, history proved to support Mordechai. Again and again in the centuries that followed, the demand for human responsibility and initiative evident in Esther allowed the Jewish people to survive where a more passive understanding of man's role would have resulted in annihilation. Politically, Mordechai created the mold from which came, for example, the successful revolt of Matityahu ben Johanan and his sons against the Seleucid Greeks—and in this case, too, the military and diplomatic daring of the Jewish leaders was accompanied by intellectual and religious responsibility, as evidenced by the Jews' decision to wage battle on the Sabbath, for if not, "they will only destroy us the sooner from the earth."[18] Intellectually, Mordechai's courage marked the beginning of the rabbinic period and the creation of the Talmud, on the remarkable thesis that the Tora was now in the hands of man and that, even if such were available, "we pay no attention to voices from heaven."[19] Ultimately, it was the flexibility and authority afforded the Jewish leadership by this stance that permitted Judaism to survive the Roman catastrophe and beyond.

These facts, however, only strengthen the challenge that was mounted in his own time against Mordechai's faith. If man can be such a success on his own, where is there room for God?

For the answer one must look back to Mordechai's theory of politics, as he expresses it to Esther when she must decide on her own fate and that of her people: (i) "Who knows whether it was not for such a time as this that you came into royalty?"; (ii) "if you insist on remaining silent at this time, … you and your father's house will perish"; and (iii) "relief and deliverance will come to the Jews from elsewhere." (4:13–14) Each of these elements represents for Mordechai an essential principle of political action—principles which, taken together, establish man in his new role, and so too define the relationship in which he now stands with his God.

(i) *The principle of investment.* It takes only a moderate familiarity with politics to see that, contrary to what is often supposed, there are no "coincidences" in the book of Esther. Every event from the moment that Esther is ushered into the care of the king's harem-keepers has its origins in the mind of a director, and that mind is not God. The events that lead to Haman's downfall are all of them orchestrated by Mordechai—except, of course, for the decisive turn, in which Esther makes good on years of her cousin's tutelage and breaks the king's allegiance to the vizier on the strength of a stratagem of her own. This is not to say that Mordechai can foresee every event precisely enough to have authored it move for move and line for line. Rather, events are directed, instigated, orchestrated. They are the consequence of a purposive action on his part which, when combined with all his other actions, succeeds in forcing reality in a given direction. Thus while even the most skilled politician cannot know beyond a doubt what will cause the king to suspect his vizier of evil intent, it may be probable that the insinuation of adultery will do the trick. If so, it is certainly no coincidence when the probable takes place as predicted.

Moreover, a gifted orchestrator of political events will have the *unpredicted* work in his favor much of the time as well. Esther does not know that Mordechai's life is in the balance when she moves to trigger the king's fear of Haman at the first banquet of wine. Yet it is the king's subsequent irritation with the vizier which saves Mordechai's life; had she stayed her move another twelve hours, Mordechai would likely have been put to death the next morning. But Esther's ignorance of her opponent's specific moves does not alter the fact that it is her purposive effort which saves him. Since strength attracts strength, while damage invites further damage, it is assumed that if she succeeds in weakening Haman's position in one way, he will be harmed in any number of unpredicted and additional ways—a lesson the rabbis emphasized by adding that Haman, as he was leading Mordechai through the streets on the king's horse, also suffered having a filthy chamber pot emptied on his head by his own daughter, who believed her father to be the rider.[20]

The degree to which probable and even unpredicted events fall in the desired direction is not a matter of chance. By far the most important factor is the degree to which the political player has invested in potentially useful assets in the relevant arena before the start of a given effort or campaign. Mordechai does not know precisely what will be the consequences of instructing Esther to hide her lineage, or of saving the king's life; he only recognizes that these moves are likely to strengthen the position of the Jews generally, and decides to invest against some future struggle he cannot foresee. They appear in the narrative not because they were his only political efforts, but because they are the ones which with hindsight can be seen to have contributed directly; unreported are the thousands of other such investments which Mordechai and Esther made over the years but which happened in the end to be of little importance to this particular conflict.

With regard to all of these moves, Mordechai's attitude was that which we recognize in his famous exhortation to Esther: "And who knows whether it was not for such a time as this that you came into royalty?"—that is, one can never be certain of the purpose of any specific investment in one's political position until great events have played themselves out. The excellent political player is one who treats every minor and apparently meaningless turn of events as an opportunity to affect the greatest of events which lie buried in the mists of the future, saying: Who knows whether hiding Esther's Jewish identity will not assist her in deflecting suspicion later on? Who knows whether saving the king's life will not prove useful at a later point? Over much time and in the aggregate, these purposive strengthenings in one's position, the constant imposition of will, purpose, design and meaning on the raw material of happenstance, tend to be the critical prerequisites for victory on the day the actual battle breaks—although only when the story is retold in the aftermath is it possible, sometimes, to see why.

In this, Mordechai was seconded by Machiavelli who, two thousand years later, prescribed this political method as the means of ensuring against the rages of fortune:

> I would compare her to an impetuous river that, when turbulent, inundates the plains, casts down the trees and buildings, removes earth from this side and places it on the other; every one flees before it, and everything yields to its fury without being able to oppose it; and yet though it is of such a kind, still when it is quiet, men can make provision against it by dykes and banks, so that when it rises it will either go into a canal or its rush will not be so wild and dangerous. So it is with fortune, which shows her power where no measures have been taken to resist her, and directs her fury where she knows that no dykes or barriers have been made to hold her.[21]

The book of Esther follows Machiavelli's message to a point: Mordechai, too, believes in the building of "dykes and barriers" against unforeseen eventualities: He builds his home and his life in the fortress of Susa rather than in the Jewish quarter; he allows Esther to leave her home and enter the court; he spends his days in calculated discussion with the courtiers to gather information and build connections; he instructs her not to reveal her lineage; he teaches her to gain favor with everyone; he saves the life of an ungrateful king. In every case, Mordechai understands that where there is an investment to be made, it is an investment that must be made. And ultimately, it is these investments which yield the resources necessary to save the Jews.

(ii) *The principle of boldness.* The political campaign may be understood as the advance of an infantryman against a sniper whom he cannot see, and whose location is known to him only as a general direction. If he tries to rush against the sniper from his initial position, he exposes himself at his weakest and gives the sniper every opportunity to take careful aim and bring him down, while he himself stands little chance of reaching his goal. By means of calculated advances, ducking from one place of cover to another, he slowly improves his own understanding of the enemy's identity and location, while at the same time decreasing the risk he will have to take in the final charge against the sniper's nest. But there is always a limit to how much time and effort can be invested in improving the position from which he will make his final assault. In the end, he must attack with what he has, either because it becomes too dangerous to wait any longer, or because he has simply reached the limit of what he can do to prepare, and usually for the former reason rather than the latter. At this point, every additional hesitation becomes a menace, and he must gather up his strength to begin the final, open assault—in which his opponent will know with certitude that he must fight for his life, and against whom.

There is no end of the investments that may be made in anticipation of action yet to come, but when the time comes one must leap into the open, or all the preparation is as though it had never been. When faced with Haman, Mordechai must make his public stand and refuse, before the watching eyes of the empire, to prostrate himself; when faced with the decree, he must take his protest to the streets of the capital; and Esther must enter to see the king, demand the elimination of her enemy, and push for the repeal of the decree. No amount of careful investment can bring these moves to life without the decision to come out from hiding and attack. In the final analysis, only the willingness to risk everything can bring victory about—"If you remain silent at this time, ... you and your father's house will perish."

This, too, is the subject of a colorful figure in Machiavelli, who similarly argues that boldness is a virtue that no amount of planning can replace: "It is better to be impetuous than cautious, for fortune is a woman, and it is necessary, if you wish to master her, to overcome her by force; and it can be seen that she lets herself be overcome by the bold rather than by those who proceed coldly."[22]

These principles, that of investment and that of boldness, the accumulation of assets, and their expenditure on effecting change, are two fundamentals of all political action. Yet every politician knows that there are three stages in any move, in any campaign, and not two. One invests, one throws oneself into the abyss—and then one falls. To land on one's feet and in a better place, this is the goal. But how one gets there is another issue, for which is required another principle of political action.

(iii) *The principle of faith.* Although they are separated by nearly twenty centuries, Mordechai lives in a world much like that of Machiavelli. God has hidden his face, and it appears that the course of human events runs on inexorably without purpose and without hope of guidance, either from heaven or earth. In such a world, there is little hope that any man can achieve any good at all, and it is against such a nihilistic view that both Mordechai and Machiavelli set forth their principles of investment and boldness. With these, even a man utterly alone in an endless, godless anarchy can hope to project his own direction onto the tides of history, at times emerging the victor. But there is a third principle of politics which fails to appear in Machiavelli, thereby crippling his politics and stunting his world: The principle of faith, submitted by Mordechai in the assertion that without Esther's intervention to save the Jews, "relief and deliverance will come to the Jews from elsewhere."

There have been those who claimed that this "elsewhere" is itself a literal reference to God, relying on a play on the Hebrew text which, if strained, permits such a reading. In this case, Mordechai is made to say: If you remain silent at this time, relief and deliverance will come from God.[23] But neither Mordechai nor the narrative needs such a device to introduce God as Esther's understudy. For this, a direct reference would have been perfectly serviceable. Rather, the point is that God seems not to appear to his people in Susa—neither before Esther's decision, nor after; nor is there reason to believe he would have been more in evidence had she remained silent and relief come from another source. Who or what, then, is "elsewhere"?

Let us consider Mordechai on the day the vizier issues the decree condemning the Jews of Persia to death. At this point he has not yet spoken to Esther, and the truth is that reaching Esther is manifestly not his first thought. He neither rushes immediately to the palace to find her, nor does he send word to her in writing. Instead, he dons mourning clothes and goes on a protest march through the city, shouting and crying up at the windows of the homes belonging to the officials of the empire, many of whom he has known in various capacities during his years as a resident of the capital and as a courtier. Thus Esther may or may not be the best card Mordechai can hope to play in the confrontation which has now erupted between him and Haman, but it is certain that he does not believe her to be his only card. Esther is one of a large number of people who have an interest in preventing Haman from seizing power in the empire and in preventing the king from abolishing his system of lawyers and advisers, and it is to all of these that Mordechai seeks to appeal. Even when he sits before the palace gate, he does not immediately send a message to her, but continues to address his protest to the many powerful men who are moving in and out in their efforts to pursue their own business.

The fact is that Mordechai does not have any way of knowing whence relief and deliverance will come at this point. And every person who has a role in the court of any kind and who tries to communicate with him in his distress receives the same message that Esther hears, although tailored to speak to him personally: Do not think you will escape because you are not a Jew. If you remain silent at this time. Who knows whether it was not for such a time as this. Deliverance will come.

At this stage, Mordechai has no idea that deliverance will come from Esther. He knows it must come from somewhere, and if not from the particular individual with whom he has only just spoken, then from "elsewhere." Only once events have run their course can he know that this "elsewhere" is, as it turns out, the queen. But had Esther failed in her task, then the story would hardly have mentioned her, if at all, and deliverance would have come from another person, another political factor, whose name we have no way of knowing, and who may not even have been known to Mordechai.

What permits Mordechai to have such confidence that he is willing to speak this readily and certainly about the existence of an "elsewhere" capable of bringing salvation? First, he believes in the investments he has made, over years establishing a series of defenses—such as the hidden presence of a Jewish queen in the palace, such as the favors owed him by the king and others—for just such a time as this. Second, he believes in the boldness of his own attack, of his public refusal to recognize Haman as having absolute authority. Taking Haman off guard within weeks or even days of his coming to power, this counteroffensive is launched well before Haman's position is consolidated and stable, and is certain to result in some kind of ill-planned responses—like the issuance of an unprecedented decree of annihilation against the Jews, and the construction of the seventy-five-foot gallows. Mordechai knows he has prepared for this battle and that his open assault was launched in time. He believes that under such conditions the chances of success are good, even though the cause might appear hopeless at first glance.

But all this is still within the realm of that which Machiavelli understands as digging canals and acting impetuously, none of which affords the philosopher a certitude that "relief will come from elsewhere." For Machiavelli is in this sense a "modern" thinker: He believes in the existence of an objective world outside of man, which is in its essence a dry and unyielding surface on which he plays and dies.

Reality does not respond to his actions, does not concern itself with his actions: At best it may be forced to submit to them. Whether fortune is a river or a lady, Machiavelli's prince wages his battle against her rages alone. He can count on the provisions he himself has made against her, the favors he has done and the allies he has acquired, the advice he has sought out and heeded, the resources he has set aside for bad times, and the contingency plans which he has laid against the possibility of catastrophe—yet all these are merely extensions of his own reach. Other men may be useful to him, but only in the sense that other things are useful: One may manipulate them according to the internal rules which govern them, and according to the dictates of one's own will. The prince ultimately believes in no one and nothing but himself, the only thing warm and alive on the cold tundra of a dead, objectified universe. Since reality is dead, it can respond to man in only two ways: It can ignore him and let him perish, or it can be forced to yield to his actions and his conscious will that he may live. In either case it is for him of necessity an opponent, an enemy.

But for all that is strange and new in Esther, Mordechai nevertheless understands reality from a vantage different from Machiavelli's, one in which all that is of interest and significance to man is to be guided aright in the subjective world in which he in practice thinks, lives and acts. In this world, reality is warm and alive, a love and a friend. It supports man from underneath and above, comprising not only objects to be manipulated, but having direction and tendency of its own as well. It gives to man his life and his consciousness, the capacities to imagine and create, to learn and to remember, freedom to make judgments, and strength and spirit to stand for them, a body responsive to his spirit, an environment that feeds it and nurtures it year upon year, and daily resurrections from sleep, forgetfulness, and pain. But more than this, reality is filled with other minds, other men, familiar and unfamiliar, who are not objects but wills, whose relationship to the subjective is responsive and giving: From those who, unbidden, choose to bring one into the world, to those who, unbidden, seek to carry on one's struggles and ideas after death. These others have their interests, but many of them are in fact interested by eternal truths, so that the more one approaches the dedication to these truths, the greater is the host of wills, future and past, which stand behind one's every effort. For those such as Mordechai, who live listening to the urgings of these wills and crying out to them in turn, it is never unexpected when one such as Esther breaks ranks with the cold and the hard, the wood and the stone, and, moved by the truth, responds—taking the initiative to be second to the true King and pursue his interest; walking in all his ways that she may grow righteous and strong; piercing the blackness and illuminating the night. As was said by R. Eleazar in the name of R. Hanina, it was the moment of Esther's decision to dress in royalty and go in to see the king in which she also cloaked herself in the spirit of God.[24]

Mordechai's certainty in the assistance of hidden others such as Esther is what moved the rabbis to portray him time and again as a teacher and friend of the children, as drawing his power from them. Thus in one parable of Resh Lakish, the day of the decree finds Mordechai walking utterly alone, while Haman celebrates with his advisers and allies. Yet even as he faces the sting of the worst, Mordechai immediately understands that his hope lies with the children. He runs to a group of them coming from school, and they repeat to him the words of Isaiah: "Take counsel together, and it will be brought to naught. Speak the word, and it will not stand, for God is with us."[25] When Haman asks him: "Why are you so glad over the words of these children?" Mordechai replies: "Because of the good tidings they have given me, that I need not fear the evil design which you have formed against us."[26]

Perhaps most telling is the argument of the rabbis that it is not Esther's efforts, but those of the children which result in Ahashverosh's nightmares on the fateful night when he turns against Haman:

Having made the gallows, Haman went to Mordechai, whom he found in the house of study with the schoolchildren before him in sackcloth, studying the Tora and crying and weeping. He counted them and found twenty-two thousand children there.

He put them in iron chains and set guards over them, saying: "Tomorrow, I will kill these children first, and then I will hang Mordechai."

Their mothers brought them bread and water, and said to them: "Children, eat and drink before you die tomorrow, and do not die of hunger."

But they put their hands on their books and swore by the life of Mordechai, their teacher, saying: "We will neither eat nor drink, but will die while still fasting."

They all wept piteously until the sound of their cries ascended to heaven, and the Holy One, may he be blessed, heard the sound of their weeping at around the second hour of the night. At that moment, the compassion of the Holy One, may he be blessed, was stirred…. He took the letters containing their doom which were signed with a seal of clay and tore them, in so doing bringing fright upon Ahashverosh in the night….[27]

Here the intention is not to detract from Esther's heroism, but to understand her might as part of another cause, broader and deeper— the turmoil of the Jewish children, Esther herself among them, fasting, praying, hoping, weeping, straining for the deliverance. As Mordechai does not truly walk alone because she is there for him, hidden in the palace, so too are these others with him, in their tens of thousands. As Esther had once been a child, learning at his feet and taking his teachings to her heart that on the black day she might be ready to stand with him, so too are there always those others who, while not yet visible, are nonetheless there for him, *with* him. Elsewhere. Elsewhen. So that he need not fear the evil design of a transient and perverse creature, an idol, an impotence which, even if it should hang him and take Esther as well, still would not succeed in laying a hand on that which is eternal, which it wishes to destroy first of all, but it cannot.

As Mordechai wanders through the streets of the capital, his cries echo up and out among the arches and balconies and parapets of a city made of a thousand thousand stones, begging for an answer. The truth is that he seeks a response not only from among the Jews,[28] not only from among men, but from anywhere his voice may reach—his cries, whether he calls them such or not, are a prayer. And when it comes, when Esther decides that she cannot permit this prayer to go unanswered, it is not only for the Jewish children that she responds, and not only for the righteous among men, although these voices are to be found in hers as well. Esther answers for all reality, for God himself, whose direction and tendency it has been to provide such Jewish children in every generation, and to provide them with the strength to redeem Israel again and again. It is she herself who decides, but in so doing she becomes God's answer to Mordechai's cries: "Then it is that the Holy One, may he be blessed, answers the world and its inhabitants, bringing forth the dawn from the darkness, and illuminating the world."

The world is in the first instance formless, directionless, anarchical, liquid, void, an utmost darkness. Not much has changed since Genesis: Man's place is perpetually to live in ships on the surface of the water, on the edge of the abyss.[29] Machiavelli's politics, and especially that of Nietzsche after him, looks out across the waves and calls on man to cease from his despair: He must impose that order which he himself decrees. He must recognize the vastness of the sea, and yet for all this, weigh anchor, engage those oarsmen whom he can command, and strive with his every fiber to give his craft direction and purpose, that it may make its way a distance across the emptiness, of its own power, before the end of it.[30] But Mordechai speaks to us of another politics, and a greater one: Of one in which a spirit blows unseen over the surface of the water, allowing it direction, tendency, order, rule, purposiveness, light. Perhaps this is no great wind; one can hardly feel it when one walks about the deck. Indeed, it is so still that when man disregards it, his ship may lie dead on the sea for a thousand years in spite of it, as though it did not exist. And yet he need only hoist a sail to see how this wind fills the world, as it has since creation. And if he has correctly aimed his craft, he then feels it shudder into motion as God answers.

In Esther, God has ceased to call man in the streets and the marketplaces, he has withdrawn from dictating political action and decreeing divine law. His shout is no more, and so our own shouts drown out his voice as a matter of course. But this does not mean we act in isolation. Beyond the investments and acts of boldness and might which the individual can muster, there is infinite strength in a living reality which seeks to move in the same direction, and which can respond ten-fold, ten-thousand-fold, if our aims are towards the true and eternal, towards that which is commanded. Reality does not need to be conquered, but it needs to be incited, ignited, pushed to erupt with all its latent powers in directions which man cannot possibly predict with accuracy, yet for which we are all of us responsible. We do not play against reality, but with it. We believe that if we do our part, everything that is possible according to powers that can be mustered on earth, the world is such that there will be others, there will be "elsewheres" which will react to our cries and our acts and do theirs. If we do our part, God will do his.

After every holocaust, and certainly the one in our time, it must be asked again whether all this is not nonsense. If there had been a Mordechai to witness the consequences of the German war, would not he have recognized that "relief and deliverance" simply does not come on every occasion, that God does not initiate and that frequently he also does not do his part?

To this there can be two answers, both possible, but neither pleasant. The first is that in Germany, as in all the previous enormities in the history of the Jews, God did respond. Relief and deliverance did come, in the form of the United States, in the form of the Soviets, and the life of the Jews as a people and as an idea was indeed saved. No one ever claimed that relief and deliverance would come to every Jew in every case. The second is that God did not do his part because we did not do ours—that there were too many such as Mordechai who were placed to invest for the crisis, but who did not bother to do so, and that there were too many such as Esther who were placed to act boldly to stem the tide, but who chose to remain silent at that time. We chose not to initiate, we chose not to walk in all his ways. And as we were not merciful, so he was not merciful.

And the truth is that these two answers are much the same. That while Mordechai insisted that relief and deliverance would come from somewhere, eventually, it seems that it was not his intention to say that if Esther chose to remain silent, it would be without terrible consequences. "You and your father's house will perish." And if the many choose to remain silent, they and many, many more may also perish before God can, with the feeble tools we have left him, find a way of bringing relief and deliverance to the remnant.

And one must wonder whether this is not the most terrible punishment that has come of the world after the exile, in which God's face remains hidden and the initiative has gone over to man in all things—that man may walk in God's ways in this as well: That as he hides his face, so too do we hide our face. And then even God cannot respond to the cries of his children.

May we in our own day learn these teachings, that they may be in our hearts and in our hands, that we may merit the lifting of the evil that has been decreed by reason of our folly and our ignorance, our impiety and our inaction, and that the Jews should have light and gladness, joy and honor as in days past.

# Notes

## INTRODUCTION

¹ Shabbat 88a.

² "The book of Esther and the Tora will never be abolished." Jerusalem Megilla 1:5.

³ According to the rabbis, the books of Ezekiel, Proverbs, and Ecclesiastes are associated with wisdom; Jeremiah, Job, and Lamentations with an understanding of punishment; Psalms and Song of Songs with piety; Kings with greatness; Isaiah with consolation. Esther, the last book mentioned, is associated with miracles. Brachot 57b.

⁴ The book of Ezra and Nehemia, originally one work, follows Esther chronologically in the sequence of the biblical canon. It is fair to say that the Bible's conclusion is actually divided up between these works: Ezra and Nehemia offering the hope of the return to Israel, while Esther speaks to the vast majority of Jews who were at this point to remain in exile.

CHAPTER 1

¹ Apparently Khshayarsha I, whom the Greeks knew as Xerxes I. Xerxes ruled the Persian empire from 485 to 464 BCE, a century after the exile of the Jews of Judah and the destruction of Jerusalem in 586. This would place the carnival in 483, and the first Purim in 473.

² Megilla 11b.

³ Megilla 11b.

⁴ Esther Rabba 2:2.

⁵ Genesis Rabba 68:13.

⁶ Genesis 1:26.

⁷ It is the desire for control in the hands of others, as a substitute for one's own control, which produced the golden calf when the Jews felt that Moses was no longer determining events; which led them to demand to return to the certainty of Pharaoh's bondage when they came to the desert; and which in the end led them to demand that a king be set over them because they could no longer stand the uncertainty of living with only God to rule them. Exodus 32:1, Numbers 3–4, 1 Samuel 8:4–9.

⁸ Joseph is described as "a man in whom is the spirit of God," Genesis 41:38; of Betzalel it is said that "he has filled him with the spirit of God in wisdom … and in all manner of crafts—and to contrive works of art…" Exodus 35:31–32; of Caleb it is said that "because he had a different spirit … him will I bring into the land…" Numbers 14:24; and Joshua is called simply "a man in whom there is spirit," Numbers 27:18.

⁹ Cf. Plato, who argues that great virtue can be achieved if and only if the power of the spirit is devoted to achieving that which is dictated by reason. This Plato refers to as "justice". See *Republic*, 441d–e.

¹⁰ Or David, ad loc., on Esther 1:1.

¹¹ Yalkut Shimoni, ad loc.

¹² Thus Zecharia associates alcohol with might and confidence on the battlefield. Zecharia 9:15, 10:7.

¹³ Megilla 12b.

¹⁴ Exodus 8:24f.

## CHAPTER 2

[1] The corresponding years during the reign of Xerxes were largely devoted to his invasion of Greece, an adventure which ended in humiliating defeat for Persia.

[2] This comparison is made explicitly by the prophets: E.g., "Hear this word which I take up against you: A lamentation, O house of Israel. The virgin of Israel is fallen, she will rise no more. She is forsaken on her land, there is none to raise her up." Amos 5:1–2. More generally, the way that Memuchan in the first chapter helps the king eliminate the supposed threat to the kingdom from all, foreshadows and parallels his decision to eliminate the threat from the Jews at Haman's urging in the third chapter.

[3] According to R. Nehemia, Esther is Ishtar, the Persian queen of heaven. Megilla 13a. Cf. Greek "aster," meaning star.

[4] Darius I, who ruled Persia during 522–486 BCE.

[5] Genesis 34:24–31, 35:22.

[6] Rashi, ad loc., on Genesis 37:2.

[7] Genesis 37:2. Rashi understands "their evil report" to refer not to a report against the younger brothers, but rather to be the report of the younger brothers against the older sons of Leah. In this case, Joseph had taken the lead in trying to build a coalition of the younger brothers and Jacob against the older brothers—all the more reason for them to have hated him. Rashi, ad loc.

[8] Genesis 37:3.

[9] Genesis 38:3–4.

[10] Genesis 38:21–23; 47:13–26.

[11] Genesis 45:16–21.

[12] Daniel 1:15, 17.

[13] Daniel 11:1.

[14] Daniel 6:3.

[15] The text explains that "the king thought to set him over the whole realm," as a result of his success as a triumvir. There follows an account of the conspiracy against Daniel by his political opponents, who oppose the promotion. The conspiracy ends with Daniel's salvation and the deaths of his enemies, as well as with Darius' proclamation recognizing the authority of the God of the Jews. But we are told nothing of Daniel's subsequent political career other than that he "succeeded in the reign of Darius...." The implication is rather strong that he received his promotion. Daniel 6:4, 26–29.

[16] R. Judan, in the name of R. Benjamin, attributes the similarities between Joseph and Mordechai to the fact that they are of common lineage, both being descended from Rachel. Genesis Rabba 87:6.

[17] Genesis 40:22.

[18] Esther Rabba 6:8.

[19] R. Eleazar's comment is recorded in Megilla 13a. Thus Memuchan incites Ahashverosh to decree "that every man should rule in his own house and speak in the language of his own people." Esther 2:22. Nehemia, too, is particularly distressed that the Jews' gentile wives are raising their children without a knowledge of Hebrew: "At that time, too, I saw Jews who had taken wives from Ashdod, Ammon, and Moav. And their children half-spoke Ashdodite and did not know how to speak the language of Judah, rather speaking the language of various other peoples. I fought with them and cursed them, and beat some of them and pulled out their hair, and made them swear to God, saying, 'You will not give your daughters to their sons, nor take their daughters to your sons nor to yourselves.'" Nehemia 13:23–25. The capacity to put all men at ease by speaking to them in their own tongue also appears with regard to Joseph and Mordechai, whom the rabbis describe as being able to speak seventy languages. See discussion in Chapter 4.

[20] Playing on the fact that her given name is Hadassa (a myrtle), he asserts that her complexion was greenish. Megilla 13a. But the majority opinion among the rabbis was that Esther was physically beautiful as well, following the plain meaning in the narrative. Megilla 15a.

[21] Megilla 13a. Other rabbinic adages on the subject of Esther's sexual virtues are even more graphic. For example, Yoma 29a.

²² Megilla 16b argues that Mordechai was opposed by some among the Jewish leadership, on which Rashi, ad loc., brings what has become the traditional understanding of their opposition: "Because Mordechai neglected Tora and went into rulership."

²³ See discussion in Chapter 11.

## CHAPTER 4

¹ Cf. Plato: "Also don't some of those who helped in setting [the tyrant] up and are in power—the manliest among them—speak frankly to him and to one another, criticizing what is happening? ... Then the tyrant must gradually do away with all of them, if he's going to rule, until he has left neither friend nor enemy of any worth whatsoever." *Republic* 567b.

² Megilla 16a.

³ Megilla 15a.

⁴ The Talmud actually renders Shmuel's opinion as: "The king above has prevailed over the king below," the reverse of anything that Mordechai might actually have said. This is apparently in the tradition of using opposites as euphemisms for expressions that men of faith should never utter. Megilla 15a; Rashi, ad loc.

⁵ Jonah 4:11. Cf. Jeremiah's crying for Moav in Jeremiah 48:31–38.

⁶ From Jeremiah's declamations against Jehoyakim, Josiah's son, who was ruler in Jerusalem. The entire passage reads: "Woe to him who builds his house without righteousness, and his upper chambers without justice, who makes his neighbor labor for free, and does not pay his worker, who says: 'I will build myself a wide house with airy upper chambers,' and he cuts himself windows, and it is raftered with cedar and painted with vermilion. Will you reign because you compete in cedar? Your father, did he not manage to eat and drink, and yet do justice and righteousness? Then it was well with him. He judged the cause of the poor and the needy. Then it was well. Is this not to know me? says the Eternal." Jeremiah 22:13–16.

⁷ Genesis 18:20–19:28. The flood in the time of Noah is a related and even earlier example. Genesis 6:1–8:22.

⁸ *Republic* 488a–e.

⁹ Proverbs 16:14. Cf. "Lips saying righteousness are the desire of kings, and he who speaks what is right will he love." Proverbs 16:13. "Whatever pleases him, he will do. For the word of the king is rule, and who will ask him 'What are you doing?'" Ecclesiastes 8:3–4.

¹⁰ To this, the school of R. Ishmael added: "Just as the hammer blow produces seventy sparks, so every word that went forth from the Holy One, may he be blessed, fragmented into seventy languages." Shabbat 88b. Cf. Pirkei d'Rabi Eliezer, ch. 24.

¹¹ Genesis 11:1, 7–9. Cf. Targum Jonathan on 11:8, ad loc.

¹² Accompanying this theory in the rabbinic literature is the ideal of understanding the seventy languages—that is, being able to understand and speak to the perspectives of all men. This R. Johanan considered to be a theoretical requirement for being appointed to the Sanhedrin, the highest legal body among the Jews, and such knowledge was also a requirement for leadership in other nations. With regard to the Sanhedrin, the Talmud also suggests that if three or four members out of the seventy men of the court are so gifted, it would be an exceptional Sanhedrin. Sanhedrin 17a, b. The reference to such a requirement among the Egyptians appears in Sota 36b. Not coincidentally, the tradition sometimes ascribes the skill of understanding the seventy languages to Joseph and to Mordechai, each of whom is considered able to gain favor with others precisely because of his talent for appreciating their personal perspectives. Joseph's knowledge of the seventy languages appears in Sota 36b. Cf. Numbers Rabba 14:5, 19:3; Ecclesiastes Rabba 7:23. Mordechai, in particular, was held by R. Johanan to have gained his knowledge of the plot against Ahashverosh through a familiarity with the "language" of the conspirators, and so was able to understand their motives, although they themselves thought them well concealed. Mordechai's knowledge of languages is mentioned in Shekalim 5:1 and Megilla 13b. Cf. R. Eleazar's image attributing much the same ability to Esther. Megilla 13a. See discussion in Chapter 2.

¹³ The passage continues: "Tomorrow two men will appear before you in a suit, a Jew and one who is a tormentor and an enemy. Can you please both of them? You will have to raise up the one and hang the other." Esther Rabba 2:14.

¹⁴ The argument that the state must balance competing interests appears later in Plato, when he argues for "a compromise between a monarchical and a democratic constitution," in which each of four property classes is to

be given equal power, since either strict equality or inequality "fills a state with quarrels among its citizens." *Laws* 756–757. Aristotle mentions other theories of the mixed state which may have predated Plato. *Politics* 1265b. But in the book of Esther the argument is not so much one of keeping the peace, but of actually finding the true course for the state, as is evident from the connotation of idolatry attributed to the state as ruled by Haman (see discussion in Chapter 5).

It is important to note, however, that the free play of competing interests in the palace is not a mechanism which in and of itself leads to justice and to the true course of the state. On the contrary, it is only a prerequisite, permitting the ruler to understand political reality in its totality so that his decisions may be informed ones. But even if all perspectives were fully represented, in the end the true state is one whose ruler is wise enough to be able to select the more important claim over the less important, and the more worthy cause over the less worthy. And this capacity for political judgment must also be wedded to a courageous spirit capable of maintaining the true course after such a judgment is made.

[15] According to R. Shmuel ben Imi, Ahashverosh's habit of consulting with his advisers should be credited as a virtue. Esther Rabba 1:15. Cf. Malbim's commentary, ad loc., on Esther 1:1, which understands the structural argument to distinguish between constitutional monarchy (the rule of the Persian king and the seven princes) and absolute rule (the rule of the king through his vizier).

[16] The rabbis assumed that the principal effect of the decree was to damage Ahashverosh's credibility among the citizens. Thus R. Pinhas suggests that it made the king the butt of humor among the citizens. Esther Rabba 4:12. Rava goes so far as to argue that the letters issued after Vashti's disobedience contributed to the failure of Haman's scheme by making the peoples doubt the seriousness of the king's subsequent edicts. Megilla 12b.

[17] Herodotus brings an additional illustration of the way Xerxes made decisions of state in describing the determination to go to war. He receives arguments on both sides from members of his own family and court, as well as from the representatives of various factions in Greece itself. Herodotus reports the king to have changed his mind several times before finally electing to pursue the venture. *The Persian Wars* (New York: Random House, 1942), pp. 494–502.

## CHAPTER 5

[1] Esther Rabba 6:2.

[2] Megilla 19a.

[3] Herodotus reports the invasion force Xerxes mustered against the Greeks to have comprised an incredible 1,700,000 men. Contemporary scholars suggest that his numbers were off by a factor of six, Herodotus apparently calculating 60,000 men to a division, when in fact these divisions commanded only 10,000 troops. If this is correct, the 76,000 casualties reported in Esther amount to a force more than a fourth the size of Persia's land power. *The Persian Wars*, pp. 522, 522n.

[4] Megilla 13a.

[5] Esther Rabba 6:2. Cf. Sanhedrin 61b. Similarly: "So terrible is idolatry that anyone who rejects it, it is as if he accepted the entire Tora." Hullin 5a. "The prohibition against idolatry is equivalent to all the commandments of the Tora." Horayot 8a.

[6] Avoda Zara 55a.

[7] According to R. Nachman in the name of R. Mana, Jerusalem Avoda Zara 4:7.

[8] An example of how idolaters perceived the locality of truth is the adoption of certain Jewish practices by the peoples brought by the Assyrians to settle in the depopulated Jewish towns of Israel: "Then they spoke to the king of Assyria, saying: 'The nations that you have removed and settled in the cities of Samaria know not the law of the God of the land. Therefore he has sent lions among them, and behold, they do not know the law of the God of the land.'" The assumption is that the law of the Jewish God is that which controls the fate of men living in the land of the Jews, but not elsewhere. II Kings 17:26.

[9] Paraphrasing the first three commandments of the decalogue. Exodus 20:2–6.

[10] Exodus 5:1–2.

[11] Deuteronomy 7:7.

¹² Deuteronomy 12:31. The rabbis, too, wrote: "One should not leave cattle in the inns of idolaters, because they are to be suspected of bestiality. And a woman should not be alone with them, because they are to be suspected of lewdness. And a man should not be alone with them, because they are to be suspected of violence." Avoda Zara 22a. The subsequent discussion in Avoda Zara 22bf. goes into the grisly details.

¹³ See discussion in Chapter 11.

¹⁴ Shabbat 88a.

¹⁵ Genesis Rabba 38:13. Nietzsche's *Twilight of the Idols* is subtitled "How to Philosophize with a Hammer."


# CHAPTER 6

¹ Genesis 22:1–13.

² Genesis 12:2–3.

³ For example, consider the following passage from the Hindu scriptures: "The whole world is kept in order by punishment. ... If the king did not, without tiring, inflict punishment on those worthy to be punished, the stronger would roast the weaker like fish on a spit: The crow would eat the sacrificial cake and the dog would lick the sacrificial viands, and ownership would not remain with anyone, and the lower ones would usurp the place of the higher ones.... Punishment alone governs all created beings, punishment alone protects them, punishment watches over them while they sleep.... Punishment is ... the king." *The Laws of Manu*, G. Bühler, trans. (Motilal Banarsidass, 1962), Book VII, sections 16–22ff., pp. 219–220ff.

⁴ Genesis 18:25.

⁵ See, for example, Numbers 14:11–25.

⁶ Genesis 32:29. See Rashi, ad loc.

⁷ Genesis 10:8–9.

⁸ Genesis 11:3–6.

[9] Genesis 12:12.

[10] Genesis 26:18.

[11] Genesis 34:1f.

[12] Exodus 1:17–19.

[13] Regarding Pharaoh's daughter, the rabbis wrote: "Why was she called a Jewess? Because she repudiated idolatry, as it is written: 'And the daughter of Pharaoh went down to bathe in the river.' (Exodus 2:5) R. Johanan said: She went down to cleanse herself from the idols of her father's house." The point is that at the moment she drew Moses from the water and disobeyed the will of her father, she renounced the essence of Egyptian idolatry. Megilla 13a.

[14] Exodus 2:1–10.

[15] Exodus 2:11–12.

[16] Exodus 5:21.

[17] Exodus 12:3–11, 21–23.

[18] Judges 8:23.

[19] "And Samuel told all the words of the Eternal to the people who asked him for a king. And he said: 'This will be the custom of the king who will reign over you: He will take your sons and post them for himself on his chariots. And he will appoint officers over battalions and officers over platoons, and he will set them to plowing his ground and reaping his harvest, and to making his instruments of war. And he will take your daughters for perfumers and cooks and bakers. And he will take your fields and your vineyards and your best orchards and give them to his servants. And he will take a tenth of your seed and of your vineyards to give to his officers and to his servants. And he will take your male and female servants and your best young men and your asses and put them to his work. He will take a tenth of your sheep, and you will be his servants. And you will cry out on that day because of the king that you have placed over you. And the Eternal will not hear you on that day.' But the people refused to heed Samuel's warning, and they said: 'No, we will have a king over us so we may be like other nations: that our king may judge us and go out before us and fight our battles.'" 1 Samuel 8:10–20.

[20] Deuteronomy 17:16–20.

[21] I Samuel 14:43–45. Similarly, when Saul had determined to have David killed, it is Jonathan and his sister Michal, David's wife, who resist the king in order to save his life. I Samuel 19:11f. Saul's servants also refuse his order to kill the priests of Nov. I Samuel 22:17.

[22] II Samuel 12:1f. The much-quoted Talmudic passage that appears to absolve David of having sinned in the affair with Batsheva (Shabbat 56a) is contradicted by a more conventional reading elsewhere that argues that David lost four loved ones prematurely as punishment for this liaison. Yoma 22b.

[23] I Samuel 15:30f., 16:1f.

[24] II Kings 9:1–10:29.

[25] Jeremiah 38:2. That such defection was illegal is clear from 37:13.

[26] Daniel 3:16–18.

[27] Daniel 6:7–11.

[28] This view was catapulted into prominence in the non-Jewish world by Henry David Thoreau in his 1848 lecture, "On the Relation of the Individual to the State," a published version of which was posthumously renamed "Civil Disobedience." In it, Thoreau argued that if government "is of such a nature that it requires you to be an agent of injustice to another, then, I say, break the law. Let your life be a counter-friction to stop the machine.... I do not hesitate to say, that those who call themselves Abolitionists should at once effectually withdraw their support, both in person and property, from the government of Massachusetts, and not wait till they constitute a majority of one, before they suffer the right to prevail through them. I think that it is enough if they have God on their side.... [E]ven suppose blood should flow. Is there not a sort of blood shed when the conscience is wounded? Through this wound a man's real manhood and immortality flow out, and he bleeds to an everlasting death. I see this blood flowing now." Henry David Thoreau, Carl Bode, ed., *The Portable Thoreau* (New York: Penguin, 1947), pp. 119–123.

[29] See discussion in Chapter 23.

[30] See discussion in Chapters 22–23.

[31] The difference between the Hebrew Bible and the New Testament in this regard is marked. While upholding the Jewish claim that the Roman emperor had no authority to determine right and wrong for his subjects,

the Christian scriptures acquiesced in the theory that so long as men were to live in this world, their relationship to worldly power should be one of submission: "Submit yourselves to every human institution for the sake of the Lord.... Servants, accept the authority of your masters with all due submission, not only when they are kind and considerate, but even when they are perverse. For it is a fine thing if a man endure the pain of undeserved suffering because God is in his thoughts.... [W]hen you have behaved well and suffer for it, your fortitude is a fine thing in the sight of God. To that you were called, because Christ suffered on your behalf, and thereby left you an example; it is for you to follow in his steps. He committed no sin ... [yet] when he suffered he uttered no threats, but committed his cause to the One who judges justly." 1 Peter 2:13, 18–23. Cf. Matthew 5:38–44; Paul 13:1–5.

[32] The text literally reads: "...one for 'we will do' and one for 'we will hear,'" the two responses of the Jewish people at Sinai in Exodus 24:7. Shabbat 88a.

[33] Midrash Tanhuma, Mishpatim 2 on Exodus 21:1.


CHAPTER 7


[1] Examples include Abraham's activities in the war of kings (Genesis 14:1–24) and his various dealings with Avimelech. (Genesis 20:1–5; 21:22–32)

[2] Ezra and Nehemia are actually a single work, which is broken up in the referencing system of chapters and verses in use today. Both parts contain much material relevant to the Esther story, but Nehemia, who was a senior adviser to the king, is of particular interest.

[3] Genesis 37:2–4. The Hebrew phrasing *ro'e et ehav* means "shepherds with his brothers," but it is worded so as to have a second meaning as well, that he "shepherds his brothers" rather than the sheep. Seforno, ad loc.

[4] Genesis 39:6.

[5] Genesis 37:6–11.

[6] Even as adults in Egypt, Joseph continues to attempt to impose order and unity on the brothers. Genesis 43:33. Also Genesis 45:24, where Joseph tells them on their way back to Canaan: "Make sure you do not fall out

along the way." This entire aspect of their relationship can be understood as foreshadowing the anarchy among the tribes in the period of the Judges, in which Joseph's efforts are parallel to the demand for the imposition of a central authority at the hands of a king.

7 Other than Joseph, the only other Jew who interprets dreams in the Bible is Daniel.

8 Genesis Rabba 84:14 on Genesis 37:20.

9 Sota 36b.

10 Genesis Rabba 87:5. The rabbis also believed that sexual appetite could itself be a false-god, dictating all value in a person's life. In this regard, they told the story of R. Eleazar ben Dordia, who could not hear of the existence of a prostitute without running to her and paying whatever she might ask. Avoda Zara 17a. But the idol that Potiphar's wife hangs before Joseph is more generally the success and power of Egypt, of which she is only one example.

11 This success is in contrast with his older brothers, Reuben and Judah, who are unable to overcome such temptation. Reuben sleeps with one of his father's concubines. Genesis 35:22. Judah becomes badly entangled because of a visit to a harlot. Genesis 38:1f.

12 Psalms 146:7.

13 Psalms 146:8.

14 Psalms 146:8.

15 Genesis 39:10.

16 The passage immediately preceding this dialogue reads: "Our rabbis taught: The poor, the rich, and the wicked come before the heavenly court…. To the wicked person they would say: Why have you not occupied yourself with the Tora? If he were to say: I was beautiful and upset by sensual passion, they would say to him: Were you more beautiful than Joseph? It was told of Joseph the righteous that the wife of Potiphar tried every day to entice him with her words. The clothes she put on for him in the morning, she did not wear in the evening; those she put on for him in the evening, she did not wear in the morning." Yoma 35b. This scene is the basis for the appellation "Joseph the righteous," which is found repeatedly in the writing of the rabbis in various contexts, e.g., Ketubot 111a, Megilla 13b, 16b.

[17] Sota 36b. It is important to note that Reuben and Judah did not have to pass such a test to remain Jews. Neither as attracted to Egypt as their brother, nor as suited to be of use to the Egyptian hierarchy, they are spared trials of this sort.

[18] "Why did Joseph die before his brothers? Rabi and the rabbis disagree. Rabi said: Because he embalmed his father. The Holy One, may he be blessed, said to him: Can I not protect my righteous ones? ... But in the opinion of the rabbis: Nearly five times did Judah say: 'Your servant, my father,' 'your servant, my father,' yet he heard it and kept silent." Genesis Rabba 100:3.

[19] Genesis Rabba 100:3. Judah says this four times himself, Genesis 44:24, 27, 30, 31, and once with his brothers, Genesis 43:28.

[20] "R. Judah said in the name of Rav: Why was Joseph referred to as 'bones' while he yet lived? (Genesis 50:25) Because he did not intervene to protect his father's honor when his brothers said to him: 'Your servant, our father,' (Genesis 44:31) but made no reply to them. R. Judah also said in the name of Rav, although others say it was R. Hama ben R. Hanina: Why did Joseph die before his brothers? Because he conducted himself with rulership." Sota 13b. Both of these criticisms are aimed at Joseph's understanding of his own place in the hierarchy of reality as a result of his position in the Egyptian state: He considered it acceptable to participate in a system in which Jacob and his God, as well as the rest of the world, were understood to be servants. See also Brachot 55a.

[21] Sota 13b. Cf. Ezekiel's comparison of the people Israel in exile to a valley filled with bones. Ezekiel 37:1f.

[22] The figure of the wine cask belongs to one of the greatest of the aggadists, R. Levi. Exodus Rabba 20:19. See discussion in Chapter 11.

[23] According to R. Hanin ben Bizna in the name of R. Shimon Hasida, Joseph sanctified God's name in private in the trial of Potiphar's wife—as opposed to Judah, who sanctified God's name in public by admitting the wrongs he had committed against Tamar. Sota 10b. It is Judah's capacity to make the right decision publicly, even at the cost of tremendous embarrassment and potential political harm to himself, which ultimately results in his meriting the leadership of the Jews, and not Joseph.

[24] See discussion in Chapter 11.

[25] Daniel 6:25.

²⁶ See discussion in Chapter 11.

²⁷ The full passage reads: "And there was no bread in the land, for the famine was severe, so that the land of Egypt and all the land of Canaan languished under the famine. Joseph collected all the money that was to be found in the land of Egypt and in the land of Canaan in exchange for the grain that they bought, and Joseph brought the money to Pharaoh's house. When the money failed in the land of Egypt and in the land of Canaan, all Egypt came to Joseph and said: 'Give us bread. Why should we die before you for lack of money?' Joseph said: 'Give your cattle, and I will trade for your cattle, if you have no money.' They brought their cattle to Joseph, and Joseph gave them bread in exchange for their horses, and for their flocks, and for their herds, and for their asses, and he fed them with bread in exchange for all their cattle that year. When the year had ended, they came to him during the second year and said to him: 'We will not hide from my lord how our money is gone. My lord also has our herds of cattle. There is nothing left in the sight of my lord but our bodies and our land. Why should we die before you, both we and our land? Buy us and our land for bread, and we and our land will be servants to Pharaoh. Give us grain that we may live and not die, that the land will not be desolate.' So Joseph bought all the land of Egypt for Pharaoh, for every Egyptian sold his field, because the famine prevailed over them, and the land became Pharaoh's. As for the people, he removed them to the cities, from one end of Egypt to the other.... Then Joseph said to the people: 'Behold, I have bought you and your land this day for Pharaoh. Here is grain for you, and you will sow the land. And it will be that at harvest times, you will give a fifth to Pharaoh, and four-fifths will be your own, for seed, and for your food, and for the members of your households, and for your little ones.' They said: 'You have saved our lives....'" Genesis 47:13–25.

²⁸ The full passage reads: "And there was a great cry of the people and of their wives against their brethren the Jews. For there were those who said, 'We, our sons, and our daughters, are many: therefore let us get corn, that we may eat, and live.' There were also those who said, 'We have mortgaged our lands, our vineyards, and our houses, that we might buy corn, because of the dearth.' There were also those who said, 'We have borrowed money for the king's tribute, and that upon our lands and vineyards. Yet now our flesh is as good as the flesh of our brethren, our children as good as their children: and lo, we press our sons and our daughters into slavery, and some of our daughters are pressed into slavery already: nor is it in our power to redeem them; for other men have our lands and vineyards.' And I was

very angry when I heard their cry and these words. Then I took counsel with myself, and I rebuked the nobles, and the rulers, and said to them, 'You make claims for debt, everyone of his brother!' And I held a great assembly against them. And I said to them, 'We after our ability have redeemed our brethren the Jews, who were sold to the heathen: and will you nevertheless sell your brethren? or shall they be sold to us?' Then they held their peace, and found nothing to answer. Also I said, 'That which you do is not good: ought you not to walk in the fear of our God because of the insult of the heathen our enemies? I likewise, and my brethren, and my servants, have lent them money and corn: I pray you, let us release this debt. Restore, I pray you, to them, even this day, their lands, their vineyards, their oliveyards and their houses, also the percentage of the money, and of the corn, the wine and the oil, that you exact of them.' Then they said, 'We will restore them, and will require nothing of them; so we will do as you say.' Then I called the priests, and took an oath of them, that they should do according to this promise. Also I shook out my lap, and said, 'So God shake out every man from his house, and from his labor, who does not perform this promise, even thus may he be shaken out, and emptied.' And all the congregation said, 'Amen, and praised be the Lord.' And the people did according to this promise. Moreover from the time that I was appointed to be their governor in the land of Judah, from the twentieth year even unto the thirty-second year of Artahshasta the king, that is, twelve years, I and my brethren have not eaten the bread of the governor. But the former governors who had been before me laid burdens upon the people, and had taken of them for bread and wine, besides forty shekels of silver; even their servants bore rule over the people: but I did not do so, because of the fear of God. For I also continued in the work of this wall, nor did we buy any land: and all my servants were gathered there to the work." Nehemia 5:1–16.

[29] Mordechai and Esther are Benjaminites, and therefore descended from Joseph's brother. Joseph and Benjamin were the only two of the twelve sons of Jacob who were born to Rachel. R. Johanan, in the name of R. Benjamin ben R. Levi, brings a long list of similarities in the personalities and in the plots of the two stories. Esther Rabba 7:7. Cf. Genesis Rabba 87:6. Moreover, the book of Esther is intentionally written in such a way as to highlight these similarities through the use of parallel wording. For example, compare Genesis 41:34–37 with Esther 2:3–4; Genesis 50:3 with Esther 2:12; Genesis 29:10 with Esther 3:4; Genesis 43:14 with Esther 4:16; Genesis 44:34 with Esther 8:6.

CHAPTER 8

[1] Another intentional association in the plot includes the deposition of Vashti in favor of "someone better than she," (1:19) the same expression used when Saul is deposed as king of the Jews for having failed to destroy Amalek. (1 Samuel 15:28) Similarly, Saul's error was in part the fact that he allowed the Jews to take spoils in their war against Amalek, (1 Samuel 15:19) whereas Mordechai makes sure that the Jews do not touch the property of the Persian anti-Semites. (9:15–16) Cf. Esther Rabba 4:9.

[2] Exodus 15:22–17:7.

[3] Exodus 17:14–16.

[4] Deuteronomy 25:17–19. According to the rabbinic tradition, this passage must be read aloud to every Jew prior to the annual reading of the book of Esther on the festival of Purim.

[5] Numbers 13:18.

[6] Numbers 13:26–33.

[7] Numbers 13:30.

[8] Numbers 14:3–4.

[9] The complete citation is: "And now, Israel, what does the Eternal your God require of you, other than to fear the Eternal your God, to walk in all his ways, and to love him, and to serve the Eternal your God with all your heart and with all your soul, to follow the instructions of the Eternal and his laws, which I instruct you this day for your good?" Deuteronomy 10:12–13.

[10] Leviticus 19:14.

[11] Deuteronomy 10:19–20.

[12] Numbers 19:32; 25:17, 36, 43.

[13] Genesis 20:11.

[14] Exodus Rabba 27:6. The enmity of Jethro the Midianite is established through an anachronism, but an important one: "How do you know that both the Amalekites and the Midianites were the enemies of Israel? Because it says: ... 'Now Midian and Amalek and all the children of the east' [lay in wait for the Jewish forces]...." Exodus Rabba 27:6 on Judges 7:12f.

[15] Exodus 1:17. Joseph also uses this expression, when, as vizier of Egypt, he seeks to assure his brothers that he will not arbitrarily destroy them although it is in his power. Genesis 42:18.

[16] Exodus Rabba 27:9.

[17] Exodus 18:21.

[18] Numbers 24:3.

[19] Numbers 24:20.

[20] Numbers 23:21, 24:5, 8.

[21] E.g., Avimelech. Genesis 20:1–5. Similarly, Bil'am. Numbers 23:7–8.

## CHAPTER 9

[1] Exodus 1:7–12, 22.

[2] Genesis Rabba 68:13. A related figure suggests that the anti-Semite, Haman, had been predestined to die being pricked to death on a thorn bush since the beginning of creation. Esther Rabba 9:2.

[3] In this passage, Resh Lakish also tells of the unspeakable cruelties which Haman describes the Jews as having committed, such as the war of liquidation against Amalek. Esther Rabba 7:13. Elsewhere, the rabbis suggested that various aspects of the Jewish tradition rendered the Jews undesirable as citizens by, for example, not working on the Sabbath, and therefore failing to pay their fair share of the tax burden. Megilla 13b. Similarly, according to R. Hisda and Raba ben R. Huna: "What is Mt. Sinai? The mountain from which came the hostility [sin'a] of the idolaters." Shabbat 89a. Cf. Jerusalem Gittin 5:7, which argues that the Romans had a tradition that the Jews had killed their national progenitor. The relevance to Christian anti-Semitism is obvious.

[4] Composed in 1905 by the Czar's secret service and still a best-selling work in the Arab world, *The Protocols of the Elders of Zion* is one of the most notorious of anti-Semitic works, claiming to contain the directives for a secret Jewish conspiracy to undermine the governments of the world.

⁵ Esther Rabba 7:23, on the verses Genesis 27:41, Exodus 1:22, Esther 3:13 and Psalms 2:2. The rabbis go further, arguing that Haman's end on the gallows is intrinsic to creation. Esther Rabba 9:2; Hullin 139b.

## CHAPTER 10

¹ "For what good are sackcloth and ashes without prayer?" Esther Rabba 10:9. See discussion in Chapter 23.

² "By the merit of the righteous women of that generation were the Jews redeemed from Egypt." Sota 11b.

³ Exodus Rabba 1:26.

⁴ Cf. Vladimir Jabotinsky: "For there is no friendship in politics: There is pressure. What tips the balance one way or another is not whether the ruler is good or bad, but the degree of pressure exerted by his subjects. If pressure is exerted solely by our opponents, with no counter-pressure applied by us, then whatever is done in Palestine will be against us, even if the hed of the government will be called Balfour, or Wedgwood, or even Theodor Herzl…. For no reformation in national conditions is attained without pressure and struggle. And whoever lacks the stamina, courage, ability and desire to fight, will not be able to achieve even the smallest adjustment [of these conditions] on our behalf." *Do'ar Hayom*, May 17, 1929. This quotation is found in Benjamin Netanyahu's essay on the subject, "The Question of Jewish Power," in *A Place among the Nations: Israel and the World* (New York: Bantam, 1993), pp. 382–383.

⁵ Exodus 3:11–12. Cf. Shabbat 88a.

## CHAPTER 11

¹ R. Sheshet also infers the ongoing nature of Mordechai's protest. Megilla 16a.

² Exodus 5:21.

³ Genesis Rabba 5:14.

⁴ It is no coincidence, either, that when the God of the Jews finally brings ruin upon Pharaoh, it is in the form of such ostensibly insignificant opponents as frogs, lice, flies, sores, hailstones and locusts—that is, grasshoppers. (But cf. Exodus Rabba 11:4, where R. Judah understands one of the plagues to be wild animals.) That the Egyptians were brought low by precisely those kinds of opponents which they thought the Jews to be is clear from the fact that the account of their increase in Egypt is referred to with the word *vayishretzu*—"they swarmed," as the narrative says: "they swarmed and multiplied and grew strong, and the land was filled with them." Exodus 1:7.

⁵ Genesis 43:32, 46:34.

⁶ Genesis 41:14, 41:28–36, 41:42, 41:43, 41:45, 42:15, 50:2, 50:26.

⁷ Genesis 41:51.

⁸ Genesis 41:37.

⁹ Genesis 39:8–9.

¹⁰ Genesis 45:5–8.

¹¹ Genesis 45:9–11.

¹² Genesis 50:20–21.

¹³ Amenemhet I, quoted in Harold Nicolson, *Monarchy* (London: Weidenfeld and Nicolson, 1962), p. 20. Amenemhet I served as vizier to the last Pharaoh of the Eleventh Egyptian Dynasty, whom he probably overthrew in order to become the founder of the Twelfth Dynasty. He ruled Egypt from 2000–1970 BCE, approximately 200 years before the time of Abraham.

¹⁴ The rabbis belittled a similar position by imagining what the Romans would say when brought before God on the day of judgment: "The Holy One, may he be blessed, will then say to them: How have you occupied yourselves? They will reply: 'Ruler of the Universe, we have established many marketplaces, we have built many bathhouses, we have accumulated much gold and silver, and all this did we do only for the sake of Israel, so that they might be able to occupy themselves with the study of Tora.' The Holy One, may he be blessed, will then answer: 'You foolish ones among peoples. All that you have done, you have done only in order to satisfy your own desires.'" Avoda Zara 2b.

[15] Genesis 47:29–31.

[16] Genesis 45:19.

[17] Genesis 46:1.

[18] Cf. "Why did he not call Reuben or Judah? Reuben was the firstborn and Judah was king, yet he disregarded them and called Joseph. Why? Because Joseph had the means of fulfilling his wish." Genesis Rabba 96:5.

[19] Genesis 50:4–5.

[20] The Moses story is written as a mirror image of Joseph's failure: When Moses approaches Pharaoh two centuries later with the request that the Jews be allowed to go up from Egypt for a religious rite, he refuses Pharaoh's offer to go without the children and herds. Exodus 10:9–12, 24–26.

[21] Genesis Rabba 100:4.

[22] Genesis Rabba 96:1.

[23] Genesis 50:24–25.

[24] Exodus Rabba 20:19.


CHAPTER 12


[1] Daniel 3:16–18.

[2] Daniel 6:7–11.

[3] Apparently Artaxerxes I, who ruled Persia from 465–424 BCE, immediately after Xerxes I. It was during his reign and under his protection, in 432, that the law of Moses was declared to be the law in a reconstructed Jerusalem under the authority of Ezra.

[4] Nehemia 1:1–3.

[5] Nehemia 2:19.

[6] Ezra 4:6–22.

[7] Nehemia 1:4–11.

[8] Nehemia 2:6. Cf. Moses' decision to take leave of Jethro's flocks after forty years or more of service: "Moses went back to Jethro, his father-in-law, and said to him: 'Let me go, I pray, and return to my brothers in Egypt, and see whether they are still alive.' Jethro said to Moses: 'Go in peace.'" Exodus 4:18.

[9] The biblical narrative does not seem to back up Joseph on this point: Unlike his forefathers, Joseph is never depicted as being spoken to by God. What understanding he does have of God's intentions seems to come from his faith and his dreams—which, while containing important truths, are problematic as well. Perhaps Joseph himself should have suspected this because they depict him, for example, as having his father, mother and brothers bow down to the ground before him, although his mother had long since died. Genesis 37:9–10. As it turns out, Joseph's brothers do end up bowing before him over and over, and referring to themselves as Joseph's servants as well, but his father Jacob never does either of these things—at least not literally. Genesis 42:6; 43:26, 28; 44:14, 16; 50:18. But perhaps his father does bow before Joseph. According to R. Joshua of Siknin in the name of R. Levi: "Jacob, too, when he was about to die, humbled himself before Joseph and said to him: 'Now if I have found favor in your eyes....'" Genesis Rabba 96:3 on Genesis 47:29.

[10] See, for example, Menahot 53b.

[11] Cf. Daniel 6:13–17, however, in which Darius tries to rescue Daniel from death by the decree he himself has issued, but is prevented by his advisers.

[12] Psalms 115:5–8, 135:16–18.

## CHAPTER 13

[1] The rabbis handed down prayers which Esther and Mordechai were supposed to have said during the crisis. Esther Rabba 8:6. Some Christian versions of the Bible incorporate the prayer of Esther into the narrative itself.

[2] "It came to pass ... that the wine was before him, and I took up the wine and gave it to the king, and I had never looked sad in front of him before then. The king said to me: 'Why is your face fallen, seeing that you are not ill? This can be nothing other than sorrow of the heart,' and I was

exceedingly afraid. And I said to the king: 'May the king live forever. Why should my face not be fallen, when the city, the place where my ancestors are buried, lies waste, and its gates are consumed with fire?'" Nehemia 2:1–3.

## CHAPTER 15

[1] According to R. Huna, Megilla 19a, and R. Eliezer of Modi'im, Megilla 15b.

[2] According to Abaye and Raba. Megilla 15b. See also Esther Rabba 10:1.

[3] Megilla 16a.

[4] According to R. Nachman in the name of R. Mana, Jerusalem Avoda Zara 4:7.

## CHAPTER 16

[1] Ahashverosh's revelation is presaged by a similar scene in the Joseph tale, in which Potiphar removes Joseph from administering his household when he comes to believe, unjustly, that his servant would take his wife from him. Although Potiphar hands control of all his affairs to Joseph, he presumes that he is still in charge so long as he feels secure in certain personal areas: as the narrative says, "He left all that he had in Joseph's hand, and he knew not what he had except for the bread he ate." Genesis 39:6. The rabbis supposed this to be a euphemism for his wife. Genesis Rabba 86:6. (The use of bread as a metaphor for sex also appears in Proverbs: "By means of a harlot, a man is brought to a piece of bread...." Proverbs 6:26.) But when Potiphar's wife claims that Joseph has made advances, the entire fiction collapses, and the master of the house is left feeling that all he has is truly in Joseph's hands, and not his own. From here Joseph's path to the dungeon is assured.

[2] Thus the rabbis compared Haman to the snake in Eden: "They set their eyes on that which was not proper for them. Therefore what they sought was not granted to them, and what they possessed was taken from them." Sota 9b.

## CHAPTER 17

[1] Genesis 40:14–15.

[2] Genesis 41:9–13.

## CHAPTER 18

[1] Haman is hanged on 16 Nisan, three days after his letters of extermination are sent out. Esther does not approach the king the second time until 23 Sivan, the day Mordechai's letters are promulgated.

[2] In Memuchan's proposed degradation of Vashti, (1:19) in Haman's initiative to have the Jews destroyed, (3:9) and in Esther's request for a renewed assault on the enemies of the Jews after the first day of battle. (9:13) A similar formulation appears where the king's youths suggest that Ahashverosh select a new queen. (2:4)

[3] "It is not, therefore, necessary for a prince to have all the above-named qualities [mercy, faith, integrity, humanity, and religion], but it is very necessary to seem to have them." Niccolò Machiavelli, *The Prince* (New York: Random House, The Modern Library, 1950), p. 65.

## CHAPTER 19

[1] From 23 Sivan to 13 Adar is a period of eight months and twenty days on the Jewish calendar, and is somewhat less on the modern, solar calendar.

[2] This is apparent from the well-developed anti-Semitic theory Haman presents the king to justify genocide, as well as the king's agreeable reaction (3:8–11); the fear of people of "Jewish descent" pervasive among Haman's advisers (6:13); the trouble members of the court make for Mordechai upon learning that he is a Jew (3:4); and his admonitions to Esther not to disclose her descent in the palace for fear that it will endanger her well-being and position (2:10). See discussion in Chapter 9.

[3] "Natural law" is a philosopher's term referring to moral principles which inhere in nature and are binding on men. Thus it may be the law of nature (i.e., "the law of the jungle") that men will always desire to steal from one another, but the natural law (i.e., the natural moral law) therefore dictates that man should not steal.

[4] "[M]any have imagined republics and principalities which have never been seen or known to exist in reality; for how we live is so far removed from how we ought to live, that he who abandons what is done for what ought to be done, will rather learn to bring about his own ruin than his preservation." Machiavelli, p. 56.

[5] 1 Kings 21:1–19.

[6] "So I hated life…. And I hated all my labor in which I had labored under the sun, because I must leave it to the man who will come after me. And who knows whether he will be a wise man or a fool, yet he will have rule over all my labor in which I have labored, and in which I have shown myself wise under the sun." Ecclesiastes 2:17–19.

[7] Jeremiah 8:10.

[8] The rabbis describe a dream of Mordechai's in which he and Haman are depicted as dragons. Esther Rabba 8:5. This dream appears as part of the narrative in some Christian editions of the book of Esther.


CHAPTER 20


[1] The description in the narrative begins with the consequences, and then works its way back to the cause. It must be read in reverse order to see the sequence of events.

[2] Machiavelli, p. 9.

[3] Machiavelli, p. 60.

[4] Daniel 6:7–25.

CHAPTER 21

[1] Isaiah 2:4; Jeremiah 31:30–33. For a discussion of the magnitude of the Jews' victory in Esther, see Chapter 5, note 3.

[2] Ecclesiastes 7:16.

[3] Ecclesiastes 7:17. R. Mani's account appears in Yoma 22b.

[4] Ecclesiastes 7:16.

[5] Leviticus 19:2. Cf. "You shall be a kingdom of priests and a holy people." Exodus 19:6. Similarly: "The commandments were given only to purify man therewith." Genesis Rabba 44:1.

[6] Deuteronomy 16:20.

[7] I Chronicles 22:8. Cf. David: "With the pure should you show yourself pure, and with the perverse should you show yourself subtle." II Samuel 22:27.

[8] Avoda Zara 18a.

[9] According to the subsequent discussion, the daughter manages to escape the house of shame, but this hardly alters the point. Avoda Zara 17b. Cf. Avoda Zara 18a, where R. Hanina's Tora study includes preaching in public, making him somewhat more of an activist than might be inferred from this account.

[10] Sota 36b. See also the opinion of R. Judah ben R. Hanina. Brachot 20a, 55b.

[11] Sanhedrin 20b. See discussion in Chapter 8.

[12] Exodus 19:6.

[13] For example, Avot 2:3. But cf. Avot 3:2.

[14] "Now an action done from duty [i.e., morality] must wholly exclude the influence of inclination, and with it every object of the will, so that nothing remains which can determine the will except objectively the law ... that I should follow this law even to the thwarting of all my inclinations.... [But] although many things are done in conformity with what duty prescribes, it is nevertheless always doubtful whether they are done strictly from duty, so as to have moral worth.... [Y]et whether this or that takes

place [in reality] is not the question ... [R]eason itself, independent of all experience, ordains what ought to take place, that accordingly actions of which perhaps the world has hitherto never been given an example ... are nevertheless inflexibly commanded by reason...." Imanuel Kant, *Fundamental Principles of the Metaphysic of Morals*, T.K. Abbott, trans. (Buffalo: Prometheus, 1987), pp. 25, 33, 35.

[15]  See Chapter 7, note 16.

[16]  Genesis 6:5. Noah is introduced as being righteous "in his generations," apparently because no one else was in his time. Genesis 6:9.

[17]  Genesis 19:1f. Lot is the proverbial righteous man to whom Abraham is referring in his argument with God in the preceding passage. Genesis 18:23–33.

[18]  Genesis 29:13–31:55. Jacob is referred to as "completely righteous" by the rabbis, Ketubot 111a; Numbers Rabba 14:5.

[19]  Megilla 13b. A parable of R. Isaac Napaha suggests that Mordechai should not be compared to Jacob but to Moses, but the line of argument is the same. He tells that when death is decreed against the Jews of Persia, the prophet Elijah runs in search of assistance for the Jews of Persia. "Abraham, Isaac and Jacob then said to him: 'If they have violated the law of the Holy One, may he be blessed, and their fate is sealed, what can we do?' Then Elijah went to Moses, saying: 'Faithful shepherd, how many times did you stand in the breach for Israel and avert their fate so that they should not be destroyed?' ... Moses said to him: 'Is there a virtuous man in that generation? ... Go and speak to him, so that he should stand and pray there, and I here, that we may together seek mercy from the Holy One, may he be blessed.'" Esther Rabba 7:13. Although the portrayal of the patriarchs is perhaps a bit unfair, the point must be well taken. For Abraham, Isaac and Jacob, worldly though they may have been in some respects, were fundamentally men of purity, whose lives were led in the hill country of Canaan, elevated both literally and figuratively, in order to be able to avoid just such direct confrontations with empire and idolatry as are the subject of the book of Esther. When it comes to delivering the Jewish nation, mired in the foulness and error of the world, they are of a type which can offer little. For such tasks one needs a man such as Moses—who grew up among the abominations of Pharaoh's court, who kills the Egyptian that justice be done, who confronts Pharaoh face to face where Abraham would have told a lie and slipped away, who rains plague and slaughter on Egypt and brings its armies to ruin. Such is a man who can contend with God over the fate of the Jewish people and

even avert that fate once it has supposedly been "sealed," because he is also a man of morality, whose acts fly in the face of fate and prevail.

²⁰ Genesis 50:20.

²¹ Deuteronomy 7:2–5, 8:25–26. See also: 12:29–31, 13:7–19. Cf. Numbers 33:55–56.

²² Daniel 6:25.

²³ Herodotus, p. 501. Even among the early Hebrews, Reuben was willing to argue for such an outcome when trying to convince his father to allow the brothers to take Benjamin down to Egypt with them: "Reuben spoke to his father, saying: 'Slay my two sons if I do not bring him back to you....'" Genesis 42:37.

²⁴ Ecclesiastes 7:15–16. The ironic usage of the word "righteous" here confuses the terms some. Kohelet achieves his effect by placing righteousness and purity on the same scale, as we tend to do, thus producing a category of "over-righteousness" for excessive purity, with the right amount of righteousness being in the balance between the extremes.

²⁵ Esther 9:10, 15, 16.

²⁶ Herodotus, pp. 258–259. Under Darius' rule, Herodotus reports that the annual income of the Persian empire was 9,540 talents of silver, plus the equivalent of another 4,680 talents levied in gold. The tribute of a relatively large province such as Egypt was 700 talents of silver annually.

²⁷ In trying to persuade Esther to act, Mordechai also sees fit to make mention of "the money that Haman had offered to pay into the royal treasuries for the Jews, to have them destroyed." Esther 4:7.

²⁸ 1 Samuel 15:9, 24.

²⁹ 1 Samuel 15:2, 18, 33.

³⁰ See discussion in Chapter 19.


CHAPTER  22


¹ The Bible does, however, refer to a number of fasts which were instituted not long before the time of Mordechai and Esther to mark the

destruction of Jerusalem in 586 BCE: "The fast of the fourth [month] and the fast of the fifth and the fast of the seventh and the fast of the tenth will be unto the house of Judah joy and gladness, and good times...." Zephania 8:19.

² The destruction of the northern kingdom of Israel by the Assyrians took place in 722 BCE. The southern kingdom, Judah, of which Mordechai's tribe of Benjamin was a part, was destroyed by the Babylonians in 586 BCE.

³ Shabbat 88a.

⁴ In the book of Nehemia, describing events some forty years after those in Esther, the Jews of Jerusalem actually take upon themselves an oath to perform the commandments of the Tora. Nehemia 10:1f.

⁵ Esther Rabba 10:10.


## CHAPTER 23

¹ "'Whither is God?' he cried; 'I will tell you. *We have killed him*—you and I. All of us are his murderers. But how did we do this? How could we drink up the sea? Who gave us the sponge to wipe away the entire horizon? What were we doing when we unchained this earth from its sun? Whither is it moving now? Away from all suns? Are we not plunging continually? Backward, sideward, forward, in all directions? Is there still any up or down? Are we not straying as through an infinite nothing? Do we not feel the breath of empty space? Has it not become colder? Is not night continually closing in on us? Do we not need to light lanterns in the morning? Do we hear nothing as yet of the noise of the gravediggers who are burying God? Do we smell nothing as yet of the divine decomposition? Gods, too, decompose. God is dead. God remains dead. And we have killed him.'" Friedrich Nietzsche, *The Gay Science*, Walter Kaufmann, trans. (Vintage Books: New York, 1974), section 125.

² Jeremiah 4:23–26.

³ Deuteronomy 31:17.

⁴ Shabbat 88a.

⁵ Jeremiah 7:22–25.

[6] Ketubot 110b.

[7] Exodus 6:6.

[8] Genesis 32:29.

[9] Passover falls on 15 Nisan, the day Esther first approaches Ahashverosh to invite him to her banquet that afternoon. Since she had requested that the Jews fast for her from 13 Nisan, this means that their seder night went by without the central aspects of the commemoration familiar to us. It is actually unclear to what degree Passover was being practiced among the Jews at the time, since the narrative reports that it had only been reinstated in the time of King Josiah, in the decades before the exile, having apparently been substantially unobserved before then. "And the king commanded all the people, saying: 'Keep the Passover to the Eternal your God, as it is written in the book of the covenant.' Surely no such Passover was held from the days of the judges who judged Israel, nor in all the days of the kings of Israel, nor the kings of Judah; but in the eighteenth year of King Josiah was this Passover held to the Eternal in Jerusalem." II Kings 23:21–23. In any case, the willingness to take responsibility for such decisions is remarkable. It bears mentioning that Nehemia also goes before the king seeking deliverance for his people in the month of Nisan. Nehemia 2:1. There is an obviously related saying of the rabbis: "In Nisan they were redeemed, and in Nisan they will be redeemed in the time to come." According to R. Eliezer, Rosh Hashana 11a; R. Joshua, Rosh Hashana 11b. But this is not true in Esther's case. The king essentially turns down her request, and the subject is not brought up again until the month of Sivan.

[10] Deuteronomy 13:1.

[11] The reference is to the public readings of the book of Esther on Purim, but the point is that all the legal provisions of Purim are added to the law. Megilla 14a.

[12] Yoma 29a.

[13] Shochar Tov 22.

[14] The very name of Esther, a star—"Ishtar," goddess of heaven to the Persians, or "aster," a star in Greek—suggests at the outset that the Persians may rely on the stars as they please, but that one of the Jews may herself be the decisive star they have simply failed to include in their calculations. The rabbis understood the plot of Esther to be making a mockery of the belief

that astrology, even if it were a true science, could be the ultimate arbiter of history. They envisioned Haman in his vain efforts to learn of a fortuitous time to attack the Jews by casting lots: "Then he turned to examining the signs of the zodiac: ... On reaching Pisces, the sign of the fishes, which shines in the month of Adar, he found no merit in it and rejoiced, saying, 'Adar has no merit and its sign has no merit, and, what is more, Moses their master died in Adar.' He did not know, however, that Moses died on the first of Adar but was also born on the first of Adar. He said: 'Just as fishes swallow one another, so will I swallow them.' The Holy One, may he be blessed, said to him: 'Fool, sometimes fishes swallow and sometimes they are swallowed.'" Esther Rabba 7:11.

[15] Seforno on Deuteronomy 11:22. Cf. Rashi, ad loc.: "He is merciful, and you should be merciful; he performs kind deeds, and you should perform kind deeds." Similarly, the Talmud on Deuteronomy 13:5 brings the opinion of R. Hama ben R. Hanina: "What is the meaning of the verse 'You will walk after the Eternal your God'? Is it then possible for a man to walk after God's presence, for has it not been said: 'For the Eternal your God is a devouring fire' (Deuteronomy 4:24)? But it means to walk after the ways of the Holy One, may he be blessed. As he clothes the naked, for it is written: 'God the Eternal made for Adam and for his wife coats of skin and clothed them,' (Genesis 3:21) so too should you clothe the naked. The Holy One, may he be blessed, visited the sick, for it is written: 'The Eternal appeared to him by the oaks of Mamre' (Genesis 18:1; see Rashi, ad loc.), so should you also visit the sick. The Holy One, may he be blessed, comforted mourners, for it is written: 'It came to pass after the death of Abraham that God blessed his son Isaac,' (Genesis 25:11) and so too should you comfort mourners. As the Holy One, may he be blessed, buried the dead, for it is written: 'He buried him [Moses] in the valley,' (Deuteronomy 34:6) so too should you bury the dead." Sota 14a.

[16] The complete passage reads: "For if you diligently keep all of this commandment which I instruct you to perform, to love the Eternal your God, to walk in all his ways and to embrace him: Then will the Eternal drive out all these nations from before you, and you will inherit nations greater and mightier than yourselves. Every place where the sole of your foot steps will be yours, from the wilderness and Lebanon, from the river, the Euphrates, to the last sea will be your border. No man will be able to stand before you, for the fear of you and the dread of you will the Eternal your God cause to fall on all the land on which you walk, as He has said to you." Deuteronomy 11:22–25. See also 10:12–13.

<sup>17</sup> The Hebrew word *rov* can be understood to mean only a majority. Megilla 16b.

<sup>18</sup> "When the news [of the massacre on the Sabbath] reached Matityahu and his compatriots, they mourned bitterly for the victims and said to one another: 'If we all do as our brothers have done and refuse to fight the pagans to defend our lives and institutions, they will only destroy us the sooner from the earth.' Then and there they came to this decision: 'If anyone attacks us on the Sabbath, whoever he may be, we will resist him. We cannot all be killed, as were our brothers in hiding.'" 1 Maccabees 2:39–41.

<sup>19</sup> In a famous passage from the Talmud, R. Joshua rejects the use of supernatural proofs in legal argumentation by relying on Deuteronomy, which says: "For this commandment which I command you this day is not hidden from you, nor is it far off. It is not in heaven, that you should say: Who will go up to heaven for us and bring it to us, that we may hear it and do it? ... But the word is very near to you, in your mouth and in your heart, that you may do it." (Deuteronomy 30:11–14) R. Jeremiah argues that decisions are properly made by the majority, and that signs and wonders have no weight, because "we pay no attention to voices from heaven." Baba Metzia 59b.

<sup>20</sup> Megilla 16a.

<sup>21</sup> Machiavelli, p. 91.

<sup>22</sup> Machiavelli, p. 94.

<sup>23</sup> The Hebrew *makom aher* ("another place") has been read by some to refer to God because the word *makom* has been an accepted designation for God. But then what can possibly be the meaning of the other word, *aher*? Cf. Esther Rabba 3:10, where references to "the king" in the narrative are understood to refer to the true King, to God. Since Ahashverosh, in his role as a human king, is also supposed to search out the correct law and execute it, even in the view of the Persians, such a reading has some interesting effects.

<sup>24</sup> Megilla 15a.

<sup>25</sup> Isaiah 8:10.

<sup>26</sup> The complete passage reads: "When this decree was signed and delivered to Haman, he and all his associates began rejoicing. As it happened, Mordechai

was just then walking in front of him. He saw three children coming from school and ran after them. So they followed Mordechai to see what he would ask the children. When Mordechai came up to the children, he asked one of them to repeat the verse he had just learned. He said: 'Be not afraid of the sudden terror, neither of the destruction of the wicked when it comes.' (Proverbs 3:25) The second followed, saying … 'Take counsel together, and it will be brought to naught. Speak the word, and it will not stand, for God is with us.' (Isaiah 8:10) Then the third spoke up with the verse: 'Even to old age am I the same, and even to silver hairs will I carry you. I have made, and I will bear. I will carry, and I will deliver.' (Isaiah 46:4) When Mordechai heard this he smiled and was exceedingly glad. Said Haman to him: 'Why are you so glad over the words of these children?' He replied: 'Because of the good tidings they have given me, that I need not fear the evil design which you have formed against us.' Thereupon the evil Haman grew angry and said: 'I will lay my hand on these children first of all.'" Esther Rabba 7:13.

[27] The passage replaced by an ellipsis reads: "At that moment, the compassion of the Holy One, may he be blessed, was stirred, and he rose from the throne of judgment and rested on the throne of mercy, and said: 'What is this loud noise I hear as the bleating of kids and lambs?' Moses our teacher stood before the Holy One, may he be blessed, and said: 'Ruler of the Universe, they are neither kids nor lambs, but the little ones of your people who have been keeping a fast now for three days and three nights, whom the enemy plans to slaughter tomorrow like kids and lambs.' At that moment the Holy One, may he be blessed, took the letters containing their doom which were signed with a seal of clay and tore them, in so doing bringing fright upon Ahashverosh in the night, as it says: 'That night,' etc." Esther Rabba 9:4 on Esther 6:1. Moses speaks for the children who are to die as he was such a one himself.

[28] That gentiles may serve as redeemers for Israel is suggested in the Bible itself, in Isaiah, where Cyrus, king of Persia and Medes, is referred to as God's anointed: "So says the Eternal to his anointed, to Cyrus, whose right hand have I held, that I might subdue nations before him…. For the sake of Jacob, my servant, and Israel, my chosen, I have called you by your name and consecrated you, though you did not know me…." Isaiah 45:1–4. Cyrus destroyed the Babylonian empire, and ordered that the Temple in Jerusalem be rebuilt at his own expense.

[29] "In the beginning, God created the heaven and the earth. And the earth was formless and void, and the darkness was on the face of the abyss. And God's wind moved over the surface of the waters. And God said: Let

there be light...." Genesis 1:1–3. The Hebrew word for wind is the same as the word for spirit. For man living on the sea in ships, cf. Baba Batra 73af.; Nietzsche, *Gay Science*, section 124.

[30] This idea is implicit in Machiavelli, but becomes an explicit and crucial theme in Nietzsche, *Gay Science*, sections 283, 289. Cf. especially 337. For Nietzsche, the meaning of humaneness itself is to be a sun, which dies at the end of its life, but which continues giving off light even at sunset, so that "even the poorest fisherman is still rowing with golden oars."

# Scriptural and Rabbinic References

## JUDGES

## I SAMUEL

## DEUTERONOMY

304 THE DAWN

# INDEX

אֲלֵיהֶ֑ם קִיְּמ֣וּ וְקִבְּל֣וּ הַיְּהוּדִים֩ ׀ עֲלֵיהֶ֨ם ׀ וְעַל־זַרְעָ֜ם וְעַ֣ל כז
כָּל־הַנִּלְוִ֣ים עֲלֵיהֶ֗ם וְלֹ֤א יַעֲבוֹר֙ לִהְי֣וֹת עֹשִׂ֔ים אֵ֥ת שְׁנֵ֖י
הַיָּמִ֣ים הָאֵ֑לֶּה כִּכְתָבָ֖ם וְכִזְמַנָּ֑ם בְּכָל־שָׁנָ֥ה וְשָׁנָֽה: וְהַיָּמִ֣ים כח
הָאֵ֡לֶּה נִזְכָּרִים֩ וְנַעֲשִׂ֨ים בְּכָל־דּ֤וֹר וָדוֹר֙ מִשְׁפָּחָ֣ה וּמִשְׁפָּחָ֔ה
מְדִינָ֥ה וּמְדִינָ֖ה וְעִ֣יר וָעִ֑יר וִימֵ֞י הַפּוּרִ֣ים הָאֵ֗לֶּה לֹ֤א יַֽעַבְרוּ֙
מִתּ֣וֹךְ הַיְּהוּדִ֔ים וְזִכְרָ֖ם לֹֽא־יָס֥וּף מִזַּרְעָֽם:

וַ֠תִּכְתֹּב אֶסְתֵּ֨ר הַמַּלְכָּ֧ה בַת־אֲבִיחַ֛יִל וּמָרְדֳּכַ֥י הַיְּהוּדִ֖י כט
אֶת־כָּל־תֹּ֑קֶף לְקַיֵּ֗ם אֵ֣ת אִגֶּ֧רֶת הַפֻּרִ֛ים הַזֹּ֖את הַשֵּׁנִֽית:
וַיִּשְׁלַ֨ח סְפָרִ֜ים אֶל־כָּל־הַיְּהוּדִ֗ים אֶל־שֶׁ֤בַע וְעֶשְׂרִים֙ וּמֵאָ֣ה ל
מְדִינָ֔ה מַלְכ֖וּת אֲחַשְׁוֵר֑וֹשׁ דִּבְרֵ֥י שָׁל֖וֹם וֶאֱמֶֽת: לְקַיֵּ֡ם אֶת־ לא
יְמֵי֩ הַפֻּרִ֨ים הָאֵ֜לֶּה בִּזְמַנֵּיהֶ֗ם כַּאֲשֶׁר֩ קִיַּ֨ם עֲלֵיהֶ֜ם מָרְדֳּכַ֣י
הַיְּהוּדִי֮ וְאֶסְתֵּ֣ר הַמַּלְכָּה֒ וְכַאֲשֶׁ֛ר קִיְּמ֥וּ עַל־נַפְשָׁ֖ם וְעַל־
זַרְעָ֑ם דִּבְרֵ֥י הַצּוֹמ֖וֹת וְזַֽעֲקָתָֽם: וּמַאֲמַ֣ר אֶסְתֵּ֔ר קִיַּ֕ם דִּבְרֵ֖י לג
הַפֻּרִ֣ים הָאֵ֑לֶּה וְנִכְתָּ֖ב בַּסֵּֽפֶר:            וַיָּ֩שֶׂם֩ הַמֶּ֨לֶךְ ו א

°אחשרש ׀ מַ֤ס עַל־הָאָ֙רֶץ֙ וְאִיֵּ֣י הַיָּ֔ם: וְכָל־מַעֲשֵׂ֤ה תָקְפּוֹ֙ ב
וּגְב֣וּרָת֔וֹ וּפָרָשַׁת֙ גְּדֻלַּ֣ת מָרְדֳּכַ֔י אֲשֶׁ֥ר גִּדְּל֖וֹ הַמֶּ֑לֶךְ הֲלוֹא־
הֵ֣ם כְּתוּבִ֗ים עַל־סֵ֙פֶר֙ דִּבְרֵ֣י הַיָּמִ֔ים לְמַלְכֵ֖י מָדַ֥י וּפָרָֽס: כִּ֣י ׀ ג
מָרְדֳּכַ֣י הַיְּהוּדִ֗י מִשְׁנֶה֙ לַמֶּ֣לֶךְ אֲחַשְׁוֵר֔וֹשׁ וְגָדוֹל֙ לַיְּהוּדִ֔ים
וְרָצ֖וּי לְרֹ֣ב אֶחָ֑יו דֹּרֵ֥שׁ טוֹב֙ לְעַמּ֔וֹ וְדֹבֵ֥ר שָׁל֖וֹם לְכָל־זַרְעֽוֹ:

יא °אֲחַשְׁוֵרוֹשׁ ק׳

וְאֵת עֲשֶׂרֶת בְּנֵי־הָמָן בִּשְׁאָר מְדִינוֹת הַמֶּלֶךְ מֶה עָשׂוּ
יג וּמַה־שְּׁאֵלָתֵךְ וְיִנָּתֵן לָךְ וּמַה־בַּקָּשָׁתֵךְ עוֹד וְתֵעָשׂ: וַתֹּאמֶר
אֶסְתֵּר אִם־עַל־הַמֶּלֶךְ טוֹב יִנָּתֵן גַּם־מָחָר לַיְּהוּדִים אֲשֶׁר
בְּשׁוּשָׁן לַעֲשׂוֹת כְּדָת הַיּוֹם וְאֵת עֲשֶׂרֶת בְּנֵי־הָמָן יִתְלוּ
יד עַל־הָעֵץ: וַיֹּאמֶר הַמֶּלֶךְ לְהֵעָשׂוֹת כֵּן וַתִּנָּתֵן דָּת בְּשׁוּשָׁן
טו וְאֵת עֲשֶׂרֶת בְּנֵי־הָמָן תָּלוּ: וַיִּקָּהֲלוּ °הַיְּהוּדִיִּים אֲשֶׁר־
בְּשׁוּשָׁן גַּם בְּיוֹם אַרְבָּעָה עָשָׂר לְחֹדֶשׁ אֲדָר וַיַּהַרְגוּ
בְּשׁוּשָׁן שְׁלֹשׁ מֵאוֹת אִישׁ וּבַבִּזָּה לֹא שָׁלְחוּ אֶת־יָדָם:
טז וּשְׁאָר הַיְּהוּדִים אֲשֶׁר בִּמְדִינוֹת הַמֶּלֶךְ נִקְהֲלוּ | וְעָמֹד עַל־
נַפְשָׁם וְנוֹחַ מֵאֹיְבֵיהֶם וְהָרֹג בְּשֹׂנְאֵיהֶם חֲמִשָּׁה וְשִׁבְעִים
יז אֶלֶף וּבַבִּזָּה לֹא שָׁלְחוּ אֶת־יָדָם: בְּיוֹם־שְׁלֹשָׁה עָשָׂר
לְחֹדֶשׁ אֲדָר וְנוֹחַ בְּאַרְבָּעָה עָשָׂר בּוֹ וְעָשֹׂה אֹתוֹ יוֹם
יח מִשְׁתֶּה וְשִׂמְחָה: °וְהַיְּהוּדִיִּים אֲשֶׁר־בְּשׁוּשָׁן נִקְהֲלוּ
בִּשְׁלֹשָׁה עָשָׂר בּוֹ וּבְאַרְבָּעָה עָשָׂר בּוֹ וְנוֹחַ בַּחֲמִשָּׁה
יט עָשָׂר בּוֹ וְעָשֹׂה אֹתוֹ יוֹם מִשְׁתֶּה וְשִׂמְחָה: עַל־כֵּן
הַיְּהוּדִים °הַפְּרוֹזִים הַיֹּשְׁבִים בְּעָרֵי הַפְּרָזוֹת עֹשִׂים אֵת
יוֹם אַרְבָּעָה עָשָׂר לְחֹדֶשׁ אֲדָר שִׂמְחָה וּמִשְׁתֶּה וְיוֹם טוֹב
כ וּמִשְׁלֹחַ מָנוֹת אִישׁ לְרֵעֵהוּ: וַיִּכְתֹּב מָרְדֳּכַי אֶת־הַדְּבָרִים
הָאֵלֶּה וַיִּשְׁלַח סְפָרִים אֶל־כָּל־הַיְּהוּדִים אֲשֶׁר בְּכָל־
כא מְדִינוֹת הַמֶּלֶךְ אֲחַשְׁוֵרוֹשׁ הַקְּרוֹבִים וְהָרְחוֹקִים: לְקַיֵּם
עֲלֵיהֶם לִהְיוֹת עֹשִׂים אֵת יוֹם אַרְבָּעָה עָשָׂר לְחֹדֶשׁ אֲדָר
כב וְאֵת יוֹם־חֲמִשָּׁה עָשָׂר בּוֹ בְּכָל־שָׁנָה וְשָׁנָה: כַּיָּמִים אֲשֶׁר־
נָחוּ בָהֶם הַיְּהוּדִים מֵאֹיְבֵיהֶם וְהַחֹדֶשׁ אֲשֶׁר נֶהְפַּךְ לָהֶם
מִיָּגוֹן לְשִׂמְחָה וּמֵאֵבֶל לְיוֹם טוֹב לַעֲשׂוֹת אוֹתָם יְמֵי
מִשְׁתֶּה וְשִׂמְחָה וּמִשְׁלֹחַ מָנוֹת אִישׁ לְרֵעֵהוּ וּמַתָּנוֹת
כג לָאֶבְיוֹנִים: וְקִבֵּל הַיְּהוּדִים אֵת אֲשֶׁר־הֵחֵלּוּ לַעֲשׂוֹת וְאֵת
כד אֲשֶׁר־כָּתַב מָרְדֳּכַי אֲלֵיהֶם: כִּי הָמָן בֶּן־הַמְּדָתָא הָאֲגָגִי
צֹרֵר כָּל־הַיְּהוּדִים חָשַׁב עַל־הַיְּהוּדִים לְאַבְּדָם וְהִפִּל פּוּר
כה הוּא הַגּוֹרָל לְהֻמָּם וּלְאַבְּדָם: וּבְבֹאָהּ לִפְנֵי הַמֶּלֶךְ אָמַר
עִם־הַסֵּפֶר יָשׁוּב מַחֲשַׁבְתּוֹ הָרָעָה אֲשֶׁר־חָשַׁב עַל־
כו הַיְּהוּדִים עַל־רֹאשׁוֹ וְתָלוּ אֹתוֹ וְאֶת־בָּנָיו עַל־הָעֵץ: עַל־כֵּן
קָרְאוּ לַיָּמִים הָאֵלֶּה פוּרִים עַל־שֵׁם הַפּוּר עַל־כֵּן עַל־כָּל־
דִּבְרֵי הָאִגֶּרֶת הַזֹּאת וּמָה־רָאוּ עַל־כָּכָה וּמָה הִגִּיעַ

טז וְשִׂמְחָה: לַיְּהוּדִים הָיְתָה אוֹרָה וְשִׂמְחָה וְשָׂשֹׂן וִיקָר:

יז וּבְכָל־מְדִינָה וּמְדִינָה וּבְכָל־עִיר וָעִיר מְקוֹם אֲשֶׁר דְּבַר־
הַמֶּלֶךְ וְדָתוֹ מַגִּיעַ שִׂמְחָה וְשָׂשֹׂן לַיְּהוּדִים מִשְׁתֶּה
וְיוֹם טוֹב וְרַבִּים מֵעַמֵּי הָאָרֶץ מִתְיַהֲדִים כִּי־נָפַל

ט א פַּחַד־הַיְּהוּדִים עֲלֵיהֶם: וּבִשְׁנֵים עָשָׂר חֹדֶשׁ הוּא־
חֹדֶשׁ אֲדָר בִּשְׁלוֹשָׁה עָשָׂר יוֹם בּוֹ אֲשֶׁר הִגִּיעַ דְּבַר־
הַמֶּלֶךְ וְדָתוֹ לְהֵעָשׂוֹת בַּיּוֹם אֲשֶׁר שִׂבְּרוּ אֹיְבֵי הַיְּהוּדִים
לִשְׁלוֹט בָּהֶם וְנַהֲפוֹךְ הוּא אֲשֶׁר יִשְׁלְטוּ הַיְּהוּדִים

ב הֵמָּה בְּשֹׂנְאֵיהֶם: נִקְהֲלוּ הַיְּהוּדִים בְּעָרֵיהֶם בְּכָל־מְדִינוֹת
הַמֶּלֶךְ אֲחַשְׁוֵרוֹשׁ לִשְׁלֹחַ יָד בִּמְבַקְשֵׁי רָעָתָם וְאִישׁ
לֹא־עָמַד לִפְנֵיהֶם כִּי־נָפַל פַּחְדָּם עַל־כָּל־הָעַמִּים:

ג וְכָל־שָׂרֵי הַמְּדִינוֹת וְהָאֲחַשְׁדַּרְפְּנִים וְהַפַּחוֹת
וְעֹשֵׂי הַמְּלָאכָה אֲשֶׁר לַמֶּלֶךְ מְנַשְּׂאִים אֶת־הַיְּהוּדִים

ד כִּי־נָפַל פַּחַד־מָרְדֳּכַי עֲלֵיהֶם: כִּי־גָדוֹל מָרְדֳּכַי
בְּבֵית הַמֶּלֶךְ וְשָׁמְעוֹ הוֹלֵךְ בְּכָל־הַמְּדִינוֹת כִּי־הָאִישׁ

ה מָרְדֳּכַי הוֹלֵךְ וְגָדוֹל: וַיַּכּוּ הַיְּהוּדִים בְּכָל־אֹיְבֵיהֶם
מַכַּת־חֶרֶב וְהֶרֶג וְאַבְדָן וַיַּעֲשׂוּ בְשֹׂנְאֵיהֶם כִּרְצוֹנָם:

ו וּבְשׁוּשַׁן הַבִּירָה הָרְגוּ הַיְּהוּדִים וְאַבֵּד חֲמֵשׁ מֵאוֹת

ז אִישׁ: וְאֵת|

פַּרְשַׁנְדָּתָא וְאֵת|

דַּלְפוֹן וְאֵת|

ח אַסְפָּתָא: וְאֵת|

פּוֹרָתָא וְאֵת|

אֲדַלְיָא וְאֵת|

ט אֲרִידָתָא: וְאֵת|

פַּרְמַשְׁתָּא וְאֵת|

אֲרִיסַי וְאֵת|

אֲרִידַי וְאֵת|

י וַיְזָתָא: עֲשֶׂרֶת
בְּנֵי הָמָן בֶּן־הַמְּדָתָא צֹרֵר הַיְּהוּדִים הָרָגוּ וּבַבִּזָּה לֹא

יא שָׁלְחוּ אֶת־יָדָם: בַּיּוֹם הַהוּא בָּא מִסְפַּר הַהֲרוּגִים בְּשׁוּשַׁן

יב הַבִּירָה לִפְנֵי הַמֶּלֶךְ: וַיֹּאמֶר הַמֶּלֶךְ לְאֶסְתֵּר הַמַּלְכָּה
בְּשׁוּשַׁן הַבִּירָה הָרְגוּ הַיְּהוּדִים וְאַבֵּד חֲמֵשׁ מֵאוֹת אִישׁ

הָמָן הָאֲגָגִי וְאֵת מַחֲשַׁבְתּוֹ אֲשֶׁר חָשַׁב עַל־הַיְּהוּדִים:

ד וַיּוֹשֶׁט הַמֶּלֶךְ לְאֶסְתֵּר אֵת שַׁרְבִט הַזָּהָב וַתָּקָם אֶסְתֵּר

ה וַתַּעֲמֹד לִפְנֵי הַמֶּלֶךְ: וַתֹּאמֶר אִם־עַל־הַמֶּלֶךְ טוֹב וְאִם־
מָצָאתִי חֵן לְפָנָיו וְכָשֵׁר הַדָּבָר לִפְנֵי הַמֶּלֶךְ וְטוֹבָה אֲנִי
בְּעֵינָיו יִכָּתֵב לְהָשִׁיב אֶת־הַסְּפָרִים מַחֲשֶׁבֶת הָמָן בֶּן־
הַמְּדָתָא הָאֲגָגִי אֲשֶׁר כָּתַב לְאַבֵּד אֶת־הַיְּהוּדִים אֲשֶׁר

ו בְּכָל־מְדִינוֹת הַמֶּלֶךְ: כִּי אֵיכָכָה אוּכַל וְרָאִיתִי בָּרָעָה
אֲשֶׁר־יִמְצָא אֶת־עַמִּי וְאֵיכָכָה אוּכַל וְרָאִיתִי בְּאָבְדַן

ז מוֹלַדְתִּי: וַיֹּאמֶר הַמֶּלֶךְ אֲחַשְׁוֵרֹשׁ לְאֶסְתֵּר
הַמַּלְכָּה וּלְמָרְדֳּכַי הַיְּהוּדִי הִנֵּה בֵית־הָמָן נָתַתִּי לְאֶסְתֵּר
וְאֹתוֹ תָּלוּ עַל־הָעֵץ עַל אֲשֶׁר־שָׁלַח יָדוֹ °בַּיְּהוּדִיים:

ח וְאַתֶּם כִּתְבוּ עַל־הַיְּהוּדִים כַּטּוֹב בְּעֵינֵיכֶם בְּשֵׁם הַמֶּלֶךְ
וְחִתְמוּ בְּטַבַּעַת הַמֶּלֶךְ כִּי־כְתָב אֲשֶׁר־נִכְתָּב בְּשֵׁם־הַמֶּלֶךְ

ט וְנַחְתּוֹם בְּטַבַּעַת הַמֶּלֶךְ אֵין לְהָשִׁיב: וַיִּקָּרְאוּ סֹפְרֵי־הַמֶּלֶךְ
בָּעֵת־הַהִיא בַּחֹדֶשׁ הַשְּׁלִישִׁי הוּא־חֹדֶשׁ סִיוָן בִּשְׁלוֹשָׁה
וְעֶשְׂרִים בּוֹ וַיִּכָּתֵב כְּכָל־אֲשֶׁר־צִוָּה מָרְדֳּכַי אֶל־הַיְּהוּדִים
וְאֶל הָאֲחַשְׁדַּרְפְּנִים וְהַפַּחוֹת וְשָׂרֵי הַמְּדִינוֹת אֲשֶׁר |
מֵהֹדּוּ וְעַד־כּוּשׁ שֶׁבַע וְעֶשְׂרִים וּמֵאָה מְדִינָה מְדִינָה
וּמְדִינָה כִּכְתָבָהּ וְעַם וָעָם כִּלְשֹׁנוֹ וְאֶל־הַיְּהוּדִים כִּכְתָבָם

י וְכִלְשׁוֹנָם: וַיִּכְתֹּב בְּשֵׁם הַמֶּלֶךְ אֲחַשְׁוֵרֹשׁ וַיַּחְתֹּם בְּטַבַּעַת
הַמֶּלֶךְ וַיִּשְׁלַח סְפָרִים בְּיַד הָרָצִים בַּסּוּסִים רֹכְבֵי הָרֶכֶשׁ
הָאֲחַשְׁתְּרָנִים בְּנֵי הָרַמָּכִים: אֲשֶׁר נָתַן הַמֶּלֶךְ לַיְּהוּדִים |

יא אֲשֶׁר | בְּכָל־עִיר וָעִיר לְהִקָּהֵל וְלַעֲמֹד עַל־נַפְשָׁם
לְהַשְׁמִיד וְלַהֲרֹג וּלְאַבֵּד אֶת־כָּל־חֵיל עַם וּמְדִינָה הַצָּרִים

יב אֹתָם טַף וְנָשִׁים וּשְׁלָלָם לָבוֹז: בְּיוֹם אֶחָד בְּכָל־מְדִינוֹת
הַמֶּלֶךְ אֲחַשְׁוֵרוֹשׁ בִּשְׁלוֹשָׁה עָשָׂר לְחֹדֶשׁ שְׁנֵים־עָשָׂר

יג הוּא־חֹדֶשׁ אֲדָר: פַּתְשֶׁגֶן הַכְּתָב לְהִנָּתֵן דָּת בְּכָל־מְדִינָה
וּמְדִינָה גָּלוּי לְכָל־הָעַמִּים וְלִהְיוֹת °הַיְּהוּדִיים עֲתוּדִים

יד לַיּוֹם הַזֶּה לְהִנָּקֵם מֵאֹיְבֵיהֶם: הָרָצִים רֹכְבֵי הָרֶכֶשׁ
הָאֲחַשְׁתְּרָנִים יָצְאוּ מְבֹהָלִים וּדְחוּפִים בִּדְבַר הַמֶּלֶךְ

טו וְהַדָּת נִתְּנָה בְּשׁוּשַׁן הַבִּירָה: וּמָרְדֳּכַי יָצָא |
מִלִּפְנֵי הַמֶּלֶךְ בִּלְבוּשׁ מַלְכוּת תְּכֵלֶת וָחוּר וַעֲטֶרֶת זָהָב
גְּדוֹלָה וְתַכְרִיךְ בּוּץ וְאַרְגָּמָן וְהָעִיר שׁוּשָׁן צָהֲלָה

ח:ו °בַּיְּהוּדִים ק׳
ח:יג °הַיְּהוּדִים
עֲתִידִים ק׳

כָּל־אֲשֶׁר קָרֵ֫הוּ וַיֹּאמְרוּ לוֹ חֲכָמָיו וְזֶ֫רֶשׁ אִשְׁתּוֹ אִם מִזֶּ֫רַע
הַיְּהוּדִים מָרְדֳּכַי אֲשֶׁר הַחִלּ֫וֹתָ לִנְפֹּל לְפָנָיו לֹא־תוּכַל לוֹ
יד כִּי־נָפוֹל תִּפּוֹל לְפָנָיו: עוֹדָם מְדַבְּרִים עִמּוֹ וְסָרִיסֵי הַמֶּלֶךְ
הִגִּיעוּ וַיַּבְהִ֫לוּ לְהָבִיא אֶת־הָמָן אֶל־הַמִּשְׁתֶּה אֲשֶׁר־
ז א עָשְׂתָה אֶסְתֵּר: וַיָּבֹא הַמֶּלֶךְ וְהָמָן לִשְׁתּוֹת עִם־אֶסְתֵּר
ב הַמַּלְכָּה: וַיֹּאמֶר הַמֶּלֶךְ לְאֶסְתֵּר גַּם בַּיּוֹם הַשֵּׁנִי בְּמִשְׁתֵּה
הַיַּ֫יִן מַה־שְּׁאֵלָתֵךְ אֶסְתֵּר הַמַּלְכָּה וְתִנָּתֵן לָךְ וּמַה־
ג בַּקָּשָׁתֵךְ עַד־חֲצִי הַמַּלְכוּת וְתֵעָשׂ: וַתַּ֫עַן אֶסְתֵּר הַמַּלְכָּה
וַתֹּאמַר אִם־מָצָ֫אתִי חֵן בְּעֵינֶ֫יךָ הַמֶּלֶךְ וְאִם־עַל־הַמֶּלֶךְ
ד טוֹב תִּנָּֽתֶן־לִי נַפְשִׁי בִּשְׁאֵלָתִי וְעַמִּי בְּבַקָּשָׁתִי: כִּי נִמְכַּ֫רְנוּ
אֲנִי וְעַמִּי לְהַשְׁמִיד לַהֲרוֹג וּלְאַבֵּד וְאִלּוּ לַעֲבָדִים
וְלִשְׁפָחוֹת נִמְכַּ֫רְנוּ הֶחֱרַ֫שְׁתִּי כִּי אֵין הַצָּר שֹׁוֶה בְּנֵ֫זֶק
ה הַמֶּלֶךְ: וַיֹּ֫אמֶר הַמֶּלֶךְ אֲחַשְׁוֵרוֹשׁ וַיֹּ֫אמֶר
לְאֶסְתֵּר הַמַּלְכָּה מִי הוּא זֶה וְאֵי־זֶה הוּא אֲשֶׁר־מְלָאוֹ לִבּוֹ
ו לַעֲשׂוֹת כֵּן: וַתֹּ֫אמֶר אֶסְתֵּר אִישׁ צַר וְאוֹיֵב הָמָן הָרָע הַזֶּה
ז וְהָמָן נִבְעַת מִלִּפְנֵי הַמֶּלֶךְ וְהַמַּלְכָּה: וְהַמֶּלֶךְ קָם בַּחֲמָתוֹ
מִמִּשְׁתֵּה הַיַּ֫יִן אֶל־גִּנַּת הַבִּיתָן וְהָמָן עָמַד לְבַקֵּשׁ עַל־נַפְשׁוֹ
מֵאֶסְתֵּר הַמַּלְכָּה כִּי רָאָה כִּי־כָלְתָה אֵלָיו הָרָעָה מֵאֵת

ח:א ᵒהַיְּהוּדִים ק׳

ח הַמֶּלֶךְ: וְהַמֶּלֶךְ שָׁב מִגִּנַּת הַבִּיתָן אֶל־בֵּית | מִשְׁתֵּה הַיַּ֫יִן
וְהָמָן נֹפֵל עַל־הַמִּטָּה אֲשֶׁר אֶסְתֵּר עָלֶ֫יהָ וַיֹּ֫אמֶר הַמֶּלֶךְ
הֲגַם לִכְבּוֹשׁ אֶת־הַמַּלְכָּה עִמִּי בַּבָּ֫יִת הַדָּבָר יָצָא מִפִּי
ט הַמֶּלֶךְ וּפְנֵי הָמָן חָפוּ: וַיֹּ֫אמֶר חַרְבוֹנָה אֶחָד מִן
הַסָּרִיסִים לִפְנֵי הַמֶּלֶךְ גַּם הִנֵּה־הָעֵץ אֲשֶׁר־עָשָׂה הָמָן
לְמָרְדֳּכַי אֲשֶׁר דִּבֶּר־טוֹב עַל־הַמֶּלֶךְ עֹמֵד בְּבֵית הָמָן
גָּבֹהַּ חֲמִשִּׁים אַמָּה וַיֹּ֫אמֶר הַמֶּלֶךְ תְּלֻ֫הוּ עָלָיו: וַיִּתְלוּ
י אֶת־הָמָן עַל־הָעֵץ אֲשֶׁר־הֵכִין לְמָרְדֳּכָי וַחֲמַת הַמֶּלֶךְ
ח א שָׁכָֽכָה: בַּיּוֹם הַהוּא נָתַן הַמֶּלֶךְ
אֲחַשְׁוֵרוֹשׁ לְאֶסְתֵּר הַמַּלְכָּה אֶת־בֵּית הָמָן צֹרֵר
ᵒהַיְּהוּדִיים וּמָרְדֳּכַי בָּא לִפְנֵי הַמֶּלֶךְ כִּי־הִגִּ֫ידָה אֶסְתֵּר מָה
ב הוּא־לָהּ: וַיָּ֫סַר הַמֶּלֶךְ אֶת־טַבַּעְתּוֹ אֲשֶׁר הֶעֱבִיר מֵהָמָן
וַיִּתְּנָהּ לְמָרְדֳּכָי וַתָּ֫שֶׂם אֶסְתֵּר אֶת־מָרְדֳּכַי עַל־בֵּית
ג הָמָן: וַתּ֫וֹסֶף אֶסְתֵּר וַתְּדַבֵּר לִפְנֵי הַמֶּלֶךְ
וַתִּפֹּל לִפְנֵי רַגְלָיו וַתֵּבְךְּ וַתִּתְחַנֶּן־לוֹ לְהַעֲבִיר אֶת־רָעַת

לֹא־הֵבִיאָה אֶסְתֵּר הַמַּלְכָּה עִם־הַמֶּלֶךְ אֶל־הַמִּשְׁתֶּה
אֲשֶׁר־עָשָׂתָה כִּי אִם־אוֹתִי וְגַם־לְמָחָר אֲנִי קָרוּא־לָהּ עִם־
הַמֶּלֶךְ: וְכָל־זֶה אֵינֶנּוּ שֹׁוֶה לִי בְּכָל־עֵת אֲשֶׁר אֲנִי רֹאֶה
אֶת־מָרְדֳּכַי הַיְּהוּדִי יוֹשֵׁב בְּשַׁעַר הַמֶּלֶךְ: וַתֹּאמֶר לוֹ
זֶרֶשׁ אִשְׁתּוֹ וְכָל־אֹהֲבָיו יַעֲשׂוּ־עֵץ גָּבֹהַּ חֲמִשִּׁים אַמָּה
וּבַבֹּקֶר | אֱמֹר לַמֶּלֶךְ וְיִתְלוּ אֶת־מָרְדֳּכַי עָלָיו וּבֹא־עִם־
הַמֶּלֶךְ אֶל־הַמִּשְׁתֶּה שָׂמֵחַ וַיִּיטַב הַדָּבָר לִפְנֵי הָמָן
וַיַּעַשׂ הָעֵץ: בַּלַּיְלָה הַהוּא נָדְדָה שְׁנַת הַמֶּלֶךְ
וַיֹּאמֶר לְהָבִיא אֶת־סֵפֶר הַזִּכְרֹנוֹת דִּבְרֵי הַיָּמִים וַיִּהְיוּ
נִקְרָאִים לִפְנֵי הַמֶּלֶךְ: וַיִּמָּצֵא כָתוּב אֲשֶׁר הִגִּיד מָרְדֳּכַי
עַל־בִּגְתָנָא וָתֶרֶשׁ שְׁנֵי סָרִיסֵי הַמֶּלֶךְ מִשֹּׁמְרֵי הַסַּף אֲשֶׁר
בִּקְשׁוּ לִשְׁלֹחַ יָד בַּמֶּלֶךְ אֲחַשְׁוֵרוֹשׁ: וַיֹּאמֶר הַמֶּלֶךְ מָה־
נַּעֲשָׂה יְקָר וּגְדוּלָּה לְמָרְדֳּכַי עַל־זֶה וַיֹּאמְרוּ נַעֲרֵי הַמֶּלֶךְ
מְשָׁרְתָיו לֹא־נַעֲשָׂה עִמּוֹ דָּבָר: וַיֹּאמֶר הַמֶּלֶךְ מִי בֶחָצֵר
וְהָמָן בָּא לַחֲצַר בֵּית־הַמֶּלֶךְ הַחִיצוֹנָה לֵאמֹר לַמֶּלֶךְ
לִתְלוֹת אֶת־מָרְדֳּכַי עַל־הָעֵץ אֲשֶׁר־הֵכִין לוֹ: וַיֹּאמְרוּ
נַעֲרֵי הַמֶּלֶךְ אֵלָיו הִנֵּה הָמָן עֹמֵד בֶּחָצֵר וַיֹּאמֶר הַמֶּלֶךְ
יָבוֹא: וַיָּבוֹא הָמָן וַיֹּאמֶר לוֹ הַמֶּלֶךְ מַה־לַעֲשׂוֹת בָּאִישׁ
אֲשֶׁר הַמֶּלֶךְ חָפֵץ בִּיקָרוֹ וַיֹּאמֶר הָמָן בְּלִבּוֹ לְמִי יַחְפֹּץ
הַמֶּלֶךְ לַעֲשׂוֹת יְקָר יוֹתֵר מִמֶּנִּי: וַיֹּאמֶר הָמָן אֶל־הַמֶּלֶךְ
אִישׁ אֲשֶׁר הַמֶּלֶךְ חָפֵץ בִּיקָרוֹ: יָבִיאוּ לְבוּשׁ מַלְכוּת אֲשֶׁר
לָבַשׁ־בּוֹ הַמֶּלֶךְ וְסוּס אֲשֶׁר רָכַב עָלָיו הַמֶּלֶךְ וַאֲשֶׁר נִתַּן
כֶּתֶר מַלְכוּת בְּרֹאשׁוֹ: וְנָתוֹן הַלְּבוּשׁ וְהַסּוּס עַל־יַד־אִישׁ
מִשָּׂרֵי הַמֶּלֶךְ הַפַּרְתְּמִים וְהִלְבִּישׁוּ אֶת־הָאִישׁ אֲשֶׁר הַמֶּלֶךְ
חָפֵץ בִּיקָרוֹ וְהִרְכִּיבֻהוּ עַל־הַסּוּס בִּרְחוֹב הָעִיר וְקָרְאוּ
לְפָנָיו כָּכָה יֵעָשֶׂה לָאִישׁ אֲשֶׁר הַמֶּלֶךְ חָפֵץ בִּיקָרוֹ: וַיֹּאמֶר
הַמֶּלֶךְ לְהָמָן מַהֵר קַח אֶת־הַלְּבוּשׁ וְאֶת־הַסּוּס כַּאֲשֶׁר
דִּבַּרְתָּ וַעֲשֵׂה־כֵן לְמָרְדֳּכַי הַיְּהוּדִי הַיּוֹשֵׁב בְּשַׁעַר הַמֶּלֶךְ
אַל־תַּפֵּל דָּבָר מִכֹּל אֲשֶׁר דִּבַּרְתָּ: וַיִּקַּח הָמָן אֶת־הַלְּבוּשׁ
וְאֶת־הַסּוּס וַיַּלְבֵּשׁ אֶת־מָרְדֳּכָי וַיַּרְכִּיבֵהוּ בִּרְחוֹב הָעִיר
וַיִּקְרָא לְפָנָיו כָּכָה יֵעָשֶׂה לָאִישׁ אֲשֶׁר הַמֶּלֶךְ חָפֵץ בִּיקָרוֹ:
וַיָּשָׁב מָרְדֳּכַי אֶל־שַׁעַר הַמֶּלֶךְ וְהָמָן נִדְחַף אֶל־בֵּיתוֹ אָבֵל
וַחֲפוּי רֹאשׁ: וַיְסַפֵּר הָמָן לְזֶרֶשׁ אִשְׁתּוֹ וּלְכָל־אֹהֲבָיו אֵת

לְמָרְדֳּכַי אֵת דִּבְרֵי אֶסְתֵּר: וַיֹּאמֶר מָרְדֳּכַי לְהָשִׁיב אֶל־ יג
אֶסְתֵּר אַל־תְּדַמִּי בְנַפְשֵׁךְ לְהִמָּלֵט בֵּית־הַמֶּלֶךְ מִכָּל־
הַיְּהוּדִים: כִּי אִם־הַחֲרֵשׁ תַּחֲרִישִׁי בָּעֵת הַזֹּאת רֶוַח יד
וְהַצָּלָה יַעֲמוֹד לַיְּהוּדִים מִמָּקוֹם אַחֵר וְאַתְּ וּבֵית־אָבִיךְ
תֹּאבֵדוּ וּמִי יוֹדֵעַ אִם־לְעֵת כָּזֹאת הִגַּעַתְּ לַמַּלְכוּת:
וַתֹּאמֶר אֶסְתֵּר לְהָשִׁיב אֶל־מָרְדֳּכָי: לֵךְ כְּנוֹס אֶת־כָּל־ טו־טז
הַיְּהוּדִים הַנִּמְצְאִים בְּשׁוּשָׁן וְצוּמוּ עָלַי וְאַל־תֹּאכְלוּ וְאַל־
תִּשְׁתּוּ שְׁלֹשֶׁת יָמִים לַיְלָה וָיוֹם גַּם־אֲנִי וְנַעֲרֹתַי אָצוּם כֵּן
וּבְכֵן אָבוֹא אֶל־הַמֶּלֶךְ אֲשֶׁר לֹא־כַדָּת וְכַאֲשֶׁר אָבַדְתִּי
אָבָדְתִּי: וַיַּעֲבֹר מָרְדֳּכָי וַיַּעַשׂ כְּכֹל אֲשֶׁר־צִוְּתָה עָלָיו יז
אֶסְתֵּר: וַיְהִי | בַּיּוֹם הַשְּׁלִישִׁי וַתִּלְבַּשׁ אֶסְתֵּר מַלְכוּת ה א
וַתַּעֲמֹד בַּחֲצַר בֵּית־הַמֶּלֶךְ הַפְּנִימִית נֹכַח בֵּית הַמֶּלֶךְ
וְהַמֶּלֶךְ יוֹשֵׁב עַל־כִּסֵּא מַלְכוּתוֹ בְּבֵית הַמַּלְכוּת נֹכַח פֶּתַח
הַבָּיִת: וַיְהִי כִרְאוֹת הַמֶּלֶךְ אֶת־אֶסְתֵּר הַמַּלְכָּה עֹמֶדֶת ב
בֶּחָצֵר נָשְׂאָה חֵן בְּעֵינָיו וַיּוֹשֶׁט הַמֶּלֶךְ לְאֶסְתֵּר אֶת־
שַׁרְבִיט הַזָּהָב אֲשֶׁר בְּיָדוֹ וַתִּקְרַב אֶסְתֵּר וַתִּגַּע בְּרֹאשׁ
הַשַּׁרְבִיט: וַיֹּאמֶר לָהּ הַמֶּלֶךְ מַה־לָּךְ אֶסְתֵּר הַמַּלְכָּה וּמַה־ ג
בַּקָּשָׁתֵךְ עַד־חֲצִי הַמַּלְכוּת וְיִנָּתֵן לָךְ: וַתֹּאמֶר אֶסְתֵּר אִם־ ד
עַל־הַמֶּלֶךְ טוֹב יָבוֹא הַמֶּלֶךְ וְהָמָן הַיּוֹם אֶל־הַמִּשְׁתֶּה
אֲשֶׁר־עָשִׂיתִי לוֹ: וַיֹּאמֶר הַמֶּלֶךְ מַהֲרוּ אֶת־הָמָן לַעֲשׂוֹת ה
אֶת־דְּבַר אֶסְתֵּר וַיָּבֹא הַמֶּלֶךְ וְהָמָן אֶל־הַמִּשְׁתֶּה אֲשֶׁר־
עָשְׂתָה אֶסְתֵּר: וַיֹּאמֶר הַמֶּלֶךְ לְאֶסְתֵּר בְּמִשְׁתֵּה הַיַּיִן מַה־ ו
שְּׁאֵלָתֵךְ וְיִנָּתֵן לָךְ וּמַה־בַּקָּשָׁתֵךְ עַד־חֲצִי הַמַּלְכוּת
וְתֵעָשׂ: וַתַּעַן אֶסְתֵּר וַתֹּאמַר שְׁאֵלָתִי וּבַקָּשָׁתִי: אִם־ ז־ח
מָצָאתִי חֵן בְּעֵינֵי הַמֶּלֶךְ וְאִם־עַל־הַמֶּלֶךְ טוֹב לָתֵת אֶת־
שְׁאֵלָתִי וְלַעֲשׂוֹת אֶת־בַּקָּשָׁתִי יָבוֹא הַמֶּלֶךְ וְהָמָן אֶל־
הַמִּשְׁתֶּה אֲשֶׁר אֶעֱשֶׂה לָהֶם וּמָחָר אֶעֱשֶׂה כִּדְבַר הַמֶּלֶךְ:
וַיֵּצֵא הָמָן בַּיּוֹם הַהוּא שָׂמֵחַ וְטוֹב לֵב וְכִרְאוֹת הָמָן אֶת־ ט
מָרְדֳּכַי בְּשַׁעַר הַמֶּלֶךְ וְלֹא־קָם וְלֹא־זָע מִמֶּנּוּ וַיִּמָּלֵא הָמָן
עַל־מָרְדֳּכַי חֵמָה: וַיִּתְאַפַּק הָמָן וַיָּבוֹא אֶל־בֵּיתוֹ וַיִּשְׁלַח י
וַיָּבֵא אֶת־אֹהֲבָיו וְאֶת־זֶרֶשׁ אִשְׁתּוֹ: וַיְסַפֵּר לָהֶם הָמָן אֶת־ יא
כְּבוֹד עָשְׁרוֹ וְרֹב בָּנָיו וְאֵת כָּל־אֲשֶׁר גִּדְּלוֹ הַמֶּלֶךְ וְאֵת
אֲשֶׁר נִשְּׂאוֹ עַל־הַשָּׂרִים וְעַבְדֵי הַמֶּלֶךְ: וַיֹּאמֶר הָמָן אַף יב

מָרְדֳּכָי וְאֶת־מַאֲמַר מָרְדֳּכַי אֶסְתֵּר עֹשָׂה כַּאֲשֶׁר הָיְתָה
כא בְאָמְנָה אִתּוֹ: בַּיָּמִים הָהֵם וּמָרְדֳּכַי יוֹשֵׁב
בְּשַׁעַר־הַמֶּלֶךְ קָצַף בִּגְתָן וָתֶרֶשׁ שְׁנֵי־סָרִיסֵי הַמֶּלֶךְ
כב מִשֹּׁמְרֵי הַסַּף וַיְבַקְשׁוּ לִשְׁלֹחַ יָד בַּמֶּלֶךְ אֲחַשְׁוֵרֹשׁ: וַיִּוָּדַע
הַדָּבָר לְמָרְדֳּכַי וַיַּגֵּד לְאֶסְתֵּר הַמַּלְכָּה וַתֹּאמֶר
כג אֶסְתֵּר לַמֶּלֶךְ בְּשֵׁם מָרְדֳּכָי: וַיְבֻקַּשׁ הַדָּבָר וַיִּמָּצֵא וַיִּתָּלוּ
שְׁנֵיהֶם עַל־עֵץ וַיִּכָּתֵב בְּסֵפֶר דִּבְרֵי הַיָּמִים לִפְנֵי
ג א הַמֶּלֶךְ: אַחַר | הַדְּבָרִים הָאֵלֶּה גִּדַּל הַמֶּלֶךְ
אֲחַשְׁוֵרוֹשׁ אֶת־הָמָן בֶּן־הַמְּדָתָא הָאֲגָגִי וַיְנַשְּׂאֵהוּ וַיָּשֶׂם
ב אֶת־כִּסְאוֹ מֵעַל כָּל־הַשָּׂרִים אֲשֶׁר אִתּוֹ: וְכָל־עַבְדֵי הַמֶּלֶךְ
אֲשֶׁר־בְּשַׁעַר הַמֶּלֶךְ כֹּרְעִים וּמִשְׁתַּחֲוִים לְהָמָן כִּי־כֵן צִוָּה־
ג לוֹ הַמֶּלֶךְ וּמָרְדֳּכַי לֹא יִכְרַע וְלֹא יִשְׁתַּחֲוֶה: וַיֹּאמְרוּ עַבְדֵי
הַמֶּלֶךְ אֲשֶׁר־בְּשַׁעַר הַמֶּלֶךְ לְמָרְדֳּכָי מַדּוּעַ אַתָּה עוֹבֵר
ד אֵת מִצְוַת הַמֶּלֶךְ: וַיְהִי °בְּאָמְרָם אֵלָיו יוֹם וָיוֹם וְלֹא שָׁמַע
אֲלֵיהֶם וַיַּגִּידוּ לְהָמָן לִרְאוֹת הֲיַעַמְדוּ דִּבְרֵי מָרְדֳּכַי כִּי־
ה הִגִּיד לָהֶם אֲשֶׁר־הוּא יְהוּדִי: וַיַּרְא הָמָן כִּי־אֵין מָרְדֳּכַי
כֹּרֵעַ וּמִשְׁתַּחֲוֶה לוֹ וַיִּמָּלֵא הָמָן חֵמָה: וַיִּבֶז בְּעֵינָיו לִשְׁלֹחַ
ו יָד בְּמָרְדֳּכַי לְבַדּוֹ כִּי־הִגִּידוּ לוֹ אֶת־עַם מָרְדֳּכָי וַיְבַקֵּשׁ
הָמָן לְהַשְׁמִיד אֶת־כָּל־הַיְּהוּדִים אֲשֶׁר בְּכָל־מַלְכוּת
ז אֲחַשְׁוֵרוֹשׁ עַם מָרְדֳּכָי: בַּחֹדֶשׁ הָרִאשׁוֹן הוּא־חֹדֶשׁ נִיסָן
בִּשְׁנַת שְׁתֵּים עֶשְׂרֵה לַמֶּלֶךְ אֲחַשְׁוֵרוֹשׁ הִפִּיל פּוּר הוּא
הַגּוֹרָל לִפְנֵי הָמָן מִיּוֹם | לְיוֹם וּמֵחֹדֶשׁ לְחֹדֶשׁ שְׁנֵים־עָשָׂר
ח הוּא־חֹדֶשׁ אֲדָר: וַיֹּאמֶר הָמָן לַמֶּלֶךְ
אֲחַשְׁוֵרוֹשׁ יֶשְׁנוֹ עַם־אֶחָד מְפֻזָּר וּמְפֹרָד בֵּין הָעַמִּים בְּכֹל
מְדִינוֹת מַלְכוּתֶךָ וְדָתֵיהֶם שֹׁנוֹת מִכָּל־עָם וְאֶת־דָּתֵי
ט הַמֶּלֶךְ אֵינָם עֹשִׂים וְלַמֶּלֶךְ אֵין־שׁוֶֹה לְהַנִּיחָם: אִם־עַל־
הַמֶּלֶךְ טוֹב יִכָּתֵב לְאַבְּדָם וַעֲשֶׂרֶת אֲלָפִים כִּכַּר־כֶּסֶף
אֶשְׁקוֹל עַל־יְדֵי עֹשֵׂי הַמְּלָאכָה לְהָבִיא אֶל־גִּנְזֵי הַמֶּלֶךְ:
י וַיָּסַר הַמֶּלֶךְ אֶת־טַבַּעְתּוֹ מֵעַל יָדוֹ וַיִּתְּנָהּ לְהָמָן בֶּן־
הַמְּדָתָא הָאֲגָגִי צֹרֵר הַיְּהוּדִים: וַיֹּאמֶר הַמֶּלֶךְ לְהָמָן
יא הַכֶּסֶף נָתוּן לָךְ וְהָעָם לַעֲשׂוֹת בּוֹ כַּטּוֹב בְּעֵינֶיךָ: וַיִּקָּרְאוּ
יב סֹפְרֵי הַמֶּלֶךְ בַּחֹדֶשׁ הָרִאשׁוֹן בִּשְׁלוֹשָׁה עָשָׂר יוֹם בּוֹ
וַיִּכָּתֵב כְּכָל־אֲשֶׁר־צִוָּה הָמָן אֶל אֲחַשְׁדַּרְפְּנֵי־הַמֶּלֶךְ וְאֶל־

ג:ד °כְּאָמְרָם ק׳

עִם־יְכָנְיָה מֶלֶךְ־יְהוּדָה אֲשֶׁר הֶגְלָה נְבוּכַדְנֶצַּר מֶלֶךְ בָּבֶל:

ז וַיְהִי אֹמֵן אֶת־הֲדַסָּה הִיא אֶסְתֵּר בַּת־דֹּדוֹ כִּי אֵין לָהּ אָב וָאֵם וְהַנַּעֲרָה יְפַת־תֹּאַר וְטוֹבַת מַרְאֶה וּבְמוֹת אָבִיהָ וְאִמָּהּ לְקָחָהּ מָרְדֳּכַי לוֹ לְבַת: ח וַיְהִי בְּהִשָּׁמַע דְּבַר־הַמֶּלֶךְ וְדָתוֹ וּבְהִקָּבֵץ נְעָרוֹת רַבּוֹת אֶל־שׁוּשַׁן הַבִּירָה אֶל־יַד הֵגָי וַתִּלָּקַח אֶסְתֵּר אֶל־בֵּית הַמֶּלֶךְ אֶל־יַד הֵגַי שֹׁמֵר הַנָּשִׁים: ט וַתִּיטַב הַנַּעֲרָה בְעֵינָיו וַתִּשָּׂא חֶסֶד לְפָנָיו וַיְבַהֵל אֶת־תַּמְרוּקֶיהָ וְאֶת־מָנוֹתֶהָ לָתֵת לָהּ וְאֵת שֶׁבַע הַנְּעָרוֹת הָרְאֻיוֹת לָתֶת־לָהּ מִבֵּית הַמֶּלֶךְ וַיְשַׁנֶּהָ וְאֶת־נַעֲרוֹתֶיהָ לְטוֹב בֵּית הַנָּשִׁים: י לֹא־הִגִּידָה אֶסְתֵּר אֶת־עַמָּהּ וְאֶת־מוֹלַדְתָּהּ כִּי מָרְדֳּכַי צִוָּה עָלֶיהָ אֲשֶׁר לֹא־תַגִּיד: יא וּבְכָל־יוֹם וָיוֹם מָרְדֳּכַי מִתְהַלֵּךְ לִפְנֵי חֲצַר בֵּית־הַנָּשִׁים לָדַעַת אֶת־שְׁלוֹם אֶסְתֵּר וּמַה־יֵּעָשֶׂה בָּהּ: יב וּבְהַגִּיעַ תֹּר נַעֲרָה וְנַעֲרָה לָבוֹא ׀ אֶל־הַמֶּלֶךְ אֲחַשְׁוֵרוֹשׁ מִקֵּץ הֱיוֹת לָהּ כְּדָת הַנָּשִׁים שְׁנֵים עָשָׂר חֹדֶשׁ כִּי כֵּן יִמְלְאוּ יְמֵי מְרוּקֵיהֶן שִׁשָּׁה חֳדָשִׁים בְּשֶׁמֶן הַמֹּר וְשִׁשָּׁה חֳדָשִׁים בַּבְּשָׂמִים וּבְתַמְרוּקֵי הַנָּשִׁים: יג וּבָזֶה הַנַּעֲרָה בָּאָה אֶל־הַמֶּלֶךְ אֵת כָּל־אֲשֶׁר תֹּאמַר יִנָּתֵן לָהּ לָבוֹא עִמָּהּ מִבֵּית הַנָּשִׁים עַד־בֵּית הַמֶּלֶךְ: יד בָּעֶרֶב ׀ הִיא בָאָה וּבַבֹּקֶר הִיא שָׁבָה אֶל־בֵּית הַנָּשִׁים שֵׁנִי אֶל־יַד שַׁעַשְׁגַז סְרִיס הַמֶּלֶךְ שֹׁמֵר הַפִּילַגְשִׁים לֹא־תָבוֹא עוֹד אֶל־הַמֶּלֶךְ כִּי אִם־חָפֵץ בָּהּ הַמֶּלֶךְ וְנִקְרְאָה בְשֵׁם: טו וּבְהַגִּיעַ תֹּר־אֶסְתֵּר בַּת־אֲבִיחַיִל ׀ דֹּד מָרְדֳּכַי אֲשֶׁר לָקַח־לוֹ לְבַת לָבוֹא אֶל־הַמֶּלֶךְ לֹא בִקְשָׁה דָּבָר כִּי אִם אֶת־אֲשֶׁר יֹאמַר הֵגַי סְרִיס־הַמֶּלֶךְ שֹׁמֵר הַנָּשִׁים וַתְּהִי אֶסְתֵּר נֹשֵׂאת חֵן בְּעֵינֵי כָּל־רֹאֶיהָ: טז וַתִּלָּקַח אֶסְתֵּר אֶל־הַמֶּלֶךְ אֲחַשְׁוֵרוֹשׁ אֶל־בֵּית מַלְכוּתוֹ בַּחֹדֶשׁ הָעֲשִׂירִי הוּא־חֹדֶשׁ טֵבֵת בִּשְׁנַת־שֶׁבַע לְמַלְכוּתוֹ: יז וַיֶּאֱהַב הַמֶּלֶךְ אֶת־אֶסְתֵּר מִכָּל־הַנָּשִׁים וַתִּשָּׂא־חֵן וָחֶסֶד לְפָנָיו מִכָּל־הַבְּתוּלוֹת וַיָּשֶׂם כֶּתֶר־מַלְכוּת בְּרֹאשָׁהּ וַיַּמְלִיכֶהָ תַּחַת וַשְׁתִּי: יח וַיַּעַשׂ הַמֶּלֶךְ מִשְׁתֶּה גָדוֹל לְכָל־שָׂרָיו וַעֲבָדָיו אֵת מִשְׁתֵּה אֶסְתֵּר וַהֲנָחָה לַמְּדִינוֹת עָשָׂה וַיִּתֵּן מַשְׂאֵת כְּיַד הַמֶּלֶךְ: יט-כ וּבְהִקָּבֵץ בְּתוּלוֹת שֵׁנִית וּמָרְדֳּכַי יֹשֵׁב בְּשַׁעַר־הַמֶּלֶךְ: אֵין אֶסְתֵּר מַגֶּדֶת מוֹלַדְתָּהּ וְאֶת־עַמָּהּ כַּאֲשֶׁר צִוָּה עָלֶיהָ

לַחֲכָמִים יֹדְעֵי הָעִתִּים כִּי־כֵן דְּבַר הַמֶּלֶךְ לִפְנֵי כָּל־יֹדְעֵי

יד דָת וָדִין: וְהַקָּרֹב אֵלָיו כַּרְשְׁנָא שֵׁתָר אַדְמָתָא תַרְשִׁישׁ
מֶרֶס מַרְסְנָא מְמוּכָן שִׁבְעַת שָׂרֵי | פָּרַס וּמָדַי רֹאֵי פְּנֵי

טו הַמֶּלֶךְ הַיֹּשְׁבִים רִאשֹׁנָה בַּמַּלְכוּת: כְּדָת מַה־לַעֲשׂוֹת
בַּמַּלְכָּה וַשְׁתִּי עַל | אֲשֶׁר לֹא־עָשְׂתָה אֶת־מַאֲמַר הַמֶּלֶךְ

טז אֲחַשְׁוֵרוֹשׁ בְּיַד הַסָּרִיסִים: וַיֹּאמֶר °מוֹמֻכָן
לִפְנֵי הַמֶּלֶךְ וְהַשָּׂרִים לֹא עַל־הַמֶּלֶךְ לְבַדּוֹ עָוְתָה וַשְׁתִּי
הַמַּלְכָּה כִּי עַל־כָּל־הַשָּׂרִים וְעַל־כָּל־הָעַמִּים אֲשֶׁר בְּכָל־

יז מְדִינוֹת הַמֶּלֶךְ אֲחַשְׁוֵרוֹשׁ: כִּי־יֵצֵא דְבַר־הַמַּלְכָּה עַל־כָּל־
הַנָּשִׁים לְהַבְזוֹת בַּעְלֵיהֶן בְּעֵינֵיהֶן בְּאָמְרָם הַמֶּלֶךְ
אֲחַשְׁוֵרוֹשׁ אָמַר לְהָבִיא אֶת־וַשְׁתִּי הַמַּלְכָּה לְפָנָיו וְלֹא־

יח בָאָה: וְהַיּוֹם הַזֶּה תֹּאמַרְנָה | שָׂרוֹת פָּרַס־וּמָדַי אֲשֶׁר
שָׁמְעוּ אֶת־דְּבַר הַמַּלְכָּה לְכֹל שָׂרֵי הַמֶּלֶךְ וּכְדַי בִּזָּיוֹן

יט וָקָצֶף: אִם־עַל־הַמֶּלֶךְ טוֹב יֵצֵא דְבַר־מַלְכוּת מִלְּפָנָיו
וְיִכָּתֵב בְּדָתֵי פָרַס־וּמָדַי וְלֹא יַעֲבוֹר אֲשֶׁר לֹא־תָבוֹא
וַשְׁתִּי לִפְנֵי הַמֶּלֶךְ אֲחַשְׁוֵרוֹשׁ וּמַלְכוּתָהּ יִתֵּן הַמֶּלֶךְ

כ לִרְעוּתָהּ הַטּוֹבָה מִמֶּנָּה: וְנִשְׁמַע פִּתְגָם הַמֶּלֶךְ אֲשֶׁר־
יַעֲשֶׂה בְּכָל־מַלְכוּתוֹ כִּי רַבָּה הִיא וְכָל־הַנָּשִׁים יִתְּנוּ יְקָר

כא לְבַעְלֵיהֶן לְמִגָּדוֹל וְעַד־קָטָן: וַיִּיטַב הַדָּבָר בְּעֵינֵי הַמֶּלֶךְ

א:טז °מְמוּכָן ק׳

וְהַשָּׂרִים וַיַּעַשׂ הַמֶּלֶךְ כִּדְבַר מְמוּכָן: וַיִּשְׁלַח סְפָרִים אֶל־
כב כָּל־מְדִינוֹת הַמֶּלֶךְ אֶל־מְדִינָה וּמְדִינָה כִּכְתָבָהּ וְאֶל־עַם
וָעָם כִּלְשׁוֹנוֹ לִהְיוֹת כָּל־אִישׁ שֹׂרֵר בְּבֵיתוֹ וּמְדַבֵּר כִּלְשׁוֹן

ב א עַמּוֹ: אַחַר הַדְּבָרִים הָאֵלֶּה כְּשֹׁךְ חֲמַת הַמֶּלֶךְ
אֲחַשְׁוֵרוֹשׁ זָכַר אֶת־וַשְׁתִּי וְאֵת אֲשֶׁר־עָשָׂתָה וְאֵת אֲשֶׁר־

ב נִגְזַר עָלֶיהָ: וַיֹּאמְרוּ נַעֲרֵי־הַמֶּלֶךְ מְשָׁרְתָיו יְבַקְשׁוּ לַמֶּלֶךְ

ג נְעָרוֹת בְּתוּלוֹת טוֹבוֹת מַרְאֶה: וְיַפְקֵד הַמֶּלֶךְ פְּקִידִים
בְּכָל־מְדִינוֹת מַלְכוּתוֹ וְיִקְבְּצוּ אֶת־כָּל־נַעֲרָה־בְתוּלָה
טוֹבַת מַרְאֶה אֶל־שׁוּשַׁן הַבִּירָה אֶל־בֵּית הַנָּשִׁים אֶל־יַד

ד הֵגֶא סְרִיס הַמֶּלֶךְ שֹׁמֵר הַנָּשִׁים וְנָתוֹן תַּמְרֻקֵיהֶן: וְהַנַּעֲרָה
אֲשֶׁר תִּיטַב בְּעֵינֵי הַמֶּלֶךְ תִּמְלֹךְ תַּחַת וַשְׁתִּי וַיִּיטַב הַדָּבָר

ה בְּעֵינֵי הַמֶּלֶךְ וַיַּעַשׂ כֵּן: אִישׁ יְהוּדִי הָיָה בְּשׁוּשַׁן
הַבִּירָה וּשְׁמוֹ מָרְדֳּכַי בֶּן יָאִיר בֶּן־שִׁמְעִי בֶּן־קִישׁ אִישׁ

ו יְמִינִי: אֲשֶׁר הָגְלָה מִירוּשָׁלַיִם עִם־הַגֹּלָה אֲשֶׁר הָגְלְתָה

# מגילת
# אסתר

א אַ וַיְהִי בִּימֵי אֲחַשְׁוֵרוֹשׁ הוּא אֲחַשְׁוֵרוֹשׁ הַמֹּלֵךְ מֵהֹדּוּ וְעַד־
ב כּוּשׁ שֶׁבַע וְעֶשְׂרִים וּמֵאָה מְדִינָה: בַּיָּמִים הָהֵם כְּשֶׁבֶת |
הַמֶּלֶךְ אֲחַשְׁוֵרוֹשׁ עַל כִּסֵּא מַלְכוּתוֹ אֲשֶׁר בְּשׁוּשַׁן
ג הַבִּירָה: בִּשְׁנַת שָׁלוֹשׁ לְמָלְכוֹ עָשָׂה מִשְׁתֶּה לְכָל־שָׂרָיו
וַעֲבָדָיו חֵיל | פָּרַס וּמָדַי הַפַּרְתְּמִים וְשָׂרֵי הַמְּדִינוֹת לְפָנָיו:
ד בְּהַרְאֹתוֹ אֶת־עֹשֶׁר כְּבוֹד מַלְכוּתוֹ וְאֶת־יְקָר תִּפְאֶרֶת
ה גְּדוּלָּתוֹ יָמִים רַבִּים שְׁמוֹנִים וּמְאַת יוֹם: וּבִמְלוֹאת | הַיָּמִים
הָאֵלֶּה עָשָׂה הַמֶּלֶךְ לְכָל־הָעָם הַנִּמְצְאִים בְּשׁוּשַׁן הַבִּירָה
לְמִגָּדוֹל וְעַד־קָטָן מִשְׁתֶּה שִׁבְעַת יָמִים בַּחֲצַר גִּנַּת בִּיתַן
ו הַמֶּלֶךְ: חוּר | כַּרְפַּס וּתְכֵלֶת אָחוּז בְּחַבְלֵי־בוּץ וְאַרְגָּמָן
עַל־גְּלִילֵי כֶסֶף וְעַמּוּדֵי שֵׁשׁ מִטּוֹת | זָהָב וָכֶסֶף עַל רִצְפַת
ז בַּהַט־וָשֵׁשׁ וְדַר וְסֹחָרֶת: וְהַשְׁקוֹת בִּכְלֵי זָהָב וְכֵלִים
ח מִכֵּלִים שׁוֹנִים וְיֵין מַלְכוּת רָב כְּיַד הַמֶּלֶךְ: וְהַשְּׁתִיָּה כַדָּת
אֵין אֹנֵס כִּי־כֵן | יִסַּד הַמֶּלֶךְ עַל כָּל־רַב בֵּיתוֹ לַעֲשׂוֹת
ט כִּרְצוֹן אִישׁ־וָאִישׁ:        גַּם וַשְׁתִּי הַמַּלְכָּה עָשְׂתָה
י מִשְׁתֵּה נָשִׁים בֵּית הַמַּלְכוּת אֲשֶׁר לַמֶּלֶךְ אֲחַשְׁוֵרוֹשׁ: בַּיּוֹם
הַשְּׁבִיעִי כְּטוֹב לֵב־הַמֶּלֶךְ בַּיָּיִן אָמַר לִמְהוּמָן בִּזְּתָא
חַרְבוֹנָא בִּגְתָא וַאֲבַגְתָא זֵתַר וְכַרְכַּס שִׁבְעַת הַסָּרִיסִים
יא הַמְשָׁרְתִים אֶת־פְּנֵי הַמֶּלֶךְ אֲחַשְׁוֵרוֹשׁ: לְהָבִיא אֶת־וַשְׁתִּי
הַמַּלְכָּה לִפְנֵי הַמֶּלֶךְ בְּכֶתֶר מַלְכוּת לְהַרְאוֹת הָעַמִּים
יב וְהַשָּׂרִים אֶת־יָפְיָהּ כִּי־טוֹבַת מַרְאֶה הִיא: וַתְּמָאֵן הַמַּלְכָּה
וַשְׁתִּי לָבוֹא בִּדְבַר הַמֶּלֶךְ אֲשֶׁר בְּיַד הַסָּרִיסִים וַיִּקְצֹף
יג הַמֶּלֶךְ מְאֹד וַחֲמָתוֹ בָּעֲרָה בוֹ:        וַיֹּאמֶר הַמֶּלֶךְ